CHIPPING NORTON SCHOOL

R17165Y0199

below.

AQA GCSE

Dance

SECOND EDITION

Pam Howard

Philip Allan Updates, an imprint of Hodder Education, an Hachette UK company, Market Place, Deddington, Oxfordshire OX15 0SE

Orders
Bookpoint Ltd, 130 Milton Park, Abingdon, Oxfordshire, OX14 4SB
tel: 01235 827720
fax: 01235 400454
e-mail: uk.orders@bookpoint.co.uk
Lines are open 9.00 a.m.–5.00 p.m., Monday to Saturday, with a 24-hour message answering service. You can also order through the Philip Allan Updates website: www.philipallan.co.uk

© Philip Allan Updates 2007, 2009

ISBN 978-0-340-98662-2

First published 2007
Second edition 2009

Impression number   5   4   3   2   1
Year   2014   2013   2012   2011   2010   2009

All rights reserved; no part of this publication may be reproduced, stored in a retrieval system, or transmitted, in any form or by any means, electronic, mechanical, photocopying, recording or otherwise without either the prior written permission of Philip Allan Updates or a licence permitting restricted copying in the United Kingdom issued by the Copyright Licensing Agency Ltd, Saffron House, 6–10 Kirby Street, London EC1N 8TS.

In all cases we have attempted to trace and credit copyright owners of material used.

Printed in Italy

Environmental information
Hachette UK's policy is to use papers that are natural, renewable and recyclable products and made from wood grown in sustainable forests. The logging and manufacturing processes are expected to conform to the environmental regulations of the country of origin.

Contents

Introduction

This textbook will help you to perform all the coursework tasks and to prepare for the written paper of AQA GCSE Dance. There are four sections:

Section 1 Performance skills
Section 2 Choreographic skills
Section 3 Appreciation skills
Section 4 Resources

The first three sections link with the three strands of the specification, and the fourth provides information on resources you can use to increase your knowledge and understanding of dance — places to go to learn and watch new styles of dance plus listings of books, music and DVDs that will give you ideas.

Section 1 on performance skills gives information on five styles of dance: classical ballet, contemporary, street, Bharat Natyam and capoeira. It includes exercises for you to try to increase your skill as a dancer, as well as phrases of movements to learn. Photographs of dance students from local schools and a capoeira dancer in performance are included. This section should help you to fulfil the requirement of the AQA GCSE Dance specification to present two practical performance-focussed controlled assessments for internal moderation:

1 A solo dance, set by AQA, lasting approximately 1 minute. Your teacher will decide which of the two set solos you will learn and perform.

2 A group performance piece (for 2–5 dancers), which your teacher or a visiting animateur will teach your class. It will be based on three links with one of the set works selected by your teacher from a list provided by AQA.

Section 2 on choreographic skills is intended to support you as you experiment, improvise and work towards making a solo dance linked with a professional work and either a solo or group dance that you choreograph yourself. These two tasks are your third and fourth practical assessments. This section is designed to support and guide you as you learn to create motifs and structure dances as a choreographer. It includes photographs of school dance students in action, plus two dancers from the Henri Oguike Dance Company in *Front Line*. The written paper for AQA GCSE Dance requires candidates to not only write about their own performance and choreographic knowledge from their practical work, but also to write about professional dance works.

Section 3 on appreciation skills is intended to help you learn specific dance terms and vocabulary, so that you can identify, describe, explain, discuss and analyse what you have seen in a visual recording (or live performance) of at least two set works. This section provides you with ways of looking at professional dance works and explains their features, which include:

- movement content (action, dynamics, space)
- choreographic devices
- styles of dance
- dance structure
- use of dancers
- subject matter/choreographer's intention
- design — lighting, set and costume
- accompaniment

You will be expected to write answers that range from one word, to sentences, paragraphs and an essay, so you need to know how to write about these features. This section provides you with specific performance and choreographic tasks and gives examples of professional works to watch. It also includes professional photographs from named professional dance works, which will help you to learn to identify performance styles, choreographic styles, design features and the subject matter (idea) or choreographer's intention within each dance.

Section 4 is on resources. Going to see professional dance live, or having the chance to participate in a dance workshop led by a dance animateur, will both make your course more exciting and add to your achievements. These activities may not always take place in your curriculum dance time but they are vital to help you achieve the highest grades in GCSE Dance. Facts about where to go to see dance performances and agencies and dance companies that run workshops and youth dance companies are included in this section. Some dance companies provide special resource packs on their dance works, designed for school dance students. Rambert Dance Company, the Royal Ballet, English National Ballet, Birmingham Royal Ballet, Henri Oguike Dance Company, Motionhouse Dance Theatre, Phoenix Dance Theatre Company, Siobhan Davies Dance and the Cholmondeleys have all published packs to support GCSE students, either in booklets, interactive CDs or on their web pages.

You need to know a number of specialist dance words, many of which are in French, and there is a comprehensive **glossary** at the back of the book. Terms defined in the glossary are highlighted in **purple** the first time they appear for easy reference. Making your own glossary of the terms you had to look up will help you revise nearer your written exam.

I hope you enjoy discovering more about the world of dance and that this book helps you to achieve the best grades you can for each part of the examination.

Acknowledgements

This book would not have been possible without the support, patience and encouragement of my husband Andy, who allowed me to get to the computer while he kept the domestic side of our lives in order.

My heartfelt thanks go to my assistant Anne Percival and her family, for their time, commitment and contributions to the photo shoots, contacts with schools, students and teachers, and their enthusiasm for all the work involved in meeting the various deadlines. Also, to Andrew Kristy for his music expertise and to Leann Janes, for her research and collation of her findings for the original Resources section of this book.

I would like to thank Horaciao Monteverdi for permission to include his photographs of Sarita Piotrowski and Anthony Kurt, dancers with the Henri Oguike Dance Company, demonstrating key body designs from *Front Line*; Emma Bucke for permission to use photographs of school students taken on three photo shoots; Catherine Ashmore, James Bell, David Buckland, Bill Cooper, Joel Chester Fildes, Anthony Crickmay, Peter Herbert, Chris Nash, Simon Richardson, Herman Sorgeloos. I am also grateful to Laura Bridges and Sarah Da Fonseca, who contributed their performance expertise in contemporary and capoeira dance styles in our various photo shoots.

My thanks also go to the young dancers and their families for permission to use their images in this book: Amie Bleek, Hannah Cahill, Catherine Cooper, Emily Cooper, Nicola Cooper, Harriet Curwood, Jess Dinler, Jon Everid, Aaron Farnel, Julie Foord, Ben Gaut, Jamie Gold, Jessica Harding, Samuel Haughton, Kathryn Hill, Kate Hollywood, Michael Hughes, Rebecca Joyce, Charlie-Beau Keepence, Samantha Kendall, Alice Knapp, David Martin, Stephen Mitchell, Annabel Newman, Raife Norman, Sellisha Oliver, Ashley-Jordan Packer, Charlie Packer, Sky Periam, Joanna Powell, Eleanor Regan, Chloe Shillibeer, Kirstie Skivington, Hollie Turner, Samuel Vennard, Natasha Wade and Rochelle Williams. These photo shoots took place in three centres in northwest Kent — Hextable Dance, the Mick Jagger Centre in Dartford and St George's Church of England School in Gravesend. I am grateful to the staff for their support.

Thanks go to the schools that provided and encouraged their students to be involved in the performing and choreographic workshops run alongside the photo shoots: Beaverwood School for Girls, Bexley Grammar School, Dartford Grammar School, Dartford Grammar School for Girls, Erith School, Hextable School, the Leigh City Technology College, North West Kent College, St George's Church of England School, Townley Grammar School for Girls and Trinity School. Various dance teachers were consulted and contributed ideas, which both encouraged and inspired me and guided the editing process. My thanks again go to Leann Janes, Clare McRoberts, Caroline Afford and Heather Austin with Arts Pool.

Dance companies and their education or marketing departments have also been hugely supportive in providing advice and resources to authenticate the book. I thank them all: Birmingham Royal Ballet, Motionhouse Dance Theatre, New Adventures, Richard Alston Dance Company, Rosas, the Royal Ballet, Shobana Jeyasingh Dance Company, Siobhan Davies Dance and Union Dance.

This book would have been impossible for me to start, let alone finish, without my training and teaching experience, my contact with the National Resource Centre for Dance, the National Dance Teachers Association and the education department of the Royal Academy of Dance, as well as my moderating and examining experiences with South East Regional Examining Board, the University of London and AQA. So, I would like to thank all the lecturers from I. M. Marsh PE College; PE advisers from Kent County Council; head teachers from Swanley School, Northfleet School for Girls and Hextable School, who gave me many opportunities to develop professionally; the education and archive departments of Rambert Dance Company; and various dance authors and examiners who have inspired, encouraged and guided me in my career as a dance teacher and lecturer, and now Penny Fisher and Elizabeth Galloway at Philip Allan Updates for their encouragement in my latest role as an author.

Pam Howard MBE

Chapter 1

How to get the most out of your course

You probably chose to study GCSE Dance because you love dancing. Perhaps you have already gained grades in **ballet**, **modern** or **tap**, achieved Latin or ballroom awards, or experienced **street** jazz performance. Maybe you are a good gymnast or games player, with a positive approach to dance but new skills to learn. Or perhaps you enjoy dancing socially. No matter what your dance history is, this book will help you to achieve your potential at GCSE.

Remember that any experience you already have as a dancer is likely to be different from the work you will be doing towards a GCSE qualification. You will need to be prepared to learn new movements, in different **styles** to those you already know. If you do not have much previous dance experience, you will have an exciting time learning new ideas and **expressive** ways of using your body.

About the subject

Performing

Dance demands the whole person to be visible, moving with skill and expression, and a sense of **rhythm** and confidence. It involves the whole of you — your body, mind and soul. You cannot think about anything else while dancing, so it can help you forget any worries and problems for a time.

Dance is different from painting, writing and film; for these subjects, the piece of work you have done is assessed, not you yourself. It is more like drama and music, for which you are assessed acting or playing an instrument. As a dancer, you too are a performer, and practice is essential for you to improve. You could be assessed at any time in your course, 'live' or on film.

Dance is exciting and fun, but physically and mentally hard work, so you need to be fit. You will learn how to dance in time to the rhythms and **themes** in the music, and how to treat other dance students thoughtfully.

During the course you will observe demonstrations of short and long **phrases** of movement, and you will need to remember these clearly enough to repeat what you saw accurately. Every dancer has to use his/her ears to listen for the 'images' the teacher describes; doing this will help you feel the movement you are watching in your own body. You must be aware of how your limbs can move and be able to imagine making the shapes and **actions** you see in a demonstration. You must train your eyes to look carefully at the movement being demonstrated, so that you understand which parts of the body are working. When you first learn a phrase of movement you will copy the teacher's actions; it is important that you try not to keep copying, but instead think through the phrase yourself. Remember: 'If your brain does not think it, your feet will not get the message!'

Remembering what to do, in the right order, in the right rhythm and correctly is the biggest hurdle you will have to clear at the beginning of the course. Some students will find this easy and not need to practise often; others will need to practise frequently between classes to show they can remember the phrases of movement on the assessment day.

Choreographing

Choreographing is a different skill to performing as a dancer, but it also requires patience, imagination and time. You are expected to create short dances for assessment throughout your course. These could be for you to dance yourself, or for you to teach others to dance, in which case you will have to demonstrate and teach other people the movements you create.

Dances are usually based on a subject, and choreographers go through various processes to finish up with a dance they like and which expresses the **subject matter**. You will learn these different layers to creating a dance, and should make notes on how you achieved each one. These will be useful for three of your final assessments: the two choreography tasks and your written paper. Doing your homework and keeping a choreographic diary right from the beginning of your course will help you to achieve a good final result.

Choreography often involves working with other people, so you will need to be good at sharing and listening to other people's ideas. This applies even when you are not in the mood, as your attitude will affect everyone else.

The written exam

Doing well in the written exam will boost your final grade, so you should be determined to improve the way you write about dance as you go through the course.

You will be expected to write about dances performed by professional dancers you see either on film or live. Being able to watch carefully is therefore vital. For the written exam you will have to learn about at least two **set works** from a list of ten, so you need to train your memory to do this as well as to remember practical dances.

Keeping notes on all the dances you watch is important, and going to live performances and taking part in workshops will help you. Watching and meeting professional dancers inspires everyone. Make sure you see lots of different styles of dance; some tell a story, others are **abstract**, and some share the joy of dancing with us.

Informal assessment

You will have many different performance assessments during your 2-year course. Your teacher will carry out some of these in an informal way. At times you may not even be aware you are being assessed.

During your first fortnight of lessons, your teacher will informally assess your potential as a candidate. He/she will look at the skills you already have as a dancer, choreographer and writer on professional dance works, as well as your attitude. Your teacher will then give you specific targets to work towards in each of these areas.

Commitment

Commitment is an attitude of mind. It can be seen and felt by other people as you stand, sit or move at any moment in the day, as well as in a dance lesson, rehearsal or performance. In the context of dance, your attitude of mind is affected by:

❖ your health
❖ your diet
❖ your emotional state
❖ the amount of sleep you have had
❖ your thoughts about the dance, the music and other dancers

When your teacher assesses you, he/she will observe your attitude in class to see whether you show commitment. Commitment to the various tasks you are set is vital to your success on this course. It also provides an audience, examiner or a video camera with a high-quality performance. Although you will not be marked on 'commitment' itself, without it your grade will be lower than it need be.

Only you can decide whether you will be committed or not bother. Remember, though, that one person's negative approach to dancing can, and does, drastically affect other people. So, you should:

❖ adopt a positive, vital and dynamic approach
❖ get involved quickly and willingly
❖ concentrate and apply energy

If you and everyone in the class do this, you will all achieve better quality dance.

Showing commitment before class starts

❖ Arrive on time.
❖ Bring any notebooks or folders you need.
❖ Get changed quickly and quietly.
❖ Know what you should wear in class and bring it to every lesson — check that your trousers are suitable (not too long, too tight or too low on the hips).
❖ Find out what sort of top you are allowed to wear. Is yours appropriate?
❖ Remove all jewellery without being reminded.
❖ Make sure your hair is off your face, and tied back if necessary.
❖ Enter the dance space calmly and with a sense of purpose.
❖ Never chew gum or eat in class.
❖ Hand in your homework on time.

Not the best kit you could wear

Showing commitment when warming up or learning new steps

❖ Watch any demonstrations carefully, making sure you are in a place where you can see what is being shown.
❖ Concentrate on what you see and hear. This will help you to perform the same actions in the same way as those being demonstrated.

❖ Listen carefully to any images, corrections and points to remember that your teacher explains to the class, and to the rhythms of the music as you start moving.

❖ Once you have watched an exercise or dance sequence, try to perform it without copying anyone else.

❖ If you don't understand exactly what you are supposed to be doing, ask the teacher.

❖ Try to think at least one move ahead of yourself — if your brain cannot think through or remember a sequence, your body will not be able to dance it.

❖ Train your own **movement memory** so that you can perform the right actions in the right order.

❖ Understand and show the difference between 'marking' a sequence and dancing it 'full out'.

❖ Be prepared to be energetic, to feel tired and breathless or pushed to your limit.

❖ Keep working and trying.

Showing commitment to a particular dance

You need to remember:

❖ the steps in the right order

❖ where you are facing

❖ where you are going

❖ the rhythm of the steps

❖ how quickly or slowly you should move

❖ how you are supposed to hold your body, move your arms and legs etc.

❖ when to come on or go off stage

❖ the **role** or **character** you are playing

❖ what the **dance idea** is

Roles: child and grandparent

Keeping in character: 'Texan Kangaroo Rat'

You must try to:

- dance in time with the music
- dance sensitively and sensibly with the other dancers, and in time with them
- dance with a sense of energy and purpose
- keep the energy going throughout the dance
- keep your character and style of dance alive in your head and your body
- concentrate on the dance, and how you are making the dance idea obvious to the audience

Showing commitment to this course

You need to:

- arrive punctually to class
- wear the right kit
- look interested and ready to start
- concentrate on the task given to you
- work with as much energy as is required
- work sensibly and safely
- want to learn
- be willing to help others

Student in close-fitting T-shirt and trousers

Listening to the task being set

Section 1

Performance

Performance

This section deals with the aspects of performance that you will need to demonstrate in practical solos and group dances, and will enable you to answer questions on this topic in your written examination. It covers:

- ❖ good studio practice
- ❖ features of different techniques and performing skills
- ❖ the technical and expressive nature of dance
- ❖ performing in the style of a professional work

Good studio practice

The body is the dancer's instrument. The way you look after yourself is crucial. You need to have a certain amount of physical strength, stamina, flexibility and **control** to perform well, and how often you dance and for how long will affect issues such as what you should eat and how much water you should drink. How you are trained, and the environment in which you learn, are therefore vitally important to your progress.

This chapter deals with issues you must consider in looking after yourself as a dancer.

Food and diet

Nutrition

Dancers use more energy than the average person, and therefore need extra calories to keep a nutritional balance within the body. These calories should be in the form of carbohydrate, as this is the most efficient type of food for muscle activity.

Springs Dance Company: 'Stag Leap' by Charlotte Brown in *Be Not Entangled*, choreographed by Andrea Martin

Carbohydrate is stored as glycogen in the liver and muscles. If these stores are low during long rehearsal sessions, the dancer becomes tired and blood sugar levels drop. He/she could then feel weak, irritable, nervous and have headaches. You must therefore take care not to cut back on carbohydrate before a rehearsal or performance. You can find carbohydrate in cereals, root vegetables, pasta, potatoes and fruit.

Fat is not such an effective or efficient source of energy as carbohydrate, so you should consider carefully the percentage and type of fat you eat. Fat is in dairy products, oily fish, nuts and eggs.

Protein contributes to the growth and sustenance of human tissue, so you should ensure you eat enough of it. Any excess protein is either stored as fat or

excreted through the kidneys. Protein can be found in lean meat, dairy products, fish and pulses.

Vitamins are vital to the normal functioning of the body. A balanced diet (i.e. the correct proportions of carbohydrate, protein, fat, vitamins, mineral salts and fibre) will usually supply all the necessary vitamins. Dancers may need to take extra iron.

Weight and diet

Before you attempt to lose weight, you should always check with your doctor whether you are medically overweight and be careful that you do not diet unnecessarily.

Increasing your energy output or cutting back on calories can lead to losing weight. If fatty foods are a big part of your diet, then these can be cut back. Dieting has to be sensible so you do not become dehydrated and tired. Make sure you include enough salt in your diet, and drink plenty of water, especially in warm studios.

Big performances require lots of energy and endurance. Starving the week before is therefore extremely unwise — glycogen loss combined with rapid weight loss will affect your muscle mass and lead to an unsatisfactory performance.

The timing of your meals is also important. Food can take 2 hours to digest, so you should eat a good-sized meal more than 2 hours before a performance. This should be non-greasy, bland, easily digestible food with high carbohydrate content, such as pasta. Avoid fat, large amounts of protein, and gas-producing food before a performance.

Warming up and cooling down

In every dance class you must warm up your body at the beginning of the lesson and cool it down at the end. This section explains why and gives examples of exercises you could do.

Warming up

When you warm up:
* your breathing gets faster
* your heart rate changes
* your body temperature gets higher
* your muscles can stretch more efficiently and effectively

Warming up properly helps prevent injuries by making the dancer alert and ready for action.

Walking, skipping, gallops and jogging provide an aerobic warm up. They:

❖ make your muscles warmer
❖ increase flow of blood
❖ make you more alert
❖ make you breathless

These activities are a general, not a specific, way of warming up the body. They are unrelated to the particular focus of the class.

After an aerobic warm-up, dancers should start on stretching exercises. Stretch slowly at first, waking up the muscles in the back, neck, arms, legs and feet. Stretching exercises should be performed slowly, then gradually more quickly; simply at first, and then with a more complex **coordination** or rhythmic **structure**. For example, a ballet or contemporary dancer would do small or demi-**pliés** (knee bends) in various **positions** — first, second in **parallel** and turnout — before attempting grand pliés (large knee bends). He/she should only jump once the legs and feet have been warmed up, working through feet exercises (e.g. pointing the toes, peeling parts of the foot off the floor) and little jumps before trying big leaps.

Warming-up exercises

The numbers in brackets refer to counts.

Moving from place to place
Moving from place to place in the dance space, whether by walking, jogging, skipping or galloping, trains dancers to think about where they are going and to see other people in the space. It also increases their heart rate and makes them aware of their breath control.

Aerobic walking
1 a 8 walks forward, 8 walks backward, 4 walks forward, 4 walks backward, 2 walks forward, 2 walks backward, 4 walks in a half circle to face upstage.

b Repeat but end with a $^3/_4$ circular **pathway**.

c Repeat with a half circle.

d Repeat and finish facing front, with only 3 walks in a $^1/_4$ circular pathway.

e Repeat whole sequence starting with left foot and turning anticlockwise.

2 a 4 long slow walks forward, 4 long slow walks backward, feeling the feet reaching out. 2 slow walks forward and 2 slow walks backward. 4 ordinary walks in a half circle, wait for 4 counts.

b Repeat with left leg leading.

c Jog the original sequence once with right leg leading.

Box 1

Warming up the trunk exercises

1a: your head should follow your hands downwards

1b: your knees should be over your feet

2a: weight-bearing position

2i: elongated **balance** (press-up position)

2j: walking hands back

Aerobic travelling

1 In a circle, travelling clockwise first and then anticlockwise:

  a Jog gently.

  b Jog lifting knees in front.

  c Jog lifting feet behind.

  d Gallop sideways facing centre of the circle.

  e Gallop facing away from centre of circle.

  f Walk stretching arms above head.

  g Walk stretching arms behind the back.

  h Walk with arms over the head.

Warming up the trunk (Box 1)

The first exercise should be done slowly and carefully as you think about the movement of your upper back and neck, and the relationship between your knees and your toes.

1 a Stand in parallel, roll head down and forwards.

  b Bend knees and follow curl till fingers touch the floor.

  c Uncurl, keeping arms straight. As arms pass knees, ensure knees are over feet. Slowly stretch as body comes upright. Lower shoulder girdle and lift head.

  d Take 8 counts to roll down and 8 to roll up, then 4 counts down and up twice, and 8 down and up to finish.

2 a As above, but take curl into a weight-bearing position on hands and balls of feet.

  b Rock back onto flat feet, curled with knees bent and start uncurling action.

  c Roll down (1, 2, 3, 4).

  d Move hands down and take weight. (5, 6).

  e Hold still (7, 8).

Chapter

f Rock back onto feet and release hands (1, 2).

g Roll up, head down, hips up, chin in, hips to centre, stretch legs and unfold upper back (3, 4, 5, 6, 7, 8).

h Roll down (1, 2).

i Slide into an elongated balance on hands and feet (a press-up position) (3, 4).

j Walk hands back to flat feet, hips to heels, knees bent, lower head and show curled shape (5, 6).

k Roll up and finish (7, 8).

3 a Roll down (1, 2, 3, 4).

b Slide into elongated balance (5, 6) and hold still (7, 8).

c Walk hands in, knees bent, hips towards heels (1, 2, 3, 4).

d Release hands, head down, hips high, chin in and roll up to finish (5, 6, 7, 8).

Warming up the head, trunk and arms

These exercises start with the neck, gradually bringing in other parts of the upper body and simple actions in the legs.

1 a Lower head forwards (1, 2).

b Lift to centre (3, 4).

c Look right (5, 6).

d Look centre (7, 8).

e Look left (1, 2).

f Look centre (3, 4).

g Bend knees (5, 6) and stretch (7, 8).

h Bend knees and tilt head to right (1, 2).

i Lower head forwards (3, 4).

j Uncurl to stand upright (5, 6, 7, 8).

k Tilt head to left as you bend knees (1, 2).

l Lower head forwards (3, 4).

m Uncurl upper back to stand upright (5, 6, 7, 8).

n Bend knees, tilt head and shoulder girdle to right (1, 2) forwards (3, 4) and left (5, 6).

o Stand upright (7, 8).

p Repeat with other side.

2 a Reach right arm to right (1, 2).

b Lift up and over to left (3, 4).

c Lower down in front of body as knees bend (5, 6).

d Unfold body as you stretch knees (7, 8).

e Repeat with other side.

3 a As for exercise (2), but bend knees and tilt upper body to right as arm reaches right (1, 2).

b Stretch legs as arm reaches high (3).

c Bend knees and tilt upper body to left as right arm curves over to left (4).

d Curve forwards as arm lowers (5, 6).

e Reach to right as legs stretch (7) and lower to side (8).

Isolations

These exercises start with the shoulders on their own, gradually bringing in the arms and the whole body.

1 a Lift and lower shoulders 4 times (1–8).

b Alternate shoulders for 6 counts (1–6).

c Lower and wait (7, 8).

d Roll right shoulder backwards (1, 2).

e Place right hand on shoulder and roll elbow backwards (3, 4).

f Long arm circle backwards (5, 6).

g Reach high and **drop** arm (7, 8).

h Repeat with other arm.

i Repeat with both arms together.

j Reverse direction of roll and repeat the exercise.

Feet

These exercises will help you train your feet to point, **flex** and show clear positions.

1 a Lift and lower heel twice keeping ball of foot on floor (1–4).
   b Lift heel (5).
   c Lift and **point** whole foot down towards the floor (6).
   d Place ball, then flat (7, 8).
   e Repeat with other leg.
2 a Lift and point right foot down to the floor and place down 3 times (1–6).
   b Bend both knees and stretch (7, 8).
   c Repeat with left.
   d Feet together, bend knees (1).
   e Lift right heel (2).
   f Stretch left leg (3).
   g Rise on left (4).
   h Lower right foot (5).
   i Bend right knee (6).
   j Lower left heel (7) and stretch legs (8).
   k Repeat on other leg.
3 a Face front, feet parallel. **Brush** right foot forwards (1).
   b Close (2).
   c Repeat (3, 4).
   d Brush off floor (5).
   e Flex ankle (6).
   f Point on floor (7).
   g Lower heel (8).
   h Rise on **demi-pointe** (1, 2).
   i Lower heels (3, 4).
   j Lift right foot to parallel retiré (5).
   k Lower to plié (6) and stretch (7, 8).
   l Then repeat with other leg.
   m Repeat in turnout.

Stretches and swings

1 Arms in parallel, high above head. Reach from ribs, right arm higher, left arm higher, right arm higher, left arm higher, then make a sweeping swinging curve with both arms travelling forwards and down as knees bend. (Hands finish level with back of knees as they straighten). Reverse arms and curve back up to standing.
2 Stand with feet in slightly wider parallel. Repeat exercise, but increase body stretch on each reach by bending same leg as arm. Narrow parallel for swing down and up, doubling the speed of the swing. Add a straight arms-backward circle to high reach, rise on demi-pointe, and lower.
3 As for exercise 2, but add a small jump at bottom of swing. Repeat reaches, but bring arms down sides of body as it rolls down and out into press-up position. Then curl back up to standing.

1: swing from high parallel to deep back

3: moving out into the press-up position

Swings with twists

1 a In parallel, arms in second, wrap arms to right (1).

  b Lift in a swinging action to wrap to left (2) to right (3) to left (4).

  c Drop arms, fold body over outside of left leg with demi-plié (5).

  d Bring body to front (6).

  e Uncurl to standing and arms back to second (7, 8).

  f Repeat with other side.

2 a Swing as above, right (1) left (2) right (3) left (4).

  b Step, close, step to right. Arms travel from side to forward to side again (5, 6).

  c Then to the left (turning as you go) (7, 8).

  d Repeat with other side.

Swinging leg

1 a In **lunge**, slide back foot forward, lifting knee up towards chest (1, 2).

  b Then stretch leg back to lunge (3, 4).

  c Repeat twice more (5–8, 1–4).

  d Then bring feet together and change legs (5–8).

2 a In lunge, slide back foot forwards, lifting knee up towards chest (1, 2).

  b Brush foot backward, lifting toe back and up (3, 4).

  c Repeat forward swing (5, 6).

  d Then step forward (7, 8).

  e Repeat whole exercise on other leg. (Note that this exercise travels forward.)

Sitting on floor

1 a Sit with legs curled, arms around knees. Place hands, one after the other, on the floor by hips (1, 2).

  b Stretch one leg forward (3) then the other (4).

  c Reach arms up sides of body to high parallel (5).

  d Reach out to second (6) and curl around knees (7, 8).

  e Lead with fingertips backwards, with palms then sliding backwards along floor, tucking chin to chest and keeping knees bent, and lie down on back (1–4).

  f Press on palms, tuck chin in and curl back up to sitting (5–8).

2 a Sit with legs straight together in front of you. Flex right knee and ankle (1, 2).

  b Point right foot, extending upper leg surface (3, 4).

  c Repeat (5–8). Heels do not move.

  d Repeat with left knee and ankle (1–8).

  e Then both legs together (1–8).

  f Reach arms to high parallel above head, palms facing forward (1–4).

  e Fingertips lead down past shoulder and sides of body to brush palms along floor, reaching forwards beyond feet, and curve back up to high stretch (5–8).

  f Do this twice more (1–7).

  g Hold high reach (8).

  h **Suspend** and flex ankles. Reverse arm pattern three times (1–8, 1–4) (i.e. four counts for each pattern) and take arms back to floor (5–8).

Performance

Ways of coming up to standing or going down to the floor

1 From sitting, fold legs to one side, kneel on both knees, put one foot forwards, stand on it, and put feet together.

2 From standing, kneel on one knee, then the other knee, put one hand on floor, sit towards it, twist legs to front.

3 From two knees and two hands, curl toes under, take weight on balls of feet, walk hands to feet as weight transfers to whole feet, roll body up.

4 From standing, lunge forwards on right foot, place hands on floor by right foot, left knee on floor, then pull right knee back to join it. Sit up and over to right hip, pull legs round to front to sit.

5 Sit on right hip, place right hand on floor to right, lift hips off floor, walk or run legs around you to stand as you pick up your hand.

Using the back

1 a Stand in parallel with arms in second. Contract arms (curl as if holding a large beach ball) to first (1, 2).

b Stretch back to centre, arms to second (3, 4).

c Arch upper back up and back, arms by sides (5, 6).

d Tilt from hips, forward to flat back (7, 8).

e Plié with arms extending to second (1, 2).

f Twist whole shape to left (3, 4).

g Back to flat back in plié, but arms in second (5, 6).

1d: flat back position

h Drop body forwards in parallel plié (7, 8).

i **Arms high parallel** above head (1, 2).

j Arms and body curve forwards (3, 4).

k Roll up to stand in parallel, arms drop to sides, then lift out to second (5–8).

l Repeat with twist (f) to other side.

m Repeat at faster speed.

Simple jogging to small jumps

1 a Rock weight from right, left, right, left (1–4).

b Jog right, left, right, left (5–8).

c Spring to right, left, right, left (ski — 2 feet to 2 feet) (1–8).

d Jump forward, feet in parallel (1–2).

e Jump back, feet together (3, 4).

f Jump feet apart with half turn, landing feet apart (5, 6).

g Jump with half turn to front, land feet together (7, 8).

Arms could be added to the sequence. It could travel, or be varied within pairs.

Other travelling ideas

1 a Four walks, four jumps side to side, stretch high, touch floor, turn to start again.

b Repeat with little jogging steps, or with long runs, jumps turning $\frac{1}{4}$ turn.

Cooling down

Cooling down means winding down for about 5 minutes at the end of a class. It prevents:

❖ blood pooling in the legs

❖ the heart slowing down too quickly

❖ waste products from staying within muscles

If you don't cool down you may experience aching joints, tired muscles and less general stamina.

Cooling-down exercises

The exercises you might do depends on your body and the activities you have done in class. You could:

❖ Perform movements done earlier in class much more slowly.

❖ Gently stretch your hamstrings and calves.

❖ Lower your body down to the floor and slowly come back up to standing.

❖ Walk slowly.

❖ Stand in parallel and slowly roll forward and down towards the floor, and then slowly roll back up.

❖ In parallel and taking arms to second, tilt slowly to the right and back to upright, then to the left and back to centre. Bring arms to the sides, unfold them upwards to high parallel, open to a V-shape, and lower them to second.

❖ Bend and stretch legs in parallel twice. Rise slowly to demi-pointe, taking arms to second, to high parallel, slowly lower heels, then take arms back to sides.

❖ Go to kneeling position in parallel. Lower hips to heels, take arms low forwards along floor, so that your back is stretched and your neck is long. Transfer weight onto knees and hands: arch back slowly (holding tummy muscles strong), then contract back slowly, making a humped-back bridge shape.

❖ Sit on the floor in second. Stretch the inner thighs as legs are straight and gently moving from a V-shape, extending them towards wider second position. Stretch your arms and body to sides and forwards.

Avoidance and care of injury

Dancing is physically demanding, so you could injure yourself as easily as a footballer, athlete or tennis player. Ankle and knee injuries in dancers are common, as are pulled muscles, strained ligaments and backs. If you hurt yourself, or are with someone who is hurt, it is vital that you know what you can do to help, as well as knowing what you must not do.

The following mnemonics are intended to help you remember what you should and should not do with acute (less than 48 hours old) dance injuries. (Mnemonics are memory aids. Each letter of the word stands for one of the rules.)

PRICED: actions to help speed up the healing of acute injuries

Protect injured body parts from further injury.

Rest the injured part.

Ice, wrapped in a cloth, should be applied for 12–20 minutes every 2 hours for the first day.

Compression (using a pad to press down onto the injury) should be applied to injuries that include swelling or inflammation.

Elevation of the injured part above the level of the heart helps to reduce swelling.

Diagnosis is essential to find out what is wrong. Seek expert advice from a school nurse, doctor or hospital.

HARM: actions that might stop the healing of acute injuries

Heat should not be applied, as this will increase any internal bleeding linked with the injury. Do not have a hot shower or bath until you have seen an expert.

Alcohol will increase blood temperature and should therefore be avoided until you have seen an expert.

Running, dancing and physical activity increase body temperature. You should rest instead.

Massage should not be used, except by a qualified practitioner, as it also increases heat.

Dehydration

Dancers sweat a lot during daily classes, rehearsals and performances. If you do not drink enough water as part of your daily diet, you could suffer from any of the following:

❖ fatigue, or deep-seated tiredness
❖ inability to concentrate
❖ muscle cramps

* inability to react appropriately
* feelings of light-headedness

Your physical performance may be affected. Drinking water at regular intervals is a vital habit every dancer should adopt.

Health and safety in the performing space

Are there rules to be followed in your school? Do you follow them?

Health

* Always warm up.
* Wear several layers of clothing, which can be safely removed.
* Wear trousers that do not drape along the floor to prevent slipping on trailing material.

A dance space

* Check your dancers are wearing appropriate clothing for rehearsing your choreography.
* Do not eat or chew gum while dancing.
* Cover any sores or foot infections so you do not pass them on to others. You could wear soft, split-sole jazz shoes.
* Remember to breathe appropriately.
* Be aware of others in the space near you, and be prepared to adapt your movements if the distance between dancers is small.
* Adapt the movements in your choreography to suit any less-skilful dancers.
* Cool down, calm down, stretch and walk out of the space. This will allow your muscles to cool and your heart rate to drop, preventing lactic acid build-up.
* You should warm up and cool down dancers before and after teaching your choreography.
* Return to exercise gradually after an injury.
* Do not repeat a particular action too frequently as this could lead to injury.
* Take a plastic, screw-top bottle of water to class to keep yourself hydrated.

Is the floor in your dance space safe?

A clean, bright and airy dance space

Safety

Conditions

* Is the floor clean, free of splinters, not too slippery, and not a solid concrete base? Is it a sprung floor, or does it have a 'sprung' harlequin floor covering?
* Is the space at a safe temperature, so dancers do not injure themselves? The minimum recommendation is 20°C. Is the space air-conditioned, or does it have fans to move the air when needed?
* Are the mirrors clean and made of safety glass?
* Are there curtains to cover mirrors when necessary? Can they be safely opened and closed?
* Are there suitable changing and washing facilities?
* Are there any objects that might injure a dancer travelling at speed?

Equipment

❖ Is the sound system placed in an accessible, secure and safe area? Are its leads out of reach and tucked away? Can it be used safely by people of different heights?

❖ Are portable CD players etc. stored safely? Are they in good working order and tested annually? When in use, are the attached wires and extension leads kept out of the dance space?

❖ Where is visual equipment (i.e. televisions, DVD/video players, data projectors) placed? Who switches the equipment on and off? If items are on wheels, who stores them? Are they situated in a safe part of the performing space?

Spot the safety hazards

Suggested safety rules

❖ Only barefoot work is to take place in the studio. No outdoor shoes are allowed.

❖ Do not switch any power sockets on until all parts of the equipment are linked together.

❖ All electrical wires must be trailed along the sides of the studio.

❖ Where necessary, use masking tape to protect dancers from wiring.

❖ Conduct regular safety spot-checks.

❖ Only water in plastic bottles is allowed in the studio.

Safe practice in developing physical skills

❖ Position yourself sensibly in class, whether travelling across the space or moving on the spot.

❖ Be aware of your core strength and use your body muscles consciously in every exercise and dance phrase.

❖ Correctly align your leg joints while running, jumping or performing pliés. You must think about what these joints are doing and where the movement happens.

❖ Use full extension through the fingertips, toes, core and head to safely sustain a balance with a clear shape.

❖ Consider other dancers during contact work. Use the appropriate touch and strength in any grip when you support or lift another dancer.

❖ Time a contact movement safely.

❖ Listen and learn how to perform actions and visualise the instruction as you move.

Chapter 3

Techniques and performing skills

For GCSE dance, you are expected to perform in at least two different styles, to different types of music, in different places, for different purposes, and with different people. You should have technical skill in at least two dance styles.

Each dance **technique** has a particular **posture** (way of holding the body), specific use of the arms and legs, particular hand and foot **gestures**, and uses of the head and face. Dance styles have their own actions, and dancers must be aware of how these are done rhythmically, energetically and in the flow of each movement. Each technique uses the space around the body (**personal space**) and around the dance space (**general space**) in an identifiable style, and involves certain ways in which dancers relate to each other, with specific types of **physical contact**, or never touching.

Dancers are trained to make their bodies move accurately in a particular style or technique, whether that be ballet, flamenco, Russian Cossack, tap or ballroom. This training has to be safe, clear and appropriate to the age, experience and attitude of the dancer. Dancers need to know how their bodies should look as they dance in a particular style — the line of the body, the shapes of the arm gestures, the size and speed of the steps. Using a mirror to observe particular actions is a good way of correcting movements.

Training takes time, energy and commitment. Each technique and style is so different that specific training to perform each accurately is vital, whether this be in workshops led by qualified dancers/teachers in your school, or in special dance studios nearby. Whichever styles you perform in, you need to acquire technical (physical) and interpretative (expressive) skills, to communicate a dance idea through that style to an audience.

Learning particular warm-up exercises will help you absorb a style of dance both physically and mentally, as they will work specific muscles or joints.

All dance styles require you to be able to dance both in your personal space and travelling through the general space. You need to be able to control your body, and have awareness of your posture and a sense of balance. You will learn to coordinate the actions of your arms with those of your legs and feet, and how to move in time with the beats, accents and flow of the music. Learning short phrases of linked movements will gradually train and extend your movement memory.

As you become more technically skilled, you will move from a high to a low **level** with exciting jumps and falls. You will learn to perform both large and small actions with good control, and how to **project** strength and gentleness, sharpness and fluid, dynamic qualities. Thinking about your head and eyes will improve your use of **focus**.

Once you can control your body, you will want to dance with a partner or group of dancers. At this stage you need to train your awareness of another's body, as well as your own. You will need to develop how you watch other dancers and how you occupy the space, along with projecting accurately the idea and style of a dance.

A dancer has to learn how to move towards, past and away from another dancer, as well as how to dance sensitively in step. Making physical contact, for example by turning, tilting, carrying, lifting, lowering, pulling or pushing another dancer, needs guidance and training. Dancers must learn to support each other appropriately during physical contact, so that injuries are avoided.

The way you present your skills as a dancer changes, depending on whether you are performing a **solo**, in which case you have to project through the whole space, or a duo or **group dance**, where you have to project your relationships with the other dancers, the subject matter of the dance and your relationship with the audience. To project your dance skills you must have understood and absorbed the relevant technique, the **accompaniment** and the dance idea, as well as your role in the performance.

Note that you must wear the clothing most appropriate to the style of dance you choose. For example, performing morris dancing barefoot would be unsafe, and attempting pointe work in ballet without the correct footwear would be exceptionally dangerous.

The five styles covered in this chapter differ from each other in many ways. The photographs will give you an idea of the technical features of each. There are, of course, many other styles that you might already dance or know about; these will also be identifiable through their distinctive and particular movements, and the posture shown by the dancers.

Some styles will be more appropriate for GCSE Dance than others. Your dance teacher will choose those most appropriate for you, your school and its facilities, and the general experience and skills of your particular class. All dance techniques and styles have identifiable features in the way the body, limbs and head are used. Figure 1 shows these features. Figures 2–6 show the features of the various dance styles.

Figure 1
Features of
dance styles
and techniques

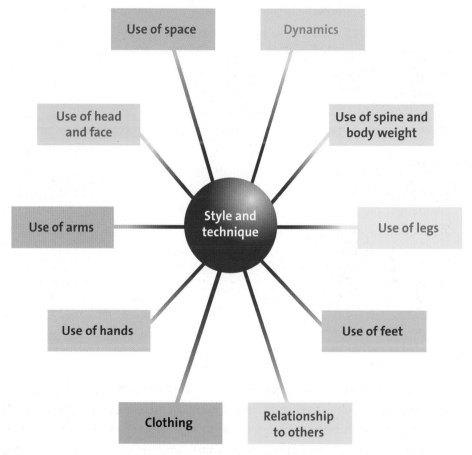

Classical ballet

Classical ballet is a style of dance you are unlikely to have experienced on a regular basis at your primary or secondary school. It is usually taught at private dancing schools by specially qualified ballet teachers; there will be at least one near where you live or go to school. This technique is centuries old and has recognisable features. Many of these are given in Figure 2.

Chapter 3

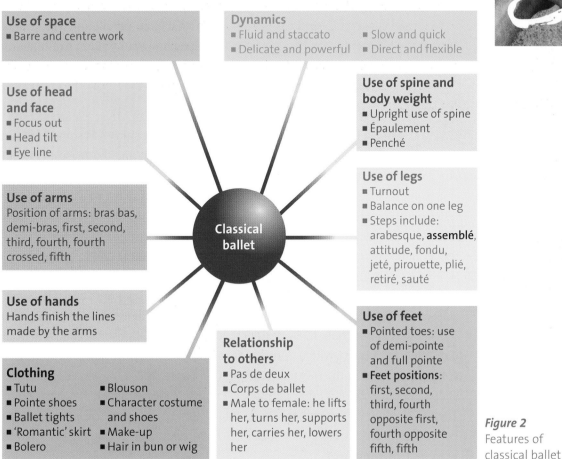

Use of space
- Barre and centre work

Dynamics
- Fluid and staccato
- Delicate and powerful
- Slow and quick
- Direct and flexible

Use of head and face
- Focus out
- Head tilt
- Eye line

Use of spine and body weight
- Upright use of spine
- Épaulement
- Penché

Use of arms
Position of arms: bras bas, demi-bras, first, second, third, fourth, fourth crossed, fifth

Use of legs
- Turnout
- Balance on one leg
- Steps include: arabesque, **assemblé**, attitude, fondu, jeté, pirouette, plié, retiré, sauté

Use of hands
Hands finish the lines made by the arms

Classical ballet

Use of feet
- Pointed toes: use of demi-pointe and full pointe
- **Feet positions:** first, second, third, fourth opposite first, fourth opposite fifth, fifth

Clothing
- Tutu
- Pointe shoes
- Ballet tights
- 'Romantic' skirt
- Bolero
- Blouson
- Character costume and shoes
- Make-up
- Hair in bun or wig

Relationship to others
- Pas de deux
- Corps de ballet
- Male to female: he lifts her, turns her, supports her, carries her, lowers her

Figure 2
Features of classical ballet

Terminology

Classical ballet has its own terms for specific positions of the arms, legs, feet and body, most of which are in the original French. These make identifying particular movements and shapes easy for you, your teacher and examiners. The terms you might hear or read most often are 'plié', **'fondu'**, **'retiré'** and **'relevé'**, all of which are described in the Glossary on pages 240–47. There are photographs of some of these positions and movements in the pages that follow.

Balletic terms also appear in the teaching of other dance styles, as most professional dancers will have experienced ballet as part of their training. The five positions of the feet, which are used in turnout in ballet, appear in parallel in **contemporary dance**. Similarly, contemporary dance varies ballet's five **arm positions** by using different **dynamic** qualities, hand shapes or degrees of bend or stretch.

It is worth knowing balance terms, such as 'attitude' and '**arabesque** en l'air', as you might want to use these recognisable shapes in parallel or with a bent supporting leg (fondu), both in your choreography and your written examination paper.

Training

How you stand in these various ballet positions — your posture — is something you should know and understand. Your spine is often upright and the muscles in your stomach (core), legs and feet have to work hard to control each action accurately.

It is all too easy to perform ballet movements incorrectly, so you should be taught by a trained ballet teacher for at least a short series of workshops in order to learn how to control your legs, feet, body and arms. You will also learn new movements you could adopt later for choreographic tasks, and terms to use in written exam papers and assessments set by your teacher.

You could find out which styles of ballet are taught in your area and if beginner classes for teenagers are available. Ballet teachers should ideally have RAD, ISTD (Cecchetti and Imperial), IDTA or BBO teaching qualifications. Alternatively, your dance teacher could invite a dancer, teacher or animateur from one of the ballet companies listed in the Resources section on pages 207–39 to lead some workshops at your school. The Royal Ballet, English National Ballet, Northern Ballet Theatre Company, Birmingham Royal Ballet, Rambert Dance Company, Scottish Ballet and Independent Ballet Wales all have education departments that run workshop programmes.

If you hope to become a dancer in any style, you would be wise to undertake ballet classes to support the physical training of your body. The photographs in this book are of students who have had ballet training.

Features of classical ballet

Positions of feet

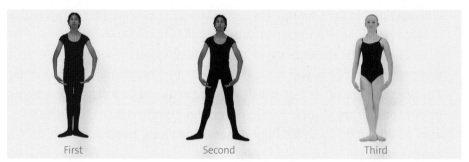

First   Second   Third

Fourth opposite first | Fourth opposite fifth | Fifth

Positions of arms

First | Second | Third

Fourth | Fourth crossed | Fifth

Bras bas | Demi-bras

Key arm shapes and steps

First arabesque

Second arabesque

Third arabesque

Arabesque penché

Attitude ordinaire en l'air

Grand fourth in open arabesque

Demi-plié

Rond de jambe á terre

Retiré

Chassé

Chapter

Contemporary dance (Graham technique)

Martha Graham formed her ideas in the USA as new way of moving in comparison to classical ballet. The spine is used differently, and the hand and feet shapes are more angular and strong. It includes work on the floor, with **contraction**, **release** and **spiral** actions, which were not part of a normal ballet class.

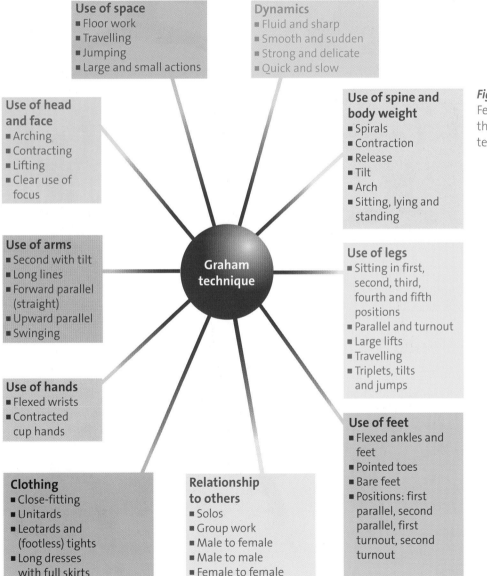

Use of space
- Floor work
- Travelling
- Jumping
- Large and small actions

Dynamics
- Fluid and sharp
- Smooth and sudden
- Strong and delicate
- Quick and slow

Use of head and face
- Arching
- Contracting
- Lifting
- Clear use of focus

Use of spine and body weight
- Spirals
- Contraction
- Release
- Tilt
- Arch
- Sitting, lying and standing

Use of arms
- Second with tilt
- Long lines
- Forward parallel (straight)
- Upward parallel
- Swinging

Graham technique

Use of legs
- Sitting in first, second, third, fourth and fifth positions
- Parallel and turnout
- Large lifts
- Travelling
- Triplets, tilts and jumps

Use of hands
- Flexed wrists
- Contracted cup hands

Use of feet
- Flexed ankles and feet
- Pointed toes
- Bare feet
- Positions: first parallel, second parallel, first turnout, second turnout

Clothing
- Close-fitting
- Unitards
- Leotards and (footless) tights
- Long dresses with full skirts

Relationship to others
- Solos
- Group work
- Male to female
- Male to male
- Female to female

Figure 3
Features of the Graham technique

Features of contemporary dance (Graham technique)

Sitting positions

First

Second

Third

Fourth

Fifth

Positions in medium level

Tilt and roll

Flat back in parallel plié

Lunge

Jumps

Split leap

Two to two on spot

Turning jump: one to the other

Stag leap

Balances

On right leg: left leg elongated

On left leg and right hand

Graham technique exercises

Sitting

Contractions

These four exercises could be linked together. The weight should be on the hip bones.

1 a Sit upright with legs bent, soles of feet touching (first position) and hands resting on front of shin bones or ankles.

b Curve over forwards, contracting tummy muscles and lowering top of head

towards feet. Bend arms outside legs
as you curve down.

  c Breathe out as you curl, taking 8 counts.

  d Return to starting position: release the light
contraction shifting weight slightly forwards, pull chin in, stretch back to upright,
and bring chin up as you look ahead.

  e Straighten arms as you breathe in over
8 counts.

2 a Sit in second position, arms in second
and legs in turnout (knees to ceiling),
toes pointed, stretching spine.

  b Curve forwards, breathing out as you
extend top of head to the floor. Rest
hands lightly on shins. Take 8 counts.

  c As for the first exercise, reverse back to
starting position taking 8 counts.

3 a Sit upright in first parallel, legs extended
straight in front of you in parallel, arms
also parallel in front of you (1–4).

  b Curve over forwards, extending top of
head to knees (5–8).

  c Arms curve towards the body as you
breathe out over 8 counts.

  d Reach arms forward away from you past
the outsides of your legs.

  e Reach up high (1–4) and back to starting
point (5–8).

4 a Sit upright, legs bent and crossed in fifth
position, arms by sides, hands just
touching the floor.

  b Roll hips under, contract muscles
and breathe out (spine curves out
backwards, lengthening) (1–4).

  c Straighten spine, shifting weight
forward slightly, breathing in (5–8).

  d Lift chest to ceiling, arching upper back
so that face is to ceiling (1–4).

  e Come back to upright (5–8).

This exercise could also be done sitting with
knees bent, legs parallel, soles of feet on floor
and hands resting on outside of knee caps.

Side stretches

1 It is important to keep both hips on the
floor throughout this exercise.

  a Sit in second, toes pointed, arms in
second, with palms facing ceiling.

  b Reach right arm out to right, with left
curving over head to right (1–4).

  c Curve forward, palms facing shins, top of
head to floor (5–8).

  d Reach left arm out to left, with right
curving over to left (1–4).

  e Bring right arm back over head to
starting position (5–8).

  f Repeat with flexed feet, going to left
first, still taking 4 counts to each stretch.

  g Then take 2 counts for each stretch, both
sides, then 1, making the flow of the arms
continuous and the breathing smooth,
with both hips staying on the floor.

Remember to keep your legs straight,
feeling the extension. Toes should be
pointed or ankles flexed.

Working leg and feet muscles, using ankle and knee joints

1 a Sit in first parallel, both legs straight and
toes pointed.

  b Bend right knee and flex ankle joint
(heel not moving on floor) (1, 2).

  c Stretch right leg and point toe (left leg
stays straight and pointed) (3, 4).

  d Repeat flex with right (5–8).

  e Repeat flex and stretch twice with left
(1–8).

Sitting with legs parallel and feet pointed

1 a Alternate legs: right flex, left flex (1–4).

  b Right flex, left flex (5–8).

  c Repeat both legs together, flex and stretch twice (1–8).

  d Flex both legs together (1, 2).

  e Rotate outwards (3, 4).

  f Stretch toes (5, 6).

  g Close (7, 8).

  h Repeat (1–8).

  i Turn legs out (1, 2).

  j Bend knees and flex ankle joints (3, 4).

  k Bring legs to parallel, knees staying bent (5, 6).

  l Straighten to first parallel with legs straight (7, 8).

Sitting with legs parallel and feet flexed

Travelling

Triplets

1 Perform these in turnout. The pattern is down, up, up.

  a Start standing on left leg, with right stretched behind you (toe on floor).

  b Take a long step forward on a bent right leg (1).

  c Step forwards onto demi-pointe (ball of foot) of left leg (2).

  d Step high on demi-pointe of right foot (both legs are in relevé) (3).

  e Repeat triplet with left leg (1–3).

  f Side step, tilt with leg in second en l'air, cross step (1–3).

  g Repeat part (f) (1–3).

Hops and leaps

1 Perform these in 3/4 rhythm.

  a Step, step, hop (1–3).

  b Repeat on same leg (1–3).

    You could try these with:

    ❖ either side of the body

    ❖ different leg shapes

    ❖ different arm shapes

    ❖ with half turns

2 Perform these in 4/4 rhythm.

  a Step, step, step (1–3).

  b Leap and land (4).

  c Repeat with same leg.

  d Do the whole sequence on other leg.

Street dance

Street dance is the name given to a style that has features of American street locking, b-boying, body popping, breakdance, **capoeira**, kung fu and other martial arts, hip-hop and pop bands. It is a high-energy form of dance that demands great concentration, a keen sense of rhythm, good coordination and a wide range of dynamics. It is academically recognised as a social and popular **dance style**, rather than as having aesthetic or artistic qualities.

Street dancers wear hoodies, cotton trousers and T-shirts, caps and trainers; girls not spinning on the floor might wear cropped tops. They dance to rap or modern pop music, and appear in pop videos, concerts, on the streets and more recently at London theatres.

Features of street dance

Street dance includes simple stepping patterns, floor work and acrobatics. It has contrasting dynamics — both fluid and staccato — and a sense of risk and excitement. Focus and timing are important. Body parts move in isolation as dancers perform **locks**, **pops** and stops, windmills, freezes and handstands. Figure 4 outlines the features of street dance.

Figure 4
Features of
street dance

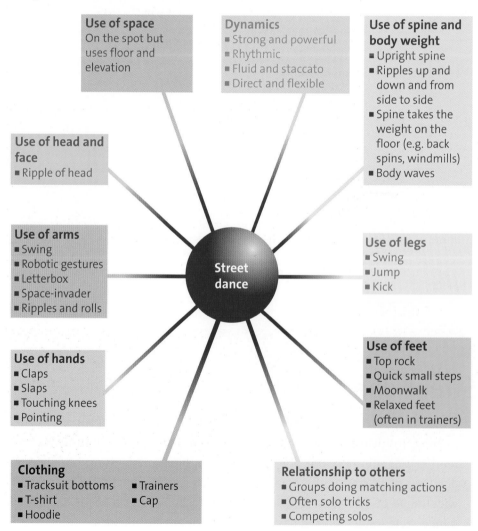

Use of space
On the spot but uses floor and elevation

Dynamics
- Strong and powerful
- Rhythmic
- Fluid and staccato
- Direct and flexible

Use of spine and body weight
- Upright spine
- Ripples up and down and from side to side
- Spine takes the weight on the floor (e.g. back spins, windmills)
- Body waves

Use of head and face
- Ripple of head

Use of arms
- Swing
- Robotic gestures
- Letterbox
- Space-invader
- Ripples and rolls

Use of legs
- Swing
- Jump
- Kick

Street dance

Use of hands
- Claps
- Slaps
- Touching knees
- Pointing

Use of feet
- Top rock
- Quick small steps
- Moonwalk
- Relaxed feet (often in trainers)

Clothing
- Tracksuit bottoms
- T-shirt
- Hoodie
- Trainers
- Cap

Relationship to others
- Groups doing matching actions
- Often solo tricks
- Competing solos

Table 1 Key moves of street dance

Source	Moves
American street locking	❖ locks ❖ points ❖ rolls ❖ freezes ❖ spins
Body popping	❖ small, slight movements ❖ pops ❖ waves — rippling movements along limbs, up and down body ❖ moonwalk ❖ high energy — gives you a buzz
Pop bands	❖ simple steps ❖ high-energy shapes ❖ intricate moves for a pop video, basic moves for a live show ❖ raw, expressive — allows you to let your hair down ❖ movements from t'ai chi, disco dancing, lyrics ❖ keep your own individuality ❖ has 'attitude' ❖ dance both in unison and canon ❖ uses lyrics
Hip-hop (American Afrocentric style)	❖ no scenery — can use any space ❖ loose arm moves and claps ❖ jumps ❖ kicks ❖ changes of direction
Breakdance	❖ imitating kung fu, marionettes, computer graphics, cartoons ❖ folding yourself in and making a new shape ❖ shuffling steps to clear a space for yourself, e.g. top rock and boxer's shuffle ❖ six step — weight on hands and feet, moving around, cutting back and forth ❖ text ❖ showing off footwork

Freeze positions

Freeze one   Freeze two   Freeze three

Freezes inspired by *Dance Tek Warriors*

Bharata Natyam

Bharata Natyam is a form of South Asian dance, and the classical dance style of southern India. It is danced to Carnatic music. Instruments used to accompany it could include a *mridangam* (drum), a *vina* (violin), a bamboo flute, *thallam* (or *manjira* — small cymbals), a *gottuvadyam* (stringed instrument) and a vocalist.

The name itself comes from the following:

❖ **BHA**va means expression
❖ **RA**ga means music
❖ **TA**la means rhythm
❖ **Natyam** means dance

Table 2 Distinctive features of Bharat Natyam (given in their Punjabi names)

Some positions of the body, legs and feet	Description
Araimandi	A half-bend from which all other movement develops.
	The body is divided into three sections as three equilateral triangles:
	1. Upper body from centre of stomach reaching out to elbows 2. From hips to knees in a wide turnout 3. In a half-bend: from the ankle joints to the knees
Aayatham	The aramandi position.
Muzhumandi	Aramandi position with knees fully bent and weight on balls of feet.
Sthaarakam	Standing feet together.
Prenkharam	One leg in half bend, the other extended to the side with weight on heel.
Swasthikam	One foot flat, the other on ball or toe of foot, crossed behind or in front of supporting leg.
	One knee bent, other extended to side but with foot turned in and weight on ball of foot.

Some positions of the hands	Description
Dola	Hand relaxed with all fingers pointing downwards.
Alapadma	All fingers spread with palm upwards.
Patāka	All fingers close together with thumb bent near to palm, which is facing forwards.
Soochi	Index finger pointing forward, all others curled into palm, with thumb resting on middle finger.
Mushti	All fingers curled into palm, with thumb resting on middle finger.
Katakamukha	Index and middle fingers touch thumb, while last two fingers extend upwards.
Sikhara	Thumb stretches upright while all fingers are curled into the palm.
Hamsasyam	Index finger on thumb, other fingers stretched and spread.
Mrigasirsha	Thumb and little finger reach strongly upward as middle three fingers bend from knuckles inward.
Pallava	Wrists of hands crossed with palms facing outwards.
Kartarimukha	Crossed wrists: index and middle fingers extended, other two fingers curled into palm and held by thumb.

There are three techniques: Nritta, Natya and Nyrta.

❖ Nritta uses movement for its own sake. It is a pure dance style.

❖ Natya is a dramatic style in which a theme is performed.

❖ Nyrta expresses emotion in a mimetic way.

It is a style of dance most often seen as a solo.

The costume and jewellery worn by Bharat Natyam dancers is colourful, ornate and often symbolic. Their costumes are brightly coloured and in one of these styles: skirt style, skirt style with crossed pleats, saree style or pyjama style. A knife-pleated fan is often used and garments can be knee- or calf-length. Jewellery adorns various parts of the body: a headset on the head, studs in the ears and nose, bangles on the wrists, a belt around the waist, anklets and bells around the ankles, and the hair is plaited. Dancers wear facial make up and decorate their hands and feet with alts (a red pigment) to emphasise the hand and feet positions.

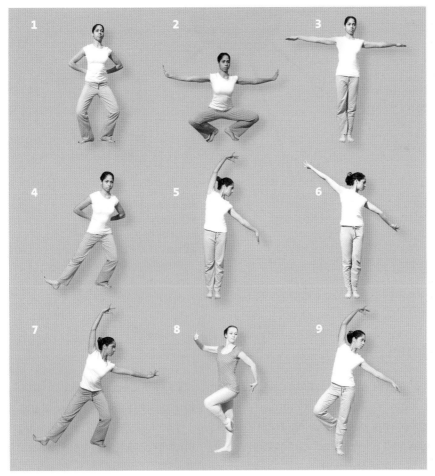

1 Aayatham: the aramandi position

2 Muzhumandi: aramandi position with knees fully bent and weight on balls of feet

3 Sthaarakam: standing feet together

4 Prenkharam: one leg in half bend, the other extended to the side with weight on heel

5 Dola: hand relaxed with all fingers pointing downwards

6 Alapadma: all fingers spread with palm upwards

7 Katakamukha: index and middle fingers touch thumb, while last two fingers extend upwards

8 Sikhara: thumb stretches upright while all fingers are curled into the palm

9 Hamsasyam: index finger on thumb, other fingers stretched and spread

The features of Bharat Natyam are outlined in Figure 5.

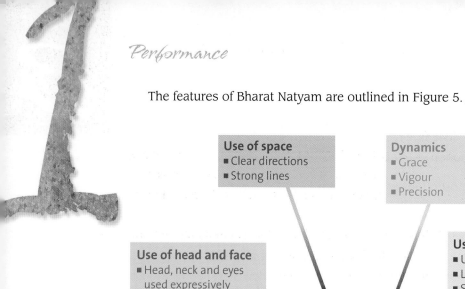
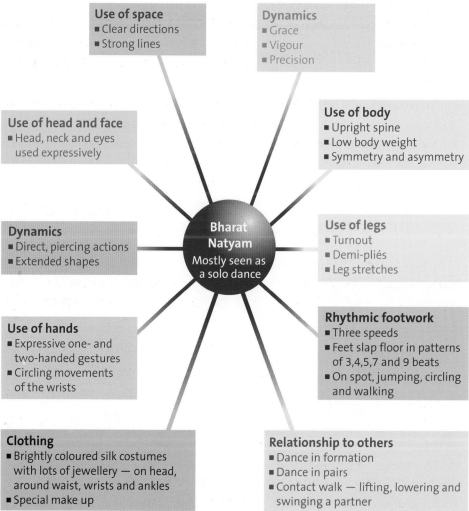

Figure 5 Features of Bharat Natyam

Capoeira

Capoeira is of Afro-Brazilian origin and embraces elements of dance, martial art, philosophy, culture, history, music and, for some practitioners, a way of life. The beauty of capoeira is that each dancer (player) is an individual. The dynamics are infinite as it allows freedom of expression, rather like contact improvisation.

Basic movements

Ginga (swing or sway)

Ginga is the essence, heartbeat, or breath of capoeira. Ginga means to swing, and the whole body swings when you ginga. When you play capoeira, or when it is improvised, ginga is performed throughout, and especially between all other movements.

Ginga is like walking; it is simple and has to be performed in as relaxed and grounded a way as possible. You may find it tricky and awkward to do at first, but with practice you will become used to the floor pattern and the coordination of your arms and legs.

Ginga parallel starting position 1

Start with the feet parallel. Remember the imaginary line at the tips of your toes — this will stop you from moving off the spot.

Ginga with right foot back 2

Take the right foot back. Drop your body down through the pelvis, so that your legs are bent and you are in a comfortable, relaxed but strong posture.

Back to parallel 3

Step the right foot back to parallel and then repeat with the other foot.

Ginga with left foot back 4

Remember:

* the heel of the back foot is never on the floor
* the legs should always be bent
* the arms swing from side to side in coordination with the legs — if the right foot is forward, the body and arms swing to the right
* when the feet come back to parallel, the arms come back to parallel in front of the chest or face

All the other movements listed and described below should be initiated out of the ginga.

Esquiva lateral (escape or dodge sideways)

Your feet should be parallel but further apart than in contemporary dance, as you have to drop your body to either side. When you drop to the right, your right hand is on the floor, just slightly behind you, your right leg is almost fully bent and your

left leg is extended (but not fully straight). Both feet are flat on the floor and your left arm and hand are in front of your face or chest to protect your personal space from any intrusion by a partner.

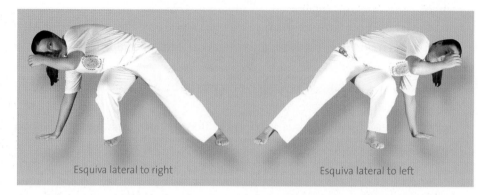

Esquiva lateral to right | Esquiva lateral to left

Negativa lateral (escape or dodge sideways press-up)

This needs more upper body strength than **esquiva lateral**, as you have to lower yourself fully to the floor, with your arms bent, in a sideways press-up position. The only parts of your body touching the floor are your feet and hands.

Again your feet should be parallel but further apart than in contemporary dance. Your body drops to the right side, then your right hand, followed by your left hand, go to the floor on your right side. Your right leg is almost fully bent (your right knee underneath your body, facing forwards) and your left leg is extended (but not fully straight). Your right heel may come off the floor and your left foot is planted on the floor.

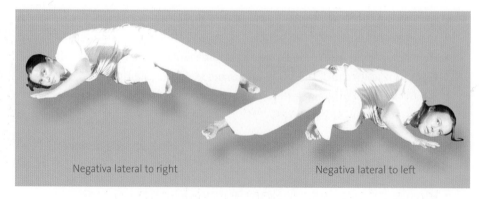

Negativa lateral to right | Negativa lateral to left

Aú (cartwheel)

There are many variations on the cartwheel. For beginners, the basic cartwheel with the legs straight and in a V, or bent and close to the body, are the best to try.

When you cartwheel in capoeira, your focus is not down to the ground, as in a gymnasts' cartwheel, but out towards your partner, keeping a long neck. You reach directly down to the ground with your hands and arms (not high into the air first, as in gymnastics).

Aú to right (1)   Aú landing (2)   Aú landing (3)

Rolê (grounded cartwheel)

This is similar to the **aú**, but the feet stay on the floor, using it and sliding, dividing the weight between the hands and feet. The head is relaxed with the back of the neck long and the focus is looking through the arms and legs at your partner. The legs are gently bent with equal weight on the arms. As you travel to the right, the left foot draws a semicircle, followed by the right foot drawing another semi-circle to end back in the parallel position.

In the photographs of a **rolê** to the left below, notice how the head looks out all the time.

Rolê to left

Meia lua de frente (half-moon kick to the front)

With your feet in parallel position, kick one leg first out to the side. Then carry it across the body at waist height to the front. To finish, bend the kicking leg at the knee and put it back down into parallel. Remember, the kicking leg cuts a curve through space, with the supporting leg bent and on a flat foot.

Kick to side   Carry it across   Bending the knee

Rabo de arraia (sting ray tail)

1. Take the right foot back (as with the ginga).
2. With both legs bent, twist body to right and place hands on the floor between the feet. Your right hand is by your right foot with your left hand next to your right hand. Your chest is wide, and you can see your partner.
3. Lean on your left leg, keeping it bent. Your right leg kicks up and around at waist height.
4. Use your hands to walk yourself back to parallel position.
5. You can then ginga to change legs.

Bênção (1) (blessing; front straight kick)

1 Take the right foot back (as with the ginga), with both legs bent in a strong and grounded stance.
2 The right foot then kicks through with a flexed foot, as if to push open a door, using the whole foot, and goes back to the starting position.
3 You can then ginga once to change legs, and the left leg will kick through and back.

This kick needs you to force the kicking leg forward, and you must counter-balance by leaning the upper body back. Pushing through the hips will help you to maintain a lifted and strong posture and kick.

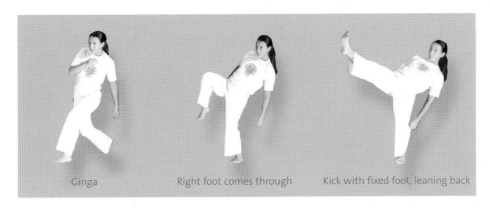

Ginga   Right foot comes through   Kick with fixed foot, leaning back

Cocorinha (escape or dodge through crouching)

1 With your feet in parallel and touching, sink to a squatting position, with your knees together and heels off the floor.
2 Keep your head lifted as you look at your partner. Your arms should stay crossed and lifted in front of your face and slightly above your head.

Queixada (step into reverse half-moon kick)

1 Take the left foot back (as with the ginga), with both legs bent in a strong and grounded stance. Turn the body 90° towards your left foot; keep your focus facing your partner.

2 Step your left foot behind your right heel.

3 Lift your right leg as a kick that travels up, out and forwards across the body, in a semi-circular air pattern, to land behind the left foot.

This can be repeated with the other leg, turning 90° to the right and then kicking with the left leg.

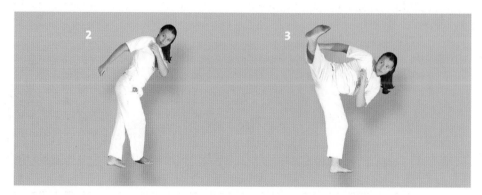

Armada (step back, turn, with reverse half moon kick)

1 Take the right foot back (as with the ginga), with both legs bent in a strong and grounded stance. Spiral by twisting on the balls of your feet towards the right foot. Turn all the way round until you can see your partner again.

2 Release the spiral by lifting the right leg, kicking all the way round to unravel the twist, and placing the right foot back in its original starting position.

3 Ginga once to change feet so that the left foot is back and you can spiral towards your left foot and repeat the kick with the other leg.

End of spiral   Kick round

Capoeira sequences

Sequence 1: Bênção and cocorinha	
Dancer A	**Dancer B**
Dancers should be mirroring each other as they ginga.	
Ginga x 4, stepping back on right leg first.	Ginga x 4, stepping back on left leg first.
On the last ginga, when your left foot is at the back, prepare for **bênção**, with the left foot kicking forwards at waist height	On the last ginga, when your right foot is at the back and you see your partner preparing to kick with bênção, bring the feet to parallel and drop down into **cocorinha**.
Once you have done the sequence on both sides, change roles.	

Remember: when performing bênção, you must try to push the hips forward, counterbalancing with your upper body. Keep a strong base and your arms to yourself. When using cocorinha, remember to make yourself as small as possible by keeping your heels off the floor, your knees together and your arms crossed above your head to protect you.

Sequence 2: Meia lua de frente, rabo de arraia, esquiva and negativa lateral	
Dancer A	**Dancer B**
Dancers should be mirroring each other as they do the ginga.	
Ginga x 4, stepping back on right leg first.	Ginga x 4, stepping back on left leg first.
On the last ginga, when your left foot steps back into parallel, kick with right leg a **meia lua de frente** at waist level towards your partner and place your right foot back to parallel.	On the last ginga, when your right foot is at the back and you see your partner's kick beginning, step back into parallel and dodge the kick by softly dropping your right hand, followed by left into **negativa lateral**.
As you place your right foot down, and see that Dancer B has dropped into negativa lateral and is performing a **rabo de arraia** kick, you gracefully lower your body down to your left to esquiva lateral.	You now respond with another kick, which unravels from your negativa lateral. You reposition, adjust your weight and perform a rabo de arraia with your right leg.

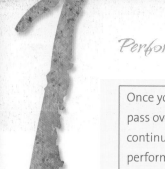

Once you have seen Dancer B's foot pass over your upper body and head, continue the momentum to the left, performing a rolê and coming back to stand in parallel.	Following the momentum of your kick, place your right foot on a parallel line. Continue by performing an aú to your right, and land standing in parallel.
Once you have completed the sequence on both sides, change roles.	

Remember: you should always be able to see your partner. Adjust your head position and relax the back of you neck so you can see between the arms and legs.

The features of capoeira are outlined in Figure 6.

Figure 6
Features of capoeira

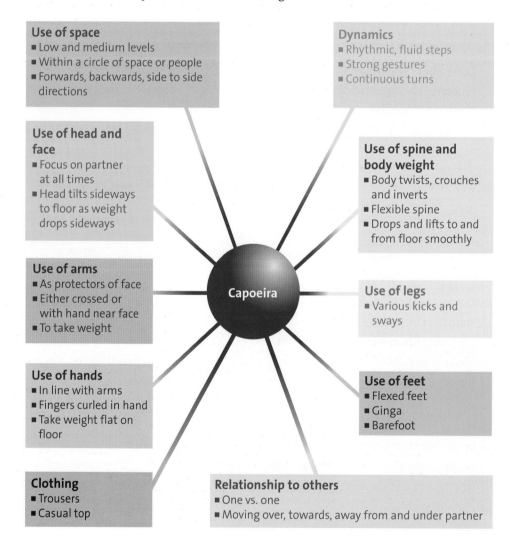

Use of space
- Low and medium levels
- Within a circle of space or people
- Forwards, backwards, side to side directions

Dynamics
- Rhythmic, fluid steps
- Strong gestures
- Continuous turns

Use of head and face
- Focus on partner at all times
- Head tilts sideways to floor as weight drops sideways

Use of spine and body weight
- Body twists, crouches and inverts
- Flexible spine
- Drops and lifts to and from floor smoothly

Use of arms
- As protectors of face
- Either crossed or with hand near face
- To take weight

Capoeira

Use of legs
- Various kicks and sways

Use of hands
- In line with arms
- Fingers curled in hand
- Take weight flat on floor

Use of feet
- Flexed feet
- Ginga
- Barefoot

Clothing
- Trousers
- Casual top

Relationship to others
- One vs. one
- Moving over, towards, away from and under partner

The technical and expressive nature of dance

This chapter looks at what dancers do, how they move, where they go, and how they relate to each other. This is different for each style of dance, but the basic vocabulary you will need for your written examination is the same. You will need to be able to name actions, dynamics, uses of **space** and **relationships**, describing each in detail and explaining how they communicate an idea within a dance you or a professional choreographer have created.

Technical nature

Each dancer has to acquire physical and interpretative (expressive) skills to show particular techniques in dance. The physical skills are listed with descriptions in Table 3. The interpretative skills are described on page 68.

Table 3
Physical skills

Skills	Description
Accuracy	Observing, interpreting and reproducing exactly the actions you see
Alignment	Positioning of body parts in relation to the whole body shape
Balance	Controlling the weight on a particular support
Body awareness	Kinaesthetic knowledge — what is moving, where and how
Control	Performing the actions with skill and sensitivity, and the appropriate muscular awareness
Coordination	Controlling all parts moving at the same time
Dynamic awareness	How you move, e.g. quickly, slowly, gently, strongly, energetically
Extension	Stretching into the space
Flexibility	The range of movement in a joint
Flow	How the energy moves from one action to the next
Movement memory	Remembering the order of actions accurately
Posture	How the body is held when sitting, lying down etc.
Spatial awareness	Knowing where you are facing, the direction of the action and its size, level and shape
Stamina	Endurance — both muscular and cardio-respiratory
Strength	Muscle power needed to perform an action

The basic technical elements of dance are shown in Figure 7.

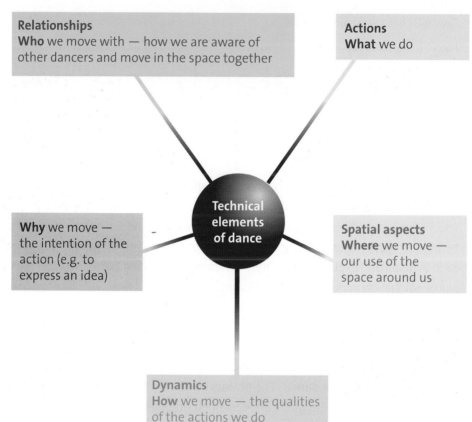

Relationships
Who we move with — how we are aware of other dancers and move in the space together

Actions
What we do

Why we move — the intention of the action (e.g. to express an idea)

Technical elements of dance

Spatial aspects
Where we move — our use of the space around us

Dynamics
How we move — the qualities of the actions we do

Figure 7
Basic technical elements

Actions: what we do

During your 2-year course you will experience ordinary everyday actions, simple combinations of stylised dance actions, and complex sequences of actions that require great physical and dynamic skill to control and perform well. Actions can be small, for example a gesture such as wagging a finger, or large, such as a grand **jeté** (split leap) with arms in extended arabesque. They can happen within your own personal space or move into the general space around you.

You need to know the difference between what action is being performed and how or where it is being danced. You will have to **identify** which part of the body is moving, and what it is doing; this could be a whole body movement, or just one arm. We have a head, neck, shoulders, arms, elbows, wrists, hands, fingers, chest, spine, waist, hips, legs, knees, ankles, feet and toes. Some of these parts are more flexible than others and some take our weight more easily.

Figure 8 shows the range of actions undertaken in dance.

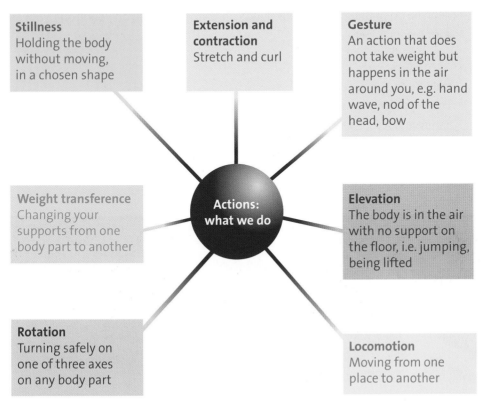

Stillness
Holding the body without moving, in a chosen shape

Extension and contraction
Stretch and curl

Gesture
An action that does not take weight but happens in the air around you, e.g. hand wave, nod of the head, bow

Weight transference
Changing your supports from one body part to another

Actions: what we do

Elevation
The body is in the air with no support on the floor, i.e. jumping, being lifted

Rotation
Turning safely on one of three axes on any body part

Locomotion
Moving from one place to another

Figure 8
Actions

Locomotion
Moving from one place to another

Locomotion can use your feet, for example walking, jogging, running or a mixture of steps and jumps. It can be rolling, curled and elongated, and on different surfaces of the body. You can slide on different parts of the body. Movement can be forwards, backwards, sideways or while turning, along any pathway you make.

Weight transference
Changing your support from one body part to another

You can transfer your weight from one part of your foot to another, or perhaps from your feet to your hands or front of your body.

Moving into rolls

For example, from standing on two feet, move one foot back and go down on the knee, then onto both knees. Sit on one hip and use one hand to support you. Then sit on both hips with your hands on your knees. Lie on your front, your side, your back and sit.

Stillness

Holding the body without moving, in a chosen shape

The supports you use to keep your body still could, for example, be a foot, two hands and a foot, or one knee and a foot. You should hold your body in an 'alive' position. The stillness can be brief or quite prolonged.

Stillness could be in the form of a balance, for instance standing still in a lunge, with your arms and head in a chosen position.

Balances, different supports and body shapes

Inspired by *Overdrive*

Inspired by *Overdrive*

A moment from *Texan Kangaroo Rat*

Inspired by *Dance Tek Warriors*

Gesture

An action that does not take weight but happens in the air around you

A gesture can be a wave, shake, point, kick, clap, click, nod, twist, curve, stretch, arch, look, push, pull, **extension** or flexion. Gestures can be large or minimal. They could involve left, right or both arms; left, right or both legs; the head; the feet; hands or fingers.

A gesture might:

❖ be outwards from the body
❖ be inwards to the body
❖ be above the body
❖ be around the **periphery**
❖ be towards other people
❖ make **air patterns**
❖ express a mood or idea

'Come on, then': a hand gesture linked with *Faultline*

Rejecting gestures: linked with *Perfect*

Elevation

The body is in the air with no support on the floor

Elevation is made up of three stages — the take-off, the moment in the air and the landing. There are five recognised basic jumps, which use the feet for the first and last stages as supports. Can you, for example, perform the two jumps shown below?

Gestures towards other people: a moment linked with *Perfect*

One foot to same foot (temps levé — **hop**)   One foot to other foot (jeté — leap)

Jumps can be:

- on the spot or travelling
- with different leg shapes
- with arched, tilted, contracted or upright use of the spine
- with a turn
- in different directions
- large or small
- with various arm gestures

The shape and size made by the body in the air, as well as the direction the jump takes, are **spatial** features.

Rotation

Turning

Turns can be:

- quarter, half, three-quarter or whole
- clockwise or anti-clockwise
- on the hips
- on the length of the body
- on the knees
- on hands and feet
- on two feet
- on one foot
- with a jump

Turns may change level, spiral, be initiated by different body parts, or go from one support to another.

Extension and contraction

Stretch and curl

You can extend and **contract** different parts of the body, reaching up, down, right, left, diagonally, forwards, backwards, towards, away, over, and onto. You can reach in different directions and at different speeds, using your spine to arch and lean.

1 Contracting forwards and low: linked with *Dance Tek Warriors*, **2** Contraction, **3** Extending in several directions: inspired by the Southern Cape Zebra in *'Still Life' at the Penguin Café*, **4** Leaning backwards

Table 4 Action vocabulary

A	arabesque, attitude
B	balance, bend, bob, bounce, brake
C	carry, cartwheel, circle, clap, clench, click, close, coil, collapse, connect, contract, couru, cower, crawl, creep, cross, crumple, curl, curve
D	dangle, dart, **développé**, **dig**, dip, dive, divide, drag, drift, droop, drop
E	elevate, elongate, enlarge, enter, exit, explode, explore, extend
F	fall, flex, flip, float, fly, fold, follow, freeze
G	gallop, gather, gesture, glide, grab, grip, grow
H	hang, hesitate, hide, hold, hop, hover, hurtle, hustle
I	indicate, invert
J	jab, jerk, jeté, join, jump
K	kick, kneel, knock
L	land, lean, leap, lengthen, lie, lift, lollop, look, lower, lunge
M	meander, melt, mime, mould, mix up, move
N	nod, notice
O	open, over
P	pad, pause, pelt, perch, perform, pierce, **pirouette**, pivot, place, play, plod, point, pop, **posé**, pounce, prance, pull, punch, push
Q	quiver
R	raise, reach, relevé, return, ripple, rise, roll, **rotate**, run
S	scatter, settle, shake, shimmy, shoot, shoulder stand, shrink, shrivel, shuffle, sink, sit, skim, skip, slide, slither, snake, soar, spin, spiral, spring, squeak, squiggle, squirm, stalk, stamp, stand, step, stretch, stroke, support, surround, suspend, sway, swerve, swing, swirl, swoop
T	tangle, tap, tilt, toss, tramp, travel, turn, twirl, twist
U	under, undo, unfold, unwind, up
V	veer, vibrate
W	wait, walk, watch, wave, whip, whirl, whiz, wind, wrap, wriggle
Z	zoom

Dynamics: how we move

We all have the choice whether to be energetic or unenergetic. For instance, if you are late for school or college and your bus is approaching, you choose either to be energetic and run as fast as you can to catch it, or not to bother, staying calm and moving slowly as the bus drives by.

The same applies to energy in dance. We choose *how* we will dance each action — the 'dynamics' we will use. There are many choices. Ordinary actions can be done slowly, quickly, gently, powerfully, jerkily, smoothly, suddenly,

sharply, fluidly or directly. In dance, the dynamic qualities used by dancers give movements their significance, importance or meaning. A sharp, rhythmic walk has a different impact to a slow, careful, loitering walk. The action of walking is the same, but how it is performed gives character and meaning.

Note that a dance without any dynamic changes will appear flat and monotonous, and will not gain a good grade at GCSE!

Features of dynamics

Rudolph Laban defined four main features of dynamics: time, weight, space and flow. Each feature has two extremes; these are given in Table 5.

Combining the first three of these features brings about particular actions, which Laban called 'effort actions'.

Table 5 Laban's features of dynamics

Factor	Qualities	Basic vocabulary
Time	sudden > sustained	quickly > slowly
Weight	firm > fine touch	strongly > gently
Space	direct > flexible	straight > winding
Flow	bound > free	tight > loose

Table 6 Laban's effort actions

Time	Weight	Space	Actions
Sudden	Firm	Direct	Punch, kick, slice, grab, slap, stamp, dig, gallop, leap
Sudden	Firm	Flexible	Whip, whisk, turning jump
Sudden	Fine touch	Direct	Dab, tap, pad, skip, hop
Sudden	Fine touch	Flexible	Flick, swirl
Sustained	Firm	Direct	Press, push, pull, contract
Sustained	Firm	Flexible	Wring, spiral
Sustained	Fine touch	Direct	Glide, stroke, release, creep
Sustained	Fine touch	Flexible	Float, drift, sway, hover, weave

These actions can be danced in a tight, controlled and bound manner, or a loose, wild and free way, giving them a sense of flow.

Jumps can be danced quickly, strongly and with a directly aimed kick in the air, or as a small, tight **shunt** with a strong, direct, sudden and sharp landing. They can be performed as a series of quick, delicate hops and skips that skim the floor on a winding, tortuous pathway. This would be more interesting and expressive than just a basic jump or series of general hops. Remember, the dynamic qualities or features of the jumps communicate with the audience. They say something about the subject matter of the dance at that moment.

1 Cupids and Clara on their journey to Sweetieland, in *Nutcracker!* by Matthew Bourne

2 A linear extended leap by Saju Hari, from *Faultline* by Shobana Jeyasingh

3 Enjoying the snow on the frozen lake, in *Nutcracker!* by Matthew Bourne

An arm gesture of reaching forwards could be danced in the following two ways:

1 The wrist is flexed and the palm presses the air forwards directly (in a straight line) and slowly (sustained).

2 The palm faces the floor, and the fingertips lead the gesture forwards directly, with fine touch (delicately) and slowly, as if gliding over or smoothing the air beneath the palms.

The tension and energy in the hands would be different for each example. In the first there would be a sense of force and strength, and in the second a sense of softness and gentleness. In each example the body would probably echo these qualities.

Paintings

Looking at paintings can help your understanding of dynamics in dance. The colours in paintings highlight images within the picture. Red, black and brown are strong colours, whereas white, blue and yellow seem more delicate.

The colourful abstract paintings of Kandinsky are excellent examples to study. A black and white picture can be stark and convey a different atmosphere, mood and theme. Picasso's *Guernica* is a good example of this.

The width and length of lines in a painting, and whether or not they are repeated, could be compared to sequences of travelling steps. A series of short black dashes could be likened to a sequence of short strong leaps, and a long, curved, thin line to a large, curved arm gesture, which takes the body from high to low, leading into a fall.

Dynamics exercises

1 Try some of the following actions with different dynamics:

a Turn your head and stare at the audience.

b Fall, roll and stand.

c Triplets across the room.

d Walking in pairs, follow the leader, who suddenly stops. The follower then has to get past and become the leader.

e Move in **counter-tension** with a partner.

f Swing, stretch and collapse.

Counter-tension by Mandeep, Yamuna and Saju, from *Faultline* by Shobana Jeyasingh

2 Discuss the dynamic qualities you can see in the following two photographs.

Springs Dance Company: reaching forwards by Charlotte Brown and Claire Talbot, in *Be Not Entangled*, by Andrea Martin

Springs Dance Company: curled jump by Charlotte Brown and Claire Talbot in *Be Not Entangled*, by Andrea Martin

Dynamics and the dance exam

Dynamics have a vital role in dance: they make a dance come alive. When you dance the solo composition task, the set study, your solo and the group piece, you must show that you can use different dynamic qualities. Without these, your dance could appear flat, lifeless and without meaning. If you have not tried to move at different speeds or changed the energy output or flow of movement, this could prevent you from achieving a high grade. Building dynamic qualities into your solo or group choreography is also important. Adding accents within a phrase, or changing a fluid phrase to a series of sharp stop-and-start actions, will create highlights and give your dance greater expressive qualities.

Use surprise stops or unexpected **acceleration**. Gradually slow down your movements or make them become more and more powerful. Controlling and incorporating dynamic changes will make your performances more expressive and improve your ability to communicate a dance idea clearly to an audience.

A	accented, allegro, angry
B	begrudging, bold, bouncy
C	calm, careful, crafty, crude, cute
D	delicate, determined
E	easy, elegant, energetic, expansive
F	fast, featherlike, firm, floating, flowing, fluid, forceful, free
G	gay, gentle, gliding, gradual
H	happy, hasty, heavy, hesitant
I	idle, immediate, impish
J	jerky
L	languid, lazy, lente, light, limp, lingering, liquid, loud
M	methodical, mild
N	naughty, neat, noisy
O	overt
P	passionate, pizzicato, powerful, precise
Q	quick, quiet
R	racing, rhythmical, rough
S	sad, sensual, sharp, shy, slow, smooth, solid, staccato, strong, sudden, sullen
T	tender
U	untidy, urgent
V	vibrant, violent
W	weighty, wild

Table 7
Dynamics vocabulary

Spatial aspects: where an action occurs

There are two kinds of space in dance. The first is personal space: the areas you can reach while staying on the spot — the big bubble around you. The second is general space: the areas outside your bubble that you move into, through, around and across.

Above | High: directly above the body

Level with | Medium: shoulder to hip level

Below | Deep (low): from hips to floor

Figure 9 Spatial levels

Spatial levels

The three spatial levels — high, medium and deep (low) — are shown in Figure 9.

You can jump, stand on tiptoe or reach up to high level. You can lunge or stand — on flat feet or kneeling — at medium level, and kneel, sit, lie, roll, or slide on the floor at deep level.

High level: inspired by *Overdrive*

Medium level: a moment from the GCSE set solo

Low level: inspired by *Dance Tek Warriors*

Directions

There are six single directions:

- high (H)
- deep (D)
- to the right (R)
- to the left (L)
- forwards (F)
- backwards (B)

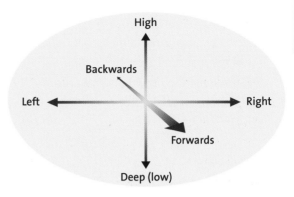

Figure 10
Spatial directions

Planes

There are three **planes** we can move in, with 12 two-dimensional directions. These are shown in Figures 11, 12 and 13.

Which two dancers are in the door plane?

Hands forward left and forward right: a moment from the GCSE set solo

High forwards

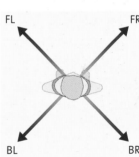

Figure 11
Spatial door plane (movements from side to side, reaching high and low)

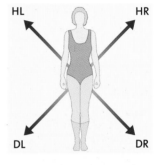

Figure 12
Spatial table plane (movements reaching forwards and backwards at waist height to right and left)

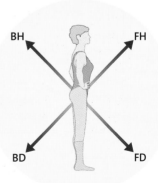

Figure 13
Spatial wheel plane (movements reach forwards and backwards with change of level – no sideways action)

Diagonals

There are also three-dimensional directions, where dancers move towards and in eight diagonal directions (see Figure 14). For example, to reach HRF, the gesture has to go up high, forwards and the right at the same time. What does a dancer do to reach DRB?

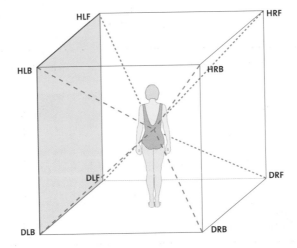

Figure 14
Three-dimensional directions

Pathways

We can travel along different-shaped pathways, from one point on the stage to another, making all sorts of floor patterns. These can be straight, horizontal, curved, zigzagged, diagonal, wavy etc. The areas of the stage have recognised names and letters to help us identify where we are moving. These are always labelled from the point of view of the dancer on the stage.

Figure 15
Stage areas

Downstage

DSL	DSR
SL	C	SR
USL	USR

Upstage

C	Centre stage
SL	Stage left
SR	Stage right
DSL	Down stage left
DSR	Down stage right
USL	Upper stage left
USR	Upper stage right

Pathways can be drawn by marking an 'O' where the dancer starts and an 'X' where the dancer finishes. We can travel forwards, sideways or backwards along any pathway, travelling at deep, medium or high level.

Chapter 4

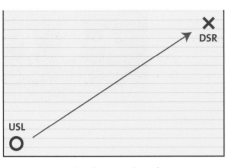

Straight diagonal pathway

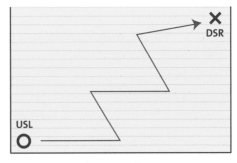

Zigzag pathway

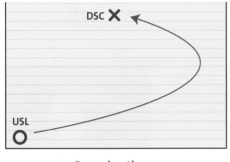

Curved pathway

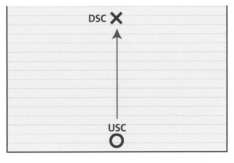

Straight pathway

Figure 16
Pathways

Size of movement

Movements can be:

* tiny, e.g. wagging a finger
* medium-sized, e.g. stretching the arm forwards and making a larger gesture with a finger
* large-sized, e.g. taking a step reaching up then forwards, and stretching both arms forward and wagging fingers in **unison**
* very large, e.g. stepping into a large hop, taking both arms high to forwards, wagging fingers and landing in balance or lunge

Shape of movement

The body can be:

* rounded
* stretched thin
* twisted
* stretched wide

Describe the shapes you can see in the photograph.

Gestures

Gestures made with the arms or legs can be:

* linear
* curved
* angular
* above, below, in front of, behind or to the side of the body
* curled and rounded

These movements, which involve limbs in the air around the body, will make air patterns.

Angular lines: inspired by *Dance Tek Warriors*

Rounded arms

Hand gestures: inspired by *Dance Tek Warriors*

Table 8 Space vocabulary

A	above, across, air, angled, angular, arch, around, arrow
B	backwards, beginning, behind, below, block
C	centre, circle, circular, corner, crooked, cross, curve
D	deep, diagonal, direction, door, down, downstage, drop
E	encircle, end, enlarge, entrance, exit, extend
F	far, flow, forwards, front
G	grand, grow
H	high
I	in, inwards
J	jagged
L	large, left, level, line, low
M	medium, middle
N	narrow, near
O	offstage, onstage, open, outwards, oval, over
P	pathway, pattern, petit, pin, place
R	right, ring, round
S	shape, side, sideways, size, small, snake, spot, square, straight
T	table, thin, through, triangular, twisted
U	under, up, upside down, upstage, up towards
V	vertical, V-shaped
W	wall, weave, wheel, wide, wings
Z	zigzag

Wide and tall gesture

Curled and rounded gesture

Relationships: who we move with

Dancers relate to the space around them, the audience, different parts of the body, props and other dancers. They are also aware of the transitions (relationship) between one movement or phrase and another.

Solo

A soloist must have the ability to dance alone, with or without a prop, in a large space. He/she must have the confidence to communicate the dance idea to an audience, which could be seated in the round or directly facing the stage. A solo performer has to be aware of:

❖ the whole performing space
❖ where he/she is in the space
❖ how he/she is relating to the audience
❖ the size and shape of his/her actions
❖ the use of directions and pathways
❖ the use of focus and body designs or shapes, which must hold the audience's attention
❖ his/her own physical skills and limitations, and performing within that range
❖ projecting a sense of confidence, boldness and concentration, to convey the dance idea clearly

Tilted balance on demi-pointe by Yamuna Devi, from *Faultline* by Shobana Jeyasingh

Dramatic reaction to shadow by Helen Parlor in *Perfect*, by Kevin Finnan

In a duo/duet

Each dancer in a duo/duet has to be aware of where the other is and what each of them is doing. They need to know:

❖ whether to look at their partner or the audience
❖ the timing of any unison **sections**
❖ the pathways each of them is travelling (to avoid collisions)
❖ when to go around, past, over or under their partner
❖ how to arrive at the right place at the right time
❖ if they are to make physical contact (e.g. turn, lift, carry, or support their partner), and how and when that will happen
❖ the character (if relevant) their partner is playing
❖ which phrases of music they might be using in **canon**
❖ their entrances and exits in relation to each other, e.g. do they lead or follow?
❖ that they can dance sensitively together

Saju held in stag leap shape by Devariaj in *Faultline*, by Shobana Jeyasingh

Possible relationships within a duo are:

- ❖ one behind the other
- ❖ side by side
- ❖ in unison
- ❖ facing towards or away from each other
- ❖ facing each other
- ❖ diagonally opposite
- ❖ close to or far from each other
- ❖ in contact

These relationships can look different according to where they are performed relative to the front of the stage, whether the dancers are facing the same or different directions, and whether they are dancing in different areas of the space (see Figure 15 on page 60.)

The dancers can move at similar or contrasting levels to each other, in unison or canon, using matching, mirroring, **complementing** or **contrasting** actions. They can pass by, move towards or away from, go over, under or around each other.

Duo performance: **1** One behind the other: a variation inspired by *Overdrive*, **2** Facing each other: trickling sand image from *Perfect*, **3** Close to each other, **4** Lifted and held: inspired by *Faultline*, **5** Are we matching?: idea inspired by *Perfect*, **6** lowered and held

Use of contact

One dancer can manipulate the other using various actions. These are:

- ❖ balancing
- ❖ dragging
- ❖ lifting
- ❖ pulling
- ❖ sliding
- ❖ swinging
- ❖ turning
- ❖ carrying
- ❖ holding
- ❖ lowering
- ❖ pushing
- ❖ supporting
- ❖ twisting

Pulling   Lowering

These actions can involve contact between different surfaces of either dancer. They can be performed slowly, quickly, rhythmically, gently or powerfully, but they must always be performed safely. Safe stance, shape, transference of

weight, use of the trunk and hands, and appropriate clothing must be adopted at all times. Preparation and recovery into and out of these actions must be safe, appropriate and well considered, with sensitivity to the required bodily tensions and use of the body with shifts of weight.

The relationship of the dancers to each other and to the front of the stage during each contact action will create different expressions and add interest to the dance. The contact can be through whole body involvement, at different levels, or by manipulating isolated parts.

The manipulator will be either stationary or travelling, with weight on selected parts of the body. The other dancer could be moved in any of the following directions:

❖ up, down, forwards, backwards, sideways
❖ diagonally, vertically, horizontally
❖ over, under, through, around
❖ in a straight line, on a curved pathway

This action could be brief, sudden, slow, rhythmical or delicate.

In a group

Dancers working in a group need to know:

❖ where they are in a group **formation**
❖ their place in a line/circle etc. as the group travels
❖ the music
❖ the order of each use of canon and their role within it
❖ that they can dance in unison with each other
❖ that they can move into and out of group shapes sensitively

A	above, against, answer, around, **asymmetric**, avoid, away
B	balance, behind, below, beneath, beside
C	canon, carry, complement, connect, contact, contrast, counter-tension
D	drag
E	elevate
F	face, far, follow, formations
G	grip, group
H	hold
I	in front of, in line
J	join in, jointly
K	knit together
L	lead, lean, lie beneath, lie on, lie over, lift, lower
M	match, mirror
N	near, next to
O	off, onto, opposite, over
P	pass, pull, push
Q	question
R	rest on
S	side by side, support, surround, symmetrical
T	through, tilt, together, towards, turn, twist
U	under, unison, upside down
W	with

Table 9
Relationships vocabulary

Close and supporting: inspired by *Dance Tek Warriors*

Awareness of others: inspired by the Gobstoppers in *Nutcracker!*

- where everyone is on the stage or in the studio
- how to adjust the size of their own gestures, leaps, turns etc. to communicate powerfully the group unison
- their own timing and that of others
- how they might move into physical contact with more than one other dancer
- how to lift, support, carry and manoeuvre other dancers safely, sensitively and sensibly
- how to be part of a team
- how to make each other feel important and needed in the dance
- how to use the stage space without blocking, knocking or getting hidden by others

Performing skills

Dancers working in a group must learn how to watch one another, keeping in time with the other dancers and the music. They need to be spatially correct in the performance space — neither too close nor too far away — and make contact with other dancers sensibly. They should use the correct focus and actions and show appropriate expression and characterisation.

Group work ideas

A group could dance together in a line in the following ways:

- positioned side by side, one behind the other or high to low
- facing the front, stage right, stage left or upstage
- from one corner to another (i.e. diagonally)
- facing alternate directions

Lifting and supporting with strength and sensitivity: inspired by *Faultline*

Facing different directions but focussed to the front: inspired by *'Still Life' at the Penguin Café*

Linear reaction – *oops!*: inspired by the Marshmallows in *Nutcracker!*

Making contact: trio in touch

Moments of contact: inspired by *Faultline*

- close to or far from each other
- at the same or different levels
- on the spot, or travelling forwards, backwards or sideways
- with or without contact
- in different areas of the stage
- in different line lengths

A group could dance together in a circle in the following ways:

- facing inwards or outwards
- with the right shoulder to the centre, or the left
- facing alternate directions
- close to or far from each other
- at the same or different levels
- on the spot or travelling forwards, backwards or sideways
- going around, in and out
- with or without contact
- in different areas of the stage
- in large or small circles

In a line: **1** In a line on a diagonal: inspired by Act 1, Scene 4 – the ballroom from *Romeo and Juliet*, **2** two levels, **3** In a line in character: based on the Marshmallows from *Nutcracker!*

Dancers in a group could move in unison or in canon, make an entrance or an exit, and dance at the same or different speeds.

Expressive nature

A dance can express joy, tragedy, excitement, beauty or ugliness. Expression is communicated through the way dancers project the dance idea through the use of their bodies.

Dancers who feel unsure of the movements, or do not understand the dance's message or idea, cannot interpret and communicate the dance to the audience. To do this, dancers must know the idea, their role and the movements; be able to dance in time with the music; use dynamics appropriately; dance in the right place; and know where to look at any time in the dance. So, physical skills have to be achieved first, and interpretative skills are gained later.

Dancers interpret what a choreographer has given them to do and communicate the choreographer's idea. The skills they need to do this are listed in

Table 10. Note that to achieve a grade C or above in GCSE Dance, you will be expected to interpret and project a dance idea with clarity and a sense of **artistry**.

Skills	Description
Focus	Use of the eyes looking at other dancers, the audience, or out across the space
Projection	Extending the inner feeling of an action clearly, with appropriate energy and use of the body into the space
Interpretation	A personal understanding of the actions projected through style, use of music and dynamics
Musicality	Awareness of the qualities of the music and projecting them, or complementing/contrasting them, effectively (phrasing, musicality and timing)
Facial expression	Projection of emotion through the use of eyes, mouth and eyebrows
Sense of rhythm	Being able to hear or feel a beat or metre and project that knowledge accurately
Sensitivity to others	This applies to space, dynamics, group formation, flow, use of contact and the audience

Table 10
Interpretative skills

Focus towards the lower hand

Focus out to the audience

Focus

Looking in a particular direction, with a specific manner and facial expression, will help you to express the dance idea clearly to both other dancers and the audience. For instance, if your eyes look down they appear 'shut' to anyone watching. This could convey shyness, tiredness, or boredom, or a lack of confidence in your own dancing ability.

Considering the line of focus for every moment in a dance is a difficult skill; it is one many people forget to even think about. You cannot contemplate how you might use your head, eyes and face until you have gained good physical control of your limbs.

Dancers playing characters in a **dance-drama** or **narrative** ballet have a particular way of holding their head and neck, moving their eyebrows and eyelids, and directing the gaze of the eyes. An angry character's facial expression should be different to that of a sad or excited character.

In classical ballet, a dancer will use focus differently to a contemporary or jazz dancer. There are particular ways a ballet dancer uses his/her head, neck and eyes — the 'eye line' is a key feature of the style. In contemporary dance, where the subject matter is abstract, there is no particular facial expression, as the focus is on areas of space around the dancer or on a particular limb. The focus can appear to be inward, as the dance idea is expressed through the whole body shape and dynamics, with the face not having an important role. In lindy hop, the focus of the eyes is outwards towards the audience and the other dancers. The face has a happy expression, with eyes wide open and an uplifting curve to the mouth.

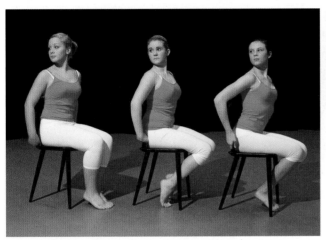

All the same: inspired by *Rosas Danst Rosas*

Focus forward: inspired by 'Texan Kangaroo Rat'

A confident Street shape: inspired by *Dance Tek Warriors*

Projection

A dancer projects a physical image, which makes a visual statement to anybody watching. Look at the messages the photographs on projection convey.

Whatever dancers think or feel, whether in a character role or their own mood, will be projected by the way they hold their bodies, heads and limbs. Extending and feeling muscular energy in the body is therefore vital. The way dancers move projects images of their energetic involvement (large or small, or not at all), their muscular awareness and their self-confidence.

Projection can only be established and improved once dancers have good control of their bodies. Dancers must therefore first gain awareness of

I am fully aware of every bone in my body: in Bharata Natyam style

their posture, whether sitting, lying, kneeling, standing, jumping, turning and so on. They must be aware of their body designs, the shape of their leg and arm gestures, and how their feet and hands are held, before they can project effectively. So, trying to dance a **motif** of difficult leaps, turns, travelling and balances could project an image of disjointed and erratic control. A motif of less demanding actions, performed with clear body, spatial and dynamic awareness and control, will project an image more clearly.

Being aware of their energy in a static position or a particular action also helps dancers to project their dance idea or theme clearly. Dancers therefore have to choose the right amount and type of energy, whether this be powerful, delicate, fluid, smooth, sharp, tight or loose. Performing actions at a particular speed makes the projection of the dance idea even more obvious. Dancers can move continuously, quickly, suddenly and then stop, slowly, rhythmically, and steadily.

To summarise, the projection of the dance idea will be communicated through body awareness, technical skill, a sense of quality (i.e. energy, speed, flow), a sense of space, and clear knowledge of the idea behind the dance being visible in the dancers as they move.

Are we all the same?: inspired by the Penguins in *'Still Life'* at the Penguin Café

Should my left arm be higher in my Gobstopper moment?: inspired by *Nutcracker!*

Tight energy in a Gobstopper moment: inspired by *Nutcracker!*

My left hand should be flat on the floor: a moment inspired by *Dance Tek Warriors*

1 Tight energy:
Saju and Deveraj
from *Faultline*, by
Shobana Jeyasingh
2 Head and arm
gesture with loose
energy, from the
scene 'Building' in
Rosas Danst Rosas,
by Anne Teresa
De Keersmaeker

Interpretation

Dancers have to be aware of the distinctive features of any dance style they may be asked to perform. They need to know how their bodies should be held and where their weight is centred. They must understand the shapes that are typically made by the limbs, feet and hands, the dynamics and flow required in the body, the use of the head and eyes, and the particular movements that characterise the style.

Sense of style:
1 contemporary
2 jazz
3 capoeira

Musicality

Music can be complex, with more than one theme and instrument being played.
Dancers need to be able to hear:

❖ rhythms: syncopated/metric and **non-metric**
❖ the themes being played
❖ changes in volume and in pitch
❖ acceleration: increase in speed

- ❖ **deceleration**: decrease in speed
- ❖ accents: emphasising particular beats
- ❖ moments when the music reaches a **climax**
- ❖ the sound's quality, through recognition of the instruments being played, e.g. voice, violin, flute, trumpet, drum, castanets
- ❖ the **time signature** (3/4, 4/4 etc.)

Once dancers can hear these distinctive features, they then have to move with control in relation to them. They need to be able to clap, walk, gesture, jump and so on in time with the music. They should be able to identify a bar or a phrase of music, which they can count or feel, from beginning to end.

If the music is 'allegro', i.e. fast and lively, dancers should be able to move with the same qualities, matching the rhythms, flow, dynamics and speed with good body control. They must keep pace with the rhythms and the beat, and not race the music or get left behind. Music in 'adagio' is more sustained and lyrical, so it requires fluid, delicate movements. Dancers are expected to be able to perform in **counterpoint**, **syncopation** and in harmony with music; this cannot happen if the dancer is unable to hear, identify and count or feel these rhythms.

Thinking one beat or two beats ahead is a skill all dancers have to acquire in order to arrive in the right place, at the right time, and with the right qualities. Having a sense of rhythm can be innate (i.e. natural), or it might have to be learnt. Dame Margot Fonteyn was especially renowned for her **musicality** as a ballerina, and the Widow Simone role in *La Fille mal gardée* requires an excellent rhythmic control and awareness, especially in the 'Clog Dance'.

Classical music, jazz, contemporary music, folk, rap, trance, hip-hop, pop, indie, rock, reggae and so on all have distinctive features that dictate the qualities dancers might bring to their performance. A dancer therefore has to be trained to hear, feel and move to different types of sound accompaniments.

Communication of the choreographer's intention

Students often perform each other's choreography, or choreography given to them by a teacher or visiting dance artist. You will also be expected to perform in a group dance based on one dance work by a professional choreographer. This will be chosen and organised by your teacher. To communicate the choreographer's intention, each dancer needs to know:

- ❖ what his/her role involves
- ❖ how this role contributes to the dance idea

- ❖ the choreographic style
- ❖ the performance style
- ❖ the specific movements
- ❖ the rhythms
- ❖ the use of space
- ❖ the dynamics
- ❖ the relationships with others on stage

With this knowledge, you can then project your understanding of your role as an outward visual image, with full body awareness, musical awareness and purposeful use of focus. The amount of practice needed to be successful in all these areas will vary from one dancer to another. You will need to understand and use your knowledge of the above points very clearly in order to achieve a good performance grade.

Communicating an idea through dance is what a dancer aims to achieve. This idea can be entertaining, humorous, **dramatic**, abstract, or simply show the beauty of dance. Knowing, feeling and dancing the idea is essential for every GCSE Dance performer. Whether through simple, short dance phrases or a complex **enchaînement**, the dancer has to be completely and personally involved in each action. Then he/she will forget everything except the dance, and breathe, move and enjoy the freedom dance can give.

Performance criteria for GCSE

For AQA GCSE Dance, the criteria for a dance performance include some of the following.

Technical (physical) skills

- ❖ High degree of technical skill and excellent coordination.
- ❖ Good level of technical skill and coordination.
- ❖ Technically competent with sound coordination.
- ❖ Technically competent at times, with some control and coordination evident.
- ❖ Limited technical competence, body coordination and control.

Use of actions, dynamics and spatial elements

- ❖ Performs these successfully and accurately.
- ❖ Shows reasonably skilful use of these elements.
- ❖ Some accurate use of these elements.

❖ Some actions are controlled, but some erratic use of dynamic and spatial elements.
❖ Some control and limited dynamic and spatial accuracy.

Interpretative skills

❖ Performs with sense of musicality, energy and style.
❖ Rhythmically accurate with clear sense of spatial design, in sustained commitment to performance.
❖ Clear projection to audience.
❖ Projects to audience throughout the dance.
❖ Communicates with the audience.
❖ Performs to audience.

Relationships to others

❖ Very sensitive to other dancers.
❖ Noticeably sensitive to other dancers.
❖ Is sensitive to other dancers.
❖ Some awareness of other dancers.
❖ Some links between self and other dancers at times.

Communication of dance idea

❖ Meaning of the dance is expressed with confidence and individual artistry.
❖ Communicates the essence of the dance imaginatively and with commitment.
❖ Some individual interpretation and projection of dance idea.
❖ Meaning of the dance is communicated at times.
❖ Tries to communicate the idea throughout the dance.

Artistic interpretation

❖ Sense of artistry, interpretation and total commitment.
❖ Some individuality visible and communicates with the audience.
❖ Some sense of performance.
❖ Occasional sense of performance and commitment.
❖ Limited sense of performance and commitment.

Section 2

Choreography

Choreography

Each candidate for GCSE Dance has to choreograph a short solo based on motifs from a set work and either a solo, duo or group dance for 3–5 dancers for final assessment. This section will help you to understand what is expected of you and enable you to achieve the best results you can. It deals with:

❖ the tools you need for choreography

❖ choosing and using different types of accompaniment

❖ using the tools to create and use motifs

❖ using choreographic devices after looking at motifs from a set work

Your solo composition based on a set work should be 1–1$\frac{1}{2}$ minutes long. It must be based on three motifs from the chosen work, which you then link together to make a clearly structured short solo. It should show the idea and style of the set work. Note that you can dance your own solo composition.

Your second choreography task will be either a solo lasting 1$\frac{1}{2}$–2 minutes or a group dance for 2–5 dancers lasting 2$\frac{1}{2}$–3 minutes. It should include:

❖ motifs that make a statement and can be repeated and developed

❖ a clear idea, topic, theme or visible subject matter

❖ accompaniment that fits with the idea

❖ actions that communicate the idea

❖ appropriate use of dynamics to communicate the idea

❖ interesting use of space to express the idea

❖ appropriate use of your dancers (or yourself in a solo)

You are expected to use a variety of choreographic devices in your dance, with a clear structure, highlights, at least one moment of contrast and clear links with the accompaniment.

As you begin the process of creating the dance you will have to make notes of what you did and how the process worked. These notes will be useful for the written examination as well as helping you to remember what you did in each lesson or week.

Tools needed for choreography

This chapter looks at the different ideas, or **stimuli**, you could consider using when creating your dances. Some are unusual and challenging, and some are more basic. The ideas you choose should suggest actions, which might link together to make a phrase of movements, or a motif that communicates the idea to an audience.

Different dance ideas

A dance could be based on a topic, story, picture, poem, prop, set, character, situation, or ideas within a set work or movement theme, e.g. diagonals, speed changes, three different actions. Knowing your dance idea thoroughly before you start **improvising** suitable actions is vital. Your first task is to choose an idea and then select which bits of it to use. Some ideas are suggested below.

Everyday life

Bread-making	Four seasons	Photo shoot
Camping	Gardening	Pop concert
Celebration	Going to the doctor/dentist	Rescue
Cinema/theatre visit	Going to the hairdresser/	Riot resolved
Conflict	barber	Shopping
Confrontation	Going to the library	Sport
Daily routine	Holiday trauma	Technology
Day at work/school	Housework	Us and them
Dining out	Journey	Visiting relatives
Disaster	London Olympics (2012)	Weather
Disaster in the kitchen	Outing or party	World Cup

Movement-based

Changing patterns
Diagonals
Lines and curves
Meeting and parting
Over, under, through, around

Slide, catch, fall
Speed changes
Turn, travel, drop, balance
Key actions or motifs from a set work

Visual media

Book
Newspaper article
Painting
Photograph

Poem
Prop
Set
Videos or DVDs of set works

How to get started

Working through the stages in the checklist below will help you to find movements that link with your dance idea and could be included in your dance. Copy the checklist and tick off the boxes as you work through the process of creating your dance.

Checklist

1 Choose a topic. .... ☐

2 Decide what the topic could involve. .... ☐

3 Group these ideas into subject boxes. .... ☐

4 Choose the subject boxes that you like and want to use. .... ☐

5 Decide how many sections your dance will have. .... ☐

6 Consider which aspect of your dance topic each section might be based on. .... ☐

7 Choose one section and list all the body actions you might include. ...... ☐

8 Start improvising. Create a motif using some of these actions for this section. .... ☐

9 Perform the motif literally, then improvise ways of enlarging it. .... ☐

10 Consider what accompaniment you might like to use. .... ☐

11 Decide whether your idea will be best shown by a solo, duo or small group dance. ..... ☐

Read through the two examples provided below and consider the decisions made. You could base your own dance on one of these topics.

Example 1: everyday life — going to the hairdresser

Decide what this topic could involve. Figure 24 shows some ideas linked with it.

- Being nagged/persuaded
- Making an appointment (diary, phone)

- Hairdryer
- Brush
- Comb

After:
- Paying
- Tipping

Hair:
- Long
- Short
- Fringe/no fringe
- Straight
- Curly
- Smooth (wavy)
- Spiky
- Blonde
- Brunette
- Auburn

- Manicure
- Ear piercing

Liking/hating haircut

Getting your hair done

- Looking in mirror
- Sitting at mirror
- Sitting at basin
- Wearing a cape

- Hair falling onto floor
- Sweeping up hair into bin

- Gossip
- Waiting
- Reading magazines
- Sitting under hairdryer

Processes:
- Cut (razor, scissors)
- Trim (number 1, 2 or 3)
- Shampoo
- Rinse
- Blow dry
- Rollers (set)

- Using gel/hairspray/lacquer
- Straightening
- Extensions
- Highlights
- Colour change

Figure 24
Getting your hair done

Cutting only this much!

Brushing long hair

Group the ideas in Figure 24 into subject boxes, as shown in Figure 25.

Getting your hair done

Before
- Short/long
- Brushing (hedgehog brush)
- Combing (with fingers)
- Gelling back (whole head of hair)
- Waxing up in spikes
- Smoothing down
- Showering
- Drying

Long
- Shave
- Curl
- Cut

Mid-length
- Restyle

After
- New style
- Brushing
- Combing
- Styling
- Gelling
- Straightening

Being the hair
- Cut
- Spiked
- Washed
- Dried
- Highlighted

Being the tools
- Scissors
- Hairdryer
- Straighteners
- Razor
- Rollers
- Cap with holes

Figure 25
Subject boxes for getting your hair done

Straightening hair

Spraying lacquer

Tools needed for choreography

Choose the subject boxes that you like and want to use. Look at the three sample choices in Figure 26.

Before: original style	Restyle	New style
■ Finger combing ■ Gelling back ■ Waxing in spikes ■ Smoothing down	■ Hairdresser ■ Hair ■ Tools	■ Doing your hair in the new style

Figure 26
Section and motif choices

The subject boxes you choose will make clear sections for your dance. You will then have to decide how many motifs, in how many sections, with how many dancers, will communicate your dance idea.

Looking in the mirror

One happy and one distressed customer

Tasks

1 Decide how many sections, motifs, music and dancers you would use from the boxes in Figure 25.

2 Using the boxes 'Being the hair' and 'Being the tools', decide the sections, motifs, music and dancers you would use to create your own dance. Refer back to the checklist on page 78 to help you.

Example 2: movement-based idea — diagonal playtime

Figure 27 shows some possible actions and shapes linked with this dance idea/topic. Some photographs and ways to consider how to create motifs based on these subject boxes are included in Chapter 7 should you want to try diagonal playtime as a choreographic task.

Figure 27
Diagonal
playtime

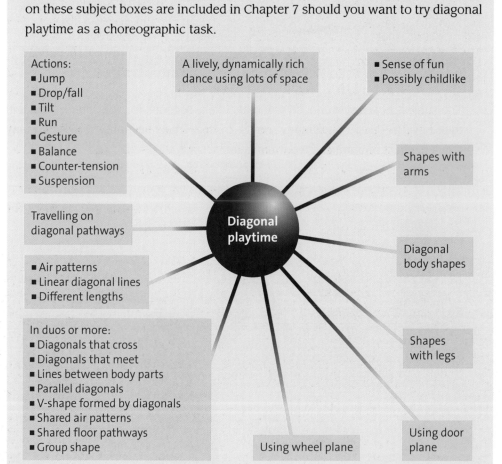

Actions:
- Jump
- Drop/fall
- Tilt
- Run
- Gesture
- Balance
- Counter-tension
- Suspension

A lively, dynamically rich dance using lots of space

- Sense of fun
- Possibly childlike

Travelling on diagonal pathways

Shapes with arms

- Air patterns
- Linear diagonal lines
- Different lengths

Diagonal playtime

Diagonal body shapes

In duos or more:
- Diagonals that cross
- Diagonals that meet
- Lines between body parts
- Parallel diagonals
- V-shape formed by diagonals
- Shared air patterns
- Shared floor pathways
- Group shape

Shapes with legs

Using wheel plane

Using door plane

Dance idea stimuli

Visual stimuli

Visual stimuli include photographs, paintings, sculptures, DVDs and videos.

Photographs

There are many types of photograph you could use as stimuli for a dance idea, for example images of dancers, historic events, sports people in action, tragedies, a holiday moment, your family, views of nature, and characters.

Views of nature: (left) a winter scene; (right) the force of water

Using photographs of dancers such as those below gives you physical shapes to try, and a central position for a motif. For example, choose an action to move into image 1, and a new action to take you into image 2; add a new action to move into image 3 and a last action to move into image 4. This is a motif. You can now vary the order of the actions, or just use the arm shapes from the photos with your own choice of leg positions.

1 Still and alert, 2 *Front Line:* gypsy swing, 3 Knuckles and toes balance, 4 *Front Line:* large lunge

You could vary the positions in the image by changing the level or the support, moving into and out of shapes at different speeds, changing the energy, arriving suddenly into the position, or getting there slowly, part by part.

Dance photographs show a moment frozen in time. Something will have happened before that moment and will happen after it. A **pure** or **abstract dance** could therefore be developed from this kind of photograph.

Narrative context

You need to identify the subject matter of a visual stimulus. Ask yourself these questions:

❖ Where is this, or where might it be?

❖ Who is involved?

❖ What seems to be happening?

❖ When is this happening: year, month, day, hour?

❖ What might have led to this situation?

❖ What might happen next?

❖ Are there particular movement patterns or actions linked with this picture?

❖ Are there any props not visible in the picture that are usually associated with this activity?

❖ Are there any gestures or actions linked with the figures?

❖ Do any of the clothes being worn indicate character, age and gender?

❖ What evidence supports your decisions?

Historic event: the French Resistance

Task

For a solo

Select one person in the visual stimulus provided by your teacher and consider his/her role prior to, within and after the image. Create a solo with an ABC structure to express the moods and feelings of this character in each situation.

For a trio or 4–5 dancers

Consider the situation in the visual stimulus provided by your teacher, the build-up to it and the repercussions afterwards. Use the dancers to express the developing situation in narrative form, with either ABC or ABCA structure.

Abstract context

You need to identify the contents of the visual stimulus provided by your teacher. This could be a painting, a sculpture, or a textile.

❖ List the shapes you can see.

❖ List the colours for each shape.

❖ Note the thickness of lines.

- ❖ How do the shapes relate to each other? (Which shape is next to which, which is highest, do shapes cross other shapes etc?)
- ❖ Which is the most striking shape for you? Draw and/or describe it.
- ❖ Which is the most delicate shape? Draw and/or describe it.
- ❖ Are any shapes repeated?
- ❖ Are they all the same size?
- ❖ Whereabouts do they appear?
- ❖ Are they always the same colour?
- ❖ Is there a shape that might be symbolic?
- ❖ Are the images natural, realistic, geometrical, atmospheric or surreal?
- ❖ Is there a sense of harmony?
- ❖ Is there a particular section of your visual stimulus that appeals to you?
- ❖ Is it a watercolour, oil painting, textile montage, or sculpture?
- ❖ Is it in a particular style?
- ❖ Who is the artist and when in his career did he/she create this work?
- ❖ Was it for a particular occasion?

Task

For a solo
Select one route through a painting provided by your teacher. Create a solo to express the shapes and patterns you encounter, with the moods inspired by the colours giving you dynamic qualities.

For a trio or 4–5 dancers
Consider the overall structure and inherent ideas of a painting provided by your teacher. Use the dancers to express the developing patterns in abstract form, using a structure that links with the route you take through the painting.

DVDs or videos of set works

You need to identify the scene of the set work you want to use. You will have to select three motifs from it. Be sure you also know the title of the work, the choreographer and the style of dance and music.

List the actions a dancer performs within each motif. You might find the charts in Chapter 3 useful in identifying whether these are steps, gestures, travelling, jumping, turning or moments of stillness. Be clear which dancer you are watching and make sure you describe how each action is danced (i.e. the dynamics). Look at the shapes made by the limbs and the body of the dancer as he/she moves.

Choreography

You should check:

❖ Which body part moves first and where it goes.

❖ The size and directions of the actions and where the dancer is moving. Is he/she moving downstage, upstage, going from stage right to stage left, etc?

❖ What style of dance is being used. Ballet? Contemporary? Release-based? Your solo will have to be in the same style.

❖ What the dancer is wearing. Is any of his/her costume vital to the motifs you might choose?

❖ If the dancer is performing a character role.

❖ The posture and facial expressions of the dancer.

❖ How the motifs link with the accompaniment.

Decide how you will adapt each motif for your body and performance skills. Find an accompaniment that links with your solo, is at a speed you can manage and is edited to the right length. You need to plan whether you will repeat the motifs in exactly the same way or vary them slightly, which order you will put them in, and how your final solo composition will link clearly with the scene from the set work.

Task

Choose three motifs from a scene in 'Still Life' at the Penguin Café by David Bintley and make a solo lasting 1–1 1/2 minutes. Give it a clear structure and link it with the style and subject matter of the scene you have chosen.

Moments inspired by '2nd movement: Chairs' from *Rosas Danst Rosas*

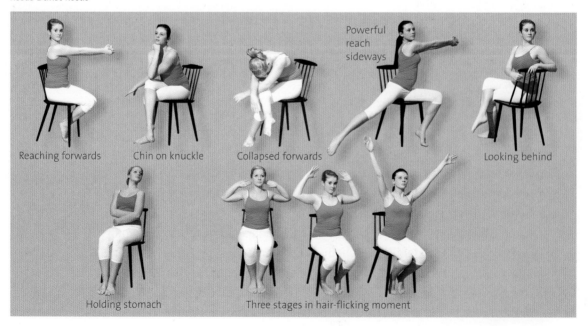

Powerful reach sideways

Reaching forwards   Chin on knuckle   Collapsed forwards   Looking behind

Holding stomach   Three stages in hair-flicking moment

Travelling on knees

Preparing to jump

The press-up position

An arresting moment

Aggression

Fighting talk

Moments inspired by the Gobstoppers from *Nutcracker!*

Literary stimuli

Literary stimuli include poems, newspaper articles, critical reviews, short stories, character sketches, and excerpts from plays or novels. They can be nonsensical, serious, dramatic or comic, and could give a critical comment, political statement or opinion.

Subject matter

You need to identify the subject matter of the stimulus:

❖ Where is this, or where might it be?
❖ Who is involved?
❖ What seems to be happening?
❖ When is this happening: year, month, day, hour?
❖ What might have led to this situation?
❖ What might happen next?
❖ Are there movement patterns or actions linked with this piece of writing?
❖ Are there gestures and actions linked with any of the figures described?
❖ What is the evidence to support your decisions?

Choreography

Characteristics of the writing

What are the words telling you? Ask yourself these questions:

- ❖ Are there any hidden meanings?
- ❖ Is there a structure you could use in your dance?
- ❖ What rhythms or rhymes are there?
- ❖ Is this a complete piece of writing or an excerpt?
- ❖ If it is an excerpt, what does it follow and what comes afterwards?
- ❖ Does it identify places, people or a situation realistically, or in an exaggerated form?
- ❖ Is it describing an imaginary atmosphere, place or creatures?
- ❖ Is it part of a conversation or an argument?
- ❖ Does it praise or criticise something or somebody?
- ❖ What is the context?
- ❖ Is it linked to a particular date?
- ❖ Is it relevant today?
- ❖ Is it an important piece of writing?

> ### Task
>
> **For a solo**
>
> Select one person or situation and consider his/her/its role prior to, within and after the piece of writing. Create a solo idea to express the moods and feelings of the character, or the atmosphere of the situation.
>
> **For a trio or 4–5 dancers**
>
> Consider a situation, the build-up to it, and the repercussions afterwards. How would you use the dancers to express the developing situation in narrative form, with either ABC or ABCA structure?

Social stimuli

Social stimuli include computers, mobile phones, MP3 players, saying 'No!', a disaster in the home, paparazzi at an event, living in an orphanage or a journey.

Props

Some props are given in the box below.

book	jewellery	newspaper	stick
briefcase	lipstick	pen/pencil	street map
cuddly toy	long scarf	photograph	sunglasses
cup and saucer	magazine	purse/wallet	train timetable
handbag	mask	ribbon/rope	umbrella
headphones	mobile phone	sponge ball	wheelie suitcase

Props can be used for a solo. For example, the dancer:

- ❖ enters the space without the prop (this is a travelling motif)
- ❖ picks up and uses the prop on the spot

Chapter 5

* travels using the prop in a different way
* struggles with it, abandons it, or hugs/keeps it
* exits with or without it

You and the prop

When using props in a dance, you should ask yourself:

* Who are you?
* How old are you?
* What mood are you in during each section?
* How do you feel about the prop?
* How are you holding it at any moment?

Take a book as an example. Are you the librarian, a borrower, a student, a senior citizen, a teacher or a car mechanic? List the actions and places associated with the prop. The box below gives actions and associated ideas for a book.

A book:	
opens and closes	is large or small
is read	is heavy or light
has pages	is thin or fat
has a subject	is on a shelf, up high, down low, or not available
can be frightening, boring etc.	has illustrations
is based on a specialist subject	is in small type
gives instructions	is found in a library

Task

Now do the same for three other props.

'Still Life' at the Penguin Café: shapes and positions inspired by the Southern Cape Zebra

Animal stance

Contracted forwards

Curves

Balance in fondu leading into a jogging step

Standing tall

Low level twisting extension

Balance in attitude

Choreography

'*Still Life' at the Penguin Café*: shapes and positions inspired by the Southern Cape Zebra and the Great Auk

The Great Auk starting position

A travelling hopping moment

'*Still Life' at the Penguin Café*: shapes and positions inspired by the social dance steps seen in the café

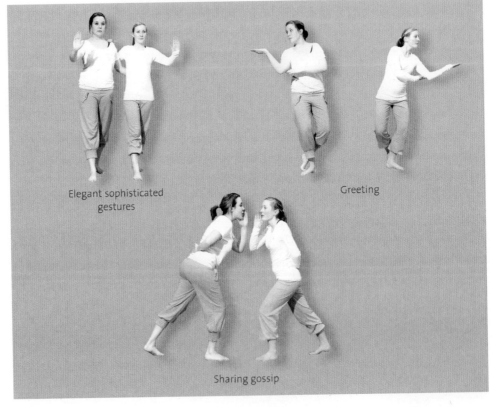

Elegant sophisticated gestures

Greeting

Sharing gossip

Chapter 6

Choosing and using accompaniment

Once you have a dance idea, your next task is to find a suitable accompaniment. This could be music, the spoken word (as in a sports commentary, or a poem spoken aloud), found sounds or natural sounds. You should start looking and listening while finalising your dance idea and improvising the movements.

Exam requirements

The range of music available to you is vast, and you may not have listened to anything other than chart music from the past few years. Remember that the exam board expects you to use music that is not simply the latest vocal hit. Ideally it should:

❖ be of the right length or properly faded at a suitable place
❖ have important moments (i.e. **highlights**)
❖ include a variety of rhythms
❖ have a clear structure — or at least a beginning, middle and end
❖ most importantly, be linked clearly in some way with your dance idea

The moods in the music must match the moods your character feels and is expressing in your dance. The structure and style of the music should fit with your idea: is a brass band recording suitable, or is a flute playing a classical tune better? Do the little ideas that inspire your movement motifs link with little tunes within the music? If the music is similar all the way through and could be used for any dance, then it is not for your dance.

So, how do you choose your accompaniment? First, you must know what you want your dance to say — your dance idea — and ideally what you think the sound should be like at particular moments of the dance.

Where to look

Music and other types of accompaniment are available to you at home, from the dance, drama, English, music, and PE departments at school, on the internet, in the local library, and in music stores.

Styles of music

Classical music

Instrumental pieces can be performed by a single instrument, or by two or more instruments in a number of combinations. Classical instruments include keyboards (e.g. piano, organ), strings (e.g. violin, viola, cello, double bass, harp), wind (e.g. clarinet, flute, recorder, piccolo, oboe, bassoon), brass (e.g. trumpet, trombone, saxophone, French horn, tuba) and percussion (e.g. timpani, drums, xylophone, bells). Combinations of instruments could be piano trios, string quartets, brass bands or a full orchestra. Opera singing, either solo or with more than one voice (soprano, alto, tenor, bass, baritone), can be used, as can choir music (hymns, psalms etc.).

Jazz

Jazz originated in the late nineteenth century in the southern states of the USA. It has features of West African rhythms, European harmony and US gospel. Jazz styles include ragtime — an instrumental style with piano, cornet and improvisations; blues from Negro spirituals; instrumental blues, with trumpet, cornet, clarinet, saxophone and trombone; Dixieland — a mix of ragtime, blues and improvisations, with trumpet, piano, trombone and saxophone; big band music and symphonic jazz, with solo cadenzas; Chicago-style and small bands with improvisation; swing; bebop, with rhythm and scat singing, trumpet, saxophone and drums, which became modern jazz. Modern jazz includes free jazz and hard rock, which has electronic instruments.

Folk music

Folk music comes from all over the world. It could feature a solo instrument or two or more instruments together. Folk can be performed with guitar, percussion, mouth organ, keyboards, pan pipes, koto, violin, concertina, taiko drums and many other instruments.

Instrumental theme tunes

You could use film themes, television themes and music from adverts.

CDs made especially for dance

These CDs have several tracks that are all the right length for a dance. Each track is in a different style, with clear structures and its own mood, tempo and rhythms. There are many CDs like this on the market, and your dance teacher probably has some of them. He/she could probably suggest tracks you might try. Some are listed in Section 4, Resource 5.

Pop, alternative, R & B etc.

Remember, only instrumental tracks should be used. These kinds of music are not always suitable, as there are often no rhythmic or melodic changes, and no change of speed or clear highlight. Most tracks are too long and would need proper editing. So although you may be most familiar with these types of music, using them may prevent you from gaining higher than a grade C for your choreography.

Listening to music

Maybe you rarely listened to a variety of music styles before starting your dance course. To choose a piece for your choreography, you will need to be able to identify the following as you listen to a track:

* the style of music (classical, jazz, folk etc.)
* the instruments making the sounds
* how long the piece is
* whether it has many different sections
* if there is a definite rhythm or beat
* if there is a difference in the volume of the music
* if it gets faster or slower
* whether the music changes in texture (staccato to melodic, or fluid, continuous notes)

If there are no real changes, the music will be unsuitable for exam purposes. Have you asked anyone other than your friends for music to go with your idea? You should listen to at least five tracks and cross-check their suitability using the list above.

Task: music timeline

You will need to do the following activities with at least **two** possible choices of music.

1 Draw a timeline for the whole piece of music, showing how many minutes and seconds a section lasts. (The whole piece of music should not be more than 3 minutes.)

Figure 30
Timeline example

| 0 | 30 sec | 1 min | 1 min 30 sec | 2 min |

| Section A | Section B | Section B2 | Section A2 |
| Curves idea | Lines: body | Lines: patterns | Curves: enlarged |

2 You could now make a graphic score of the sound you can hear in each section. You may have to listen to each 30-second section many times to identify what you can hear. You can use all sorts of symbols to match the sound; some ideas are given in the table below. You could use your own too.

Sound symbols

Table 11 shows some symbols you might use in a graphic score.

Table 11
Matching sounds to symbols of your choice

Sound	Symbols
Single, sharp, loud beats — 4 beats to a bar	I - - - - I - - - - I - - - - I - - - -II (4 bars)
Quiet, flowing tune — 3 beats to a bar	I~ ~ ~ I ~ ~ ~ I ~ ~ ~ I ~ ~ ~II (4 bars)
Low and high notes	I / / ^^^^ I / / ^^^^ I / / ^^^^ I / / ^^^^ II (4 bars)
Loud and soft notes	I > * >* I > * >* I > * >* I > * >*II (4 bars)
Continuous flowing music	~~~~~~~~~~~~~ (10 seconds)
Accents	!
Getting louder	<
Getting softer	>
Pauses	•
Instruments	Flute (F), Violin (V), Piano (Pi), Drum (Dr) etc.

Figure 31 shows a possible graphic score in three sections, A1, B and A2. Each section has 16 bars. The symbols indicate the qualities in the sounds, and show us that B sounds are different from A1 and A2 sounds.

Section A1	/•••/•••/•••/•••/•••/•••/•••/••• /•••/•••/•••/•••/•••/•••/•••/•••
Section B	ⅤⅤⅤⅤ ,,,, ⅤⅤⅤⅤ ,,,, ⅤⅤⅤⅤ ,,,, ⅤⅤⅤⅤ ,,,, ⅤⅤⅤⅤ ,,,, ⅤⅤⅤⅤ ,,,, ⅤⅤⅤⅤ ,,,, ⅤⅤⅤⅤ ,,,,
Section A2	/•••/•••/•••/•••/•••/•••/•••/••• /•••/•••/•••/•••/•••/•••/•••/•••

Figure 31
A possible
graphic score

Section A	/•••/•••/•••/•••/•••/•••/•••/••• Travelling on, steps and turns, with two important gestures /•••/•••/•••/•••/•••/•••/•••/••• Using the gestures, changing level and size of the actions
Section B	ⅤⅤⅤⅤ ,,,, ⅤⅤⅤⅤ ,,,, ⅤⅤⅤⅤ ,,,, ⅤⅤⅤⅤ ,,,, Mood change, contrasts, indecision, music loud and soft ⅤⅤⅤⅤ ,,,, ⅤⅤⅤⅤ ,,,, ⅤⅤⅤⅤ ,,,, ⅤⅤⅤⅤ ,,,, New gestures linking with moods, changes in direction
Section A	/•••/•••/•••/•••/•••/•••/•••/••• Original actions in new order, other side of body /•••/•••/•••/•••/•••/•••/•••/••• Travelling slowly off, interesting pathways, retrograde motif

Figure 32 Adding
words describing
movement ideas
to symbols in the
graphic score in
Figure 31

Common features in music

Table 12 Sound
features

Instrumental music		Vocal music	
Solo instrument: piano, guitar, flute etc.	Waltz	Solo	Aria
Orchestra	March	Duet	Speech
String quartet	Concerto	Quartet	Operetta
Brass band	Television theme tune	Choir	Commentary
Jazz band	Movement from a	Opera company	Ballad
Rock band	symphony, quartet etc.	Speaker	Song with lyrics
Electronic sounds	Film soundtrack	Actor	Pop song
Synthesised sounds		Rock band	Chant
Folk group		Jazz singers	Club mix
Percussion		Spoken verse	Folk song
Found sounds		**Natural sounds**	
Sound effects	Work-related sounds	Water	Fire
Noise of domestic appliances	Communication sounds: bells, sirens	Air	Animal and bird calls

Time signature/metre

Each piece of music has a certain number of beats to a bar, counted in whole, half or quarter beats (minims, crotchets, quavers, semi-quavers etc.). Common metres are 4/4, 3/4, 6/8 and 2/4. We would count a 4/4 metre of four bars as: **1** 2 3 4, **2** 2 3 4 , **3** 2 3 4, **4** 2 3 4. A 3/4 metre of four bars would be: **1** 2 3, **2** 2 3, **3** 2 3, **4** 2 3.

These beats could be played sharply or smoothly, or with an accent on a beat other than the first beat in the bar. The half beats could be heard played on a different instrument. For instance, a 4/4 could be heard as: 1 & **2** & 3 & **4**, & 2 2 3 & 4 &, **3** 2 3 4, 4 & **2** & **3** & **4**.

Task

1 Try clapping the 4/4 rhythm described above. Use this or a 4/4 rhythm of your own with your feet on the spot, and then travelling.
2 Add some arm gestures.
3 Repeat the motif, varying the accent in one bar (clap, feet on spot, then travel).
4 Take out one bar and repeat it four times (clap, feet on spot, then travel).
5 Link the four stages together. Perform the original travel with the arms gestures. Then repeat the motif, varying the accent. Next repeat one of the bars four times, and finish with the original travel using a new pathway.

Other sounds

Silence

When there are no sounds other than those made by the dancer, the dance has its own rhythms, speed, pauses and accents, as chosen by the choreographer. The dance is unlikely to have a metric rhythm, but will instead flow with the breath of the dancer and the natural in-built rhythms of the chosen movements. A professional example of this is *Soda Lake* by Richard Alston.

The human voice

The human voice could be heard live or on a recording. It might make sounds, such as crying, grunting, humming, laughing, shouting, sneezing and whistling. The rhythms are likely to be erratic and free-flowing, and an audience could hear the sounds unpredictably or unexpectedly.

The human voice could also use words in all sorts of spoken accompaniment. A few selected words, spoken as isolated words or phrases, could initiate actions, accompany actions, or follow an action. *Rainbow Bandit* by Richard Alston uses

the spoken word as accompaniment. A poem could be read by a professional, teacher or another student; the rhythms and accents in the lines and verses could be heard in time with the actions of the dance. The meanings of the words could influence the choreography, and the structure of the poem could influence the structure of the dance.

Prose, such as a story, newspaper article or television commentary, could be read out. This would dictate the subject matter and structure of the dance. The rhythms and meanings of the words would influence the choreography. However, mime is a temptation that needs to be avoided. Instead, use the way the dance relates to the sound, with counterpoint, **juxtaposition** and **mutual coexistence**, to create interesting highlights and contrasts. *Square Leg* by Janet Smith uses a sports commentary.

Chants can be religious, tribal, linked to football, rugby and so on. A chant would be a good accompaniment to a ritualistic dance, which would have a specific context and subject matter. You would need to check that the timing of the reading is within the limit for your dance. If it were read live, then the speed of the reading and the pauses would need to be practised many times.

Making a script with choreographic ideas would be a useful way of structuring your dance to link with the ideas in a poem, story, commentary or chant. This could include sung lyrics, although this often leads to mime and the use of popular songs and dance styles. These are the least appropriate for GCSE students to choose, and are therefore not recommended if you are aiming for a high grade.

Natural sounds

You could make a collage of recordings of natural sounds, or record the sounds themselves. These might be birdsong (e.g. a woodpecker or cuckoo), leaves rustling, a dog barking, frogs croaking, water running, wind blowing, thunder and so on. Timing these sounds and ordering them in a way that supports your dance idea is vital. The sounds' own rhythm and texture will influence the dynamics, flow and energy in a dance. How each natural sound links to the next will affect the dance's **transitions**. Making a script that links actions, sounds and your dance idea is therefore an important task. *Bird Song* by Siobhan Davies uses the song of the Australian pied butcher bird.

Found sounds

You can obtain found sounds from sound-effect CDs and sound collages you record yourself. These sounds could be a telephone ringing, a doorbell, a spoon rattling in a saucepan, machinery working, an aeroplane flying, taking off or landing, a car

or motorbike starting up, stalling or screeching to a halt, or a clock ticking. All of these sounds have inherent rhythms, flow and dynamics, which can influence the choreography. You would need to organise a list of the order each sound appears, how long each sounds lasts, and what this order might contribute to the dance. *Strong Language* by Richard Alston and *Cross Channel* by Lea Anderson are examples of professional works that use found sounds.

Relating music and dance

Music and dance relate to one another in a number of ways:

- **Correlation**: the music and dance are in harmony with each other; for instance, quiet music with gentle movements. *Swansong* by Christopher Bruce is an example of this.
- Counterpoint: the dance fills out the music; the dancers make stamping and clapping rhythms, which are sometimes on the beat, and at other times are heard in silences between notes (e.g. *Faultline* by Shobana Jeyasingh).
- Syncopation: dancers place accents differently to the accents in the music. *'Still Life' at the Penguin Café* by David Bintley contains both counterpoint and syncopation.
- **Disassociation**: the dance has contrasting qualities to the music; they have little in common and seem to oppose each other. Look at works by Merce Cunningham.
- Juxtaposition: a musical theme is echoed in the dance to another phrase of music. Look at *Rosas Danst Rosas* by Anne Teresa De Keersmaeker.
- Mutual coexistence: the dance and the music exist alongside each other at the same time. They occupy the same time and space and are not dependent on each other. 'Four Corners 1' in *Bird Song* by Siobhan Davies is an example of this.
- Narrative: this entails identification of:
  - Character: a musical theme is linked to a certain character, e.g. the 'Trio to Panpipes' in *Ghost Dances*.
  - Mood: for instance, an evil mood is heard in the music and seen in the action on set. An example is a male duet building to a fight in *Perfect* by Kevin Finnan.
  - Situation: an example is children in an orphanage in 'Presents and Party Pieces' in Act 1 of *Nutcracker!* by Matthew Bourne.
- **Visualisation**: the dance 'speaks' to the music. A high note/phrase would be matched with an upward gesture or a dancer being lifted up high; quick short notes would be seen as fast, tiny running steps. The music is the inspiration for the dance, which is a moving, visual representation of what is heard. A good example is *Overdrive* by Richard Alston.

Graphic score

Figure 33 is a graphic score of music composed by Andrew Kristy. It is followed by a chart describing the sounds heard and a choreographic structure you might like to try. This could be danced as a trio. You might want to link the sound and actions differently — feel free to do so, and enjoy! This music is available for your teacher to use.

Ternary form (ABA): classical, techno-dance, classical

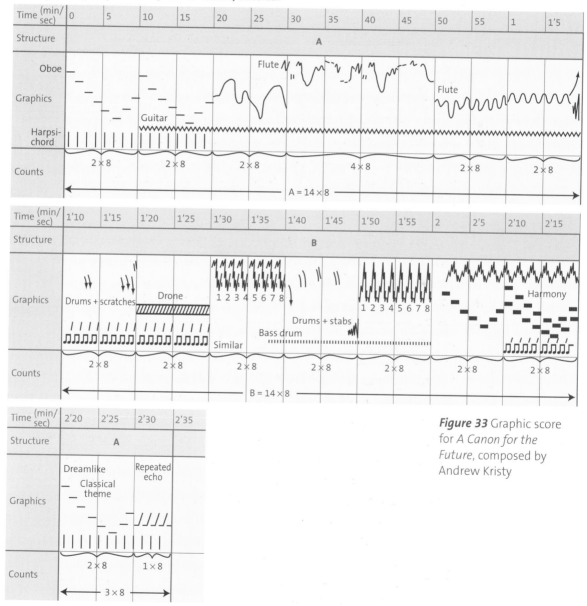

Figure 33 Graphic score for *A Canon for the Future*, composed by Andrew Kristy

Choreography

Table 13 Choreographic task using *A Canon for the Future* in ternary form (ABA)

Structure	Counts	Time	Instruments	Choreography	Use of dancers
A: classical	2 x 8	0 sec	Theme: oboe and harpsichord	Step, reach contract motif x 4	Two enter in canon
	2 x 8	10 sec	Guitar joins in, first phrase repeats	Running pathway	Third dancer enters
	2 x 8	20 sec	Melody with more movement	Circular, fluid gestures	Unison on spot
	4 x 8	30 sec	High, quirky flute motifs	Travel and skipping	Pathway of third dancer
	4 x 8	50 sec	Flowing flute	Circular, fluid gestures	In contact — under, over, through, around
		1 min 8 sec	Ascending cue	Break away	Dancers split
B: techno dance	2 x 8	1 min 10 sec	Drums and scratches	Top rock and reverse	Facing different directions
	2 x 8	1 min 20 sec	Drums and low drone	Locking moves	All face front
	2 x 8	1 min 30 sec	High, spiky lead sound, 8 repeats	Floor work and freezes	Use of canon and moving towards, through, and away from each other
		1 min 39 sec	Repeated bass (kick) drum cue	Sharp gestures and jumps	
	2 x 8	1 min 40 sec	Repeated bass and 'stabs'		
	2 x 8	1 min 50 sec	High, spiky lead sound, 8 repeats	Floor work and freezes	Unison
	2 x 8	2 min	High spiky lead and original theme from A	Reverse floor work and freezes	Solo
				Step, reach contract, motif x 4	Third dancer
	2 x 8	2 min 10 sec	Add drums and original theme and melody	Locking Step, reach, contract motif Circular gestures	Three motifs — one to each dancer
A: classical	2 x 8	2 min 20 sec	Original theme, dreamlike	Lifts using mix of classical motifs	Done as a three: two dancers lift the other
	1 x 8	2 min 30 sec	Four echoes	Exit Four gestures repeated	Two dancers Third dancer

Creating and using dance motifs and phrases

You need to decide which actions, uses of space and dynamics would be relevant to your dance idea so you can make dance motifs. Remember, a motif is a sequence of movements that makes a statement, which is linked with your dance idea. Motifs have actions and positions that can be repeated, varied and developed. Look back at Chapter 4 to remind yourself of the range of actions, uses of space and dynamics available to you.

Creating motifs

Chance charts

Choosing the final order of your actions within each motif could come about by **chance**, elimination or through improvisation. You can use the example of Figure 27 (diagonal playtime) in Chapter 5 as a prototype to help you choose the method that suits you best.

Tilts

Table 14 Actions linked with diagonals via a chance chart

1 Leaps/jumps: 1 foot to the other, 2 feet to 1 foot, 1 foot to 2 feet, 1 foot to the same foot. They could be into any diagonal direction, with a diagonal body shape, or a diagonal arm gesture.
2 Drops/falls: whole body or one part falls into a diagonal direction, with a change of level, a change of body part taking the weight.
3 Tilts: going off-balance into low diagonals — one, two or three dimensional, different levels, successive or simultaneous, with different supports.
4 Running: diagonal pathways forwards, sideways, backwards, from corner to corner, to centre and away, or zigzagging.
5 Gestures: arms or legs moving into different diagonals, with varying dynamics, speeds and flow.
6 Balances: in different diagonal shapes, on various supports.
7 Counter-tension: between two diagonal points.
8 Suspension: hovering, hanging over or swaying towards a diagonal area of the room.

This section will show you how to use a chance chart for actions taken from Figure 27 on page 82 that would communicate the two ideas — diagonals and playtime. The actions are listed in Table 14 above.

The order of the actions will be decided by the turn of a card. Take an ace, 2, 3, 4, 5, 6, 7 and 8 from a suit of playing cards, shuffle them, and lay them face down in a line in front of you. Then turn over each card — the number on the card corresponds with a step in the table. My order came out as:

❖ first card: 4 = running
❖ second card: 6 = balances
❖ third card: 2 = drops/falls

These three actions could become your first motif. Perform them in that order as a practice task before you try a task set by your teacher.

You would then make some decisions about these movements. For my card order, you would first need to decide the type of run, how long you will run for, in which direction you will run, what types of running steps you will use, and which pathway you will follow as you run. Improvise (try out) a few different ways:

❖ running for 4 counts, or 8, or more
❖ running forwards, sideways or backwards
❖ long runs, bounding runs, jogging, tiny running steps
❖ travelling diagonally from **USR** to **DSL**, or **DSR** to **USL**, or a zigzag pathway

Select the way you like best and which links with the dance idea (diagonals), and possibly a phrase in your accompaniment, if you have already chosen or been given one to use as a class.

Two tilted moments: inspired by *Overdrive*

For the example card order, you would then improvise possible balances, trying different body shapes that express a diagonal line and using different parts of the body to support your weight in a diagonal shape. Think about arm and leg shapes, as well as your spine. Experiment with the direction of your balance — sideways, forwards and so on. Once you have selected two balances you like, you could improvise how you might move into and out of each balance. For example, you might turn into and step out of the balance, or you might gesture and extend your limbs into the balance and turn out of it. Then choose whether to keep both balances, with a transition between them, or to just use one of them.

To continue the example card order, you then need to improvise ideas for the drop/fall actions. Decide which part of you drops (an arm, the whole body etc.), at what sort of speed, into what diagonal pathway, perhaps into a diagonal shape, and with what sort of energy (delicately, violently etc.).

Once you have selected your drop/fall, improvise linking the run to the balance(s), and the balance(s) to the fall, selecting the speed, energy, flow and rhythm of each link (transition) and action. You will then have your first motif — a statement that expresses the idea of diagonals, and can be varied in your dance.

Remember, this dance idea also includes another word: 'playtime'. This has dynamic implications, with maybe other actions that spring to mind. Turning over the next three cards of your line of eight will help. Mine came out as:

❖ fourth card: 1 = leaps/jumps
❖ fifth card: 5 = gestures
❖ sixth card: 8 = suspension

Choreography

Bearing in mind the idea of playtime as well as diagonals:

❖ Try improvising leaps/jumps to find at least two that seem playful and light-hearted, but still have a diagonal element to them. You could try big and little jumps, from two feet to two feet.

❖ Hopscotch — hop from one foot to one foot, then from one foot to two feet.

❖ Do split and stag leaps, from one foot to the other.

Moments inspired by *Overdrive*. **1** A landing, **2** Variations on one tilt, **3** Variations on a balance, **4** A low-level position with slow arm gesture

Then decide in which direction you will leap. What will be your body shape at take off, in the air and landing? Which dynamics will convey 'playful' as you take off etc.? How many leaps/jumps will you do, and in what rhythm?

You would then go through the same process with the gesture. Is it the hand, arm, leg, head or finger that will make the gesture? Decide what shape and how big the gesture will be. In which direction will it go? Will it be strong, delicate, fluid, sharp, tight or loose? Should it be done quickly or slowly? Are you kneeling, standing or lying down as you make the gesture?

Go through a similar process with the suspension. Decide whether you will be hanging forwards or sideways, the direction you will be looking in, what your arms will be doing, whether you will be standing or kneeling, if you will be on one leg or both, or taking weight on your hands. How will you express 'playful' in the pause? How long will the suspension be? One or two or more counts? Check that your suspension is not actually a balance.

Now link the three actions — leaps/jumps, gestures and suspension to finish in a shape and cross-check that you can dance them in a playful manner, and you have a motif to use.

Motif development and variation

You now have two motifs to use in your dance:

❖ run, link, balance, link, drop/fall to a shape — linked firmly with diagonals
❖ leaps/jumps, link, gestures, link, suspension to a new shape — linked with playtime

You now have new decisions to make, which will link with the accompaniment you choose. These are:

❖ when each motif first comes in the dance
❖ how each motif is varied and when
❖ how often each motif will be repeated
❖ whether you might mix the two motifs together

You need to know some ways you could repeat, vary and develop your two motifs or any part of each. Read the ideas provided below and choose which would best convey your dance idea.

Repetition (dancing the motif again)

You could perform the motif exactly the same as before:

❖ using the other side or another part of the body, e.g. starting with the other leg or arm
❖ using different supports (feet to knees, to hips, to one foot)
❖ **changing the order** (run, balance, drop becomes balance, run, drop)
❖ facing a different front, e.g. upstage instead of downstage
❖ performing in **retrograde** (backwards)
❖ performing in a different area of the stage
❖ changing the focus at any point in the motif

Variation (changing part or the whole motif)

Changes you might try could be applied to the whole motif or just one action:

❖ speed: e.g. a slow drop becomes sharp and quick
❖ **direction**: e.g. a run forwards becomes a run sideways and then backwards
❖ level: e.g. balance on one foot becomes balance on side of body on the floor
❖ size: e.g. a small gesture on the spot becomes a large gesture while travelling
❖ energy: a delicate loose suspension becomes a powerful tight suspension

Development

You could:

❖ add in a new action

❖ 'take away' one or more actions and repeat them at least twice, e.g. leap gesture, leap gesture, leap gesture

❖ try changing the floor or air patterns

❖ keep the arm actions but vary the leg and foot actions, e.g. balance with new support, use gesture while running

❖ change the speed (the motif accelerates or decelerates)

❖ change the rhythms of the actions

❖ add/take away the accent of an action

A photograph or a piece of 2-D or 3-D art

As an alternative to the chance charts, use the stimulus of a photograph or a piece of 2-D or 3-D art, either chosen by you or provided by your teacher, to develop motifs. From these you could:

❖ reflect the shapes made with your arms and link them together in a motif of your choice, showing air patterns and physical shapes linked with the stimulus

❖ add your own use of legs to this arm motif — the arm motif could be danced on the spot and then travel in floor pathways that link with the stimulus

❖ vary the dynamics of this travelling arm motif

You could then vary the actions made by the legs while keeping the same floor pathways and link them into a new motif, or choose new arm actions to accompany the original leg motif. You could develop a different pathway for the arms-based motif — this could be a larger or shorter pathway, or in a different rhythm.

You will then have an arm-gesture focused motif and at least one variation. These would form the basis for an abstract solo dance, which would last at least $1^{1}/_{2}$ minutes, and be clearly linked to the visual stimulus.

Character

A dramatic task could involve using a character doing a particular activity, a historical event, or a very recent topical activity to develop motifs. Some characters/character situations are given in the box below.

❖ Choose one character from the box and find three positions in which they might 'freeze'.

❖ Develop a motif by linking these three positions and making sure they express the character accurately and dramatically.

* Decide how this character might travel within the situation in which they find themselves.
* When would the travelling motif appear in your dance?

Angry teenager rebelling against a time limit	Driver with road rage
A solo sport	Teenager worrying whether they have passed an exam
Anne Boleyn awaiting execution	Late for school/work
Gangster being caught out	Little boy/girl lost on holiday
Criminal on the run	Losing a mobile phone
Distraught mother who has lost a child	Stuck in a particular situation

Creating a solo composition based on a professional dance work

For this task, you are expected to choose **3 motifs** from a professional dance work, with guidance from your teacher. These motifs could be a position, a short motif and a longer phrase. You must then develop the three motifs into a solo dance that has a clear structure. You will need to choose the accompaniment for your dance, for which your teacher may give you guidance, but you will have to decide on any editing of the music. The finished piece should be $1–1^1/_2$ minutes long and your own work.

In this book there are photos of students in positions from some of the listed works for you to consider as starting points for your motifs (see pages 86, 87, 89, 90, 103, 104 and 113).

You would be expected to dance your solo in the style of the professional work, but you do not have to perform exactly the actions of the professional dancers. You can see from the photographs of the student dancers that the styles of dance vary hugely from one work to another. *Dance Tek Warriors* by Doug Elkins, for example, has an opening scene that uses street dance, whereas *'Still Life' at the Penguin Café* by David Bintley has several different styles within it: the penguins use classical steps; there is a ballroom scene; a hoe down is performed by the Texan Kangaroo Rat; and you can see contemporary and gymnastic actions from the Southern Cape Zebra. More everyday actions and gestures can be seen in *Faultline* by Shobana Jeyasingh and in *Rosas Danst Rosas* by Anne Teresa De Keersmaeker, while complex pure contemporary dance is evident in *Overdrive* by Richard Alston.

Choreography

Once you have chosen your three motifs you need to decide the order in which they will appear; what type of repetition, variations or developments you might use; and how your solo will be structured. You should consider:

* The sound that will accompany your solo — its rhythms, speeds, accents and length.
* The type of solo. For example, one based on *Rosas Danst Rosas* will be different to one based on *Swansong*. Although both works include dancers using chairs, their ideas are very different; for instance, the sound links with the characters in *Swansong* and the sense of monotony in *Rosas Danst Rosas*.
* How you will give your solo a clear structure and make good use of choreographic devices.
* Whether you have included your own original, but relevant, ideas.
* How to link your ideas with the three motifs in an imaginative and logical manner.
* Whether the final solo has a beginning, middle and ending, as well as a climax appropriate to your structure and the idea behind each of your chosen motifs.

Deciding the order of movements

A chance chart is a good tool for ordering movements. You could throw a dice or use playing cards to reveal a number, identify the action that goes with it, and the order the numbers turn up is the order of the actions in a motif. You could then decide (if you wish) your use of space or dynamics by throwing the dice again. You would then improvise ways of linking your motif to the idea of your dance.

Table 15 A chance chart to use for improvisation

	Action	Space 1	Space 2	Dynamics	Relationships
1	Travel	Low	Medium	Strongly	Side by side
2	Extend	High	Small	Gently	Close
3	Balance	Large	Round	Sharply	Far
4	Tilt	Thin	Wide	Smoothly	Facing
5	Jump	Twisted	Forwards	Quickly	In contact
6	Turn	Backwards	Sideways	Slowly	Back to back
7	Fall	Diagonal (HRF–DLB)	Diagonal (HR–DL)	Strongly and quickly	In two different levels
8	Twist	Up	Down	Gently and quickly	One behind the other
9	Curl	Circular	Angular	Fluidly	Diagonally in the space
10	Kick	Zigzag pattern	Semicircle	Rhythmically	One surrounds the other

Use cards, dice, telephone numbers, and birth dates to choose the order of the movement. A birth date, e.g. 26.07.93, would equal: 2 – extend, 6 – turn, 0 – kick, 7 – fall, 9 – curl, 3 – balance. The first two numbers of your telephone number, e.g. 54, could suggest: 5 – forwards, 4 – wide. This chart can therefore give you some more ways of finding actions, dynamics or uses of space to link with your dance idea.

Choreographing solo, duo and group dances

At this stage, you have developed some choreographic skills for solo dances. You can build a motif that expresses an idea; repeat a motif with simple variations; develop a motif through addition (inserting new material within the motif) or subtraction (taking part of a motif and developing that part separately); and use chance or other random methods to decide the order of the movements.

Other choreographic devices

Look back to this chapter's earlier sections on repetition, variation and development and consider the following devices as your dance starts to grow:

* including little highlights
* building up to a climax, the most important part of your dance
* acceleration: a motif starts slowly and gradually gets faster
* deceleration: a motif starts powerfully and rhythmically fast, and gradually slows down to stillness
* contrasts: in speed, level, energy, focus
* unison and canon
* contact: visual and tactile

Highlights and climax

It is vital that you include highlights or a climax (a special, important moment) in your dance. A dance without highlights or a climax will appear monotonous, have little sense of drama, and be likely to fail in conveying a dance idea within a structure, which means it would not gain more than a grade D. Highlights you could consider in a solo or group dance include:

* changing the speed unexpectedly, e.g. from slow to fast
* changing the dynamics, e.g. from fluid to sharp actions, or powerful actions to soft movements

❖ making one action important by showing it repeatedly, e.g. starting small on the spot, and eventually dancing it with a huge travelling pathway
❖ stopping unexpectedly, becoming totally still.

There are other highlights possible for a duo/group dance. You might use:
❖ a special lift of a dancer
❖ a special use of focus — towards each other or sharply to the audience
❖ travelling rhythmically in unison, with strongly accented rhythms
❖ fragmentation, where each dancer stops at a different moment in the group dance, as the dancers do in 'Muybridge 2' from *Bird Song* by Siobhan Davies
❖ accumulation, where each dancer gradually joins in performing the motif
❖ dancing separately and then meeting suddenly, staying in contact and moving slowly
❖ 'question and answer' movements, with contrasting actions, after a quiet section of your dance

Building up to and moving away from a highlight or climax should be the most important part of your dance. When choreographing this, you could consider:
❖ acceleration: a motif starts slowly and gradually gets faster, leading to a dramatic pause
❖ deceleration: a motif starts powerfully and rhythmically fast, gradually slowing down to a beautiful, quiet, gentle gesture
❖ contrast: in different speeds, levels, use of energy or focus
❖ unison and canon: a motif performed by three dancers in canon, in different areas of the stage, which is then repeated in unison, more powerfully and with extra accents, makes a strong climax
❖ a dramatic beginning, middle or end
❖ contact, both visual and tactile: a sudden change of focus towards each other, followed by movement towards each other, indicates that an important moment is about to happen; making physical contact unexpectedly or breaking away from each other will create a dramatic moment

Contrast

In a solo, you could perform a slow motif followed by a quick, lively motif; a fluid, smooth, travelling motif followed by a sharp, jerky motif on the spot; a high-level motif followed by a low-level motif; large movements followed by tiny movements; or a rhythmic, accented motif followed by a non-metric motif. You could change directions, movement upstage being followed by sudden travel downstage, or a linear pathway being followed by a curving, sinuous pathway.

Table 16 gives some contrasts you could use in small groups.

One part of the group	The rest of the group
At high level upstage	At low level downstage
On the spot	Travelling around the dancers that are on the spot
Moving quickly and rhythmically	Moving slowly and fluidly
Jumping strongly from side to side	Lifting and lowering each other slowly
In a tight group formation	In an elongated line
Travelling as a block, forwards to down stage	Travelling in a circle, towards and away from centre

Table 16
Contrasts

Unison

Varieties of unison within a solo include:

* **matching unison**: e.g. both arms do the same gesture at same time; both legs land at the same time from a jump; the head turns to the left as you lunge to the left with a punching gesture (all parts arrive and freeze at the same time)
* **contrasting unison**: e.g. both arms do contrasting gestures — perhaps one punches high as the other reaches gently forwards
* **complementary unison**: e.g. both arms do complementary gestures — for instance, one reaches forwards and high, and the other reaches forwards and low

Examples of unison within a group are:

* matching unison: e.g. all dancers travel doing identical steps at the same time in the same direction
* contrasting unison: e.g. in a circle, half of the group travel into the centre with steps and hops, as the other dancers travel away from the centre with a sliding and **rolling** motif
* complementary unison: e.g. all dancers travel doing identical steps at the same time in different directions

Canon

Canon in a solo could be:

* **continuous canon**: e.g. a circular gesture by the right arm, repeated by the left arm, and again by both arms together
* **contrasting canon**: e.g. a circular gesture by the right arm is followed by a sharp, slicing gesture by the left arm
* **complementary canon**: e.g. a circular gesture by the right arm is answered by a **rond de jambe** made by the left leg

Choreography

Within a group, one dancer could start the motif and the others gradually join in. Each starts the motif either when the previous dancer finishes the motif; when the previous dancer completes the first movement of the motif; or at any time during the motif, so that each dancer starts at a different action in the motif. In a trio starting the motif at different actions, the movements would be:

❖ Dancer A: 1 2 3 4 5 6
❖ Dancer B: 5 6 1 2 3 4
❖ Dancer C: 3 4 5 6 1 2

Alternatively, all the dancers could start together and gradually stop in turn. For a trio, all three dancers could do the motif together, then two dancers repeat it, then one dancer alone repeats it. Or, all three could start together; Dancer A repeats only the first action as other two dancers carry on to repeat the whole motif; Dancer B repeats only the first two actions of the third repeat, and Dancer C continues to the end of the third repeat. Finally, each dancer could perform part of the motif in a different order in canon:

❖ All dance: 1 2 3 4 5 6
❖ A dances: 1 only while B and C repeat the whole motif
❖ B dances: 1, 2 while C finishes the motif. Then all dance in unison
❖ A dances: 1 3 5 6 2
❖ B dances: 4 6 2 1
❖ C dances: 2 4 6

Options for group dances

You can now learn to have fun with motifs using two, three, four or five dancers. This is the exciting skill of choreography: using the dancers and how they relate to each other, and various motifs, to express a dance idea.

Many options are open to you. Your dancers could at any moment be:

❖ moving in unison
❖ moving in canon
❖ making an entrance
❖ making an exit
❖ moving at the same speeds as each other or at different speeds

SIMON RICHARDSON

Springs Dance Company: stepping in contact by Charlotte Brown and Naomi Cook, in *Living the Eucharist*, choreographed by Suzannah McCreight

* moving towards, away from, around or past each other
* moving at different levels or all at the same level
* doing the same movement, but one is performing it large and the other small
* in different areas of the stage
* facing different directions or all facing the same way
* in two or more group shapes
* in contact physically with each other

For every action and motif throughout your dance, you will need to choose where and how your dancers are performing on the stage. Your choice should depend on the part of the dance idea being expressed at each moment in your dance. If you have three, four or five dancers, then they can dance into and out of group shapes or group formations. You could choose to have your dancers in a line or in a circle.

Support and hold: Wendy Hesketh and Junior Cunningham, from *Perfect* by Kevin Finnan

All facing the same way: inspired by the Marshmallows in *Nutcracker*!

Double lift by Junior, Wendy, Brian and Vanessa, from *Perfect* by Kevin Finnan

Group positions in a line	Group positions in a circle
❖ Side by side, one behind the other	❖ Facing inwards, outwards
❖ Facing front, stage right, stage left or upstage	❖ Right or left shoulder to centre
❖ From one corner to another (diagonally)	❖ Facing alternate directions
❖ From upstage to downstage (see above)	❖ Close to or far from each other
❖ Facing alternate directions	❖ At the same or different levels
❖ Close to or far from each other	❖ On the spot or travelling
❖ At the same or different levels	❖ Travelling forwards, backwards or sideways
❖ On the spot or travelling	❖ Going around, in and out
❖ Travelling forwards, backwards or sideways	❖ With or without contact
❖ With or without contact	❖ In different areas of the stage
❖ In different areas of the stage	❖ In large or small circles
❖ In different line lengths	❖ Curves can be linked to make other
❖ If in a group of four or five, some dancers could be in a line separate from the other dancer(s)	formations, such as a spiral, a semicircle
❖ Other combinations of lines to make group formations, e.g. wedge, triangle, square	

Table 17 Group positions

Observation and viewpoint

You will create the most interesting and expressive group dances if you watch and make every decision from the spectator's viewpoint. For your final choreography assessment, you personally must be able to see what your dance is about — that is, the dance idea. If you cannot see it, then there is little chance that your teacher or a visiting **moderator** will be able to either.

Once you place yourself as a dancer within your choreography, your understanding of what the dance expresses changes. You become involved in showing your own dancing ability, rather than focusing on the overall expression of the dance idea, and you are therefore unable to see what the dance is conveying to an audience. It is therefore best to spend time demonstrating and teaching your dancers the actions you want performed. You must then stand back, and watch not only that they are doing accurately the movements you chose, but also that the movements express your dance idea.

You may find that you need to adapt your original choreography. The energy the dancers are using might need changing to get the dynamic impact you want, or a movement could give a clearer image of a group shape if it faced a different direction. Experiment, almost play around, with different versions of your motifs and the placing of your dancers in the space, to see which way best conveys your dance idea. This takes time and patience, for you and your dancers, but it is time well spent that will help you gain a higher grade.

Duos

Let us consider some ideas from the 'diagonal playtime' theme as a duo, rather than as a solo. Figure 27 (in Chapter 5) includes the following duo actions:

- diagonals that cross
- diagonals that meet
- lines between body parts
- parallel diagonals
- V-shape formed by diagonals
- shared air patterns
- shared floor pathways
- group shape

Improvisation on the idea leads to two motifs (see Chapter 6):

1 run, link, balances, link, drops/falls to a shape
2 leaps/jumps, link, gestures, link, suspension to a new shape

How could two dancers use motif (1) or (2) or a mixture?

Diagonals that pass each other

The dancers' pathways could start from opposite corners as they run in a straight line past each other. They could in unison balance individually, facing the new corner (away from each other), then drop/fall in canon, to finish facing each other.

Front

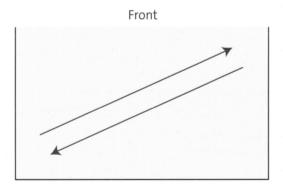

Figure 34
Diagonals that
pass each other

Diagonals that meet

Two dancers stand side-by-side, facing the front. They lunge in towards each other, with the inside arm reaching high to their side, till it touches their partner's fingertips. They then release the outside leg from the floor so that they are balancing.

Alternatively, the two dancers could drop to the floor to finish lying on their sides, facing the front, their feet near each other. They lift the leg furthest from the front diagonally sideways and up, till they touch toes or soles of feet.

Diagonals showing lines between body parts

Both the above ideas do this. Another method would be for one dancer to make part of a diagonal line with his/her right side and arms, while sitting on the walk. The partner stands on tiptoe, elongating the diagonal line with his/her arms. The dancers could be holding wrists and then drop away from each other.

Parallel diagonals

The two dancers could run side by side as a parallel pathway; they could make diagonal arm gestures at different levels in a balance; or one dancer could lie on the floor in a diagonal whole body shape, with the other standing behind in a complementary body shape in a higher level.

V-shape formed by diagonals

The dancers start at DSR and DSL. They run to centre stage, to meet in an extended balance with contact. Or they could start centre stage and use two leaps and a gesture to suspend as they turn to retrace their pathway.

Figure 35 V-shapes formed by diagonal pathways

Group

Using more than two dancers allows even more possibilities. Dancers in group shapes could face any direction or the same direction, close to or far from each other, and with or without contact. They could arrive and leave in canon or unison; arriving strongly, quickly, and holding still could be a highlight of the dance.

Group exercises: unison and canon

These exercises are for a group of four. They use the two 'diagonal playtime' motifs and their various parts.

1 Simple version

a All four dancers perform motif (1). They enter stage in canon, each starting as previous dancer goes into the balance.

b Two dancers repeat the motif together, travelling away from each other and from the remaining two. The remaining pair repeats the motif in contact, centre stage, probably moving at a different speed to the travelling couple.

c All four repeat the motif in unison to meet in a diagonal line.

d The gesture from motif (2) is performed by Dancers 1 and 3 in the line first, and then by Dancers 2 and 4 in the line.

e They all run in unison to form a circle. Three lift or support one dancer in the suspension shape.

2 More complex version

Each dancer performs a mixture of each motif:

❖ Dancer 1: run, leap, drop, gesture, suspend, balance

❖ Dancer 2: balance, suspend, gesture, drop, leap, run

❖ Dancer 3: drop, leap, run, balance, gesture, suspend

❖ Dancer 4: leap, drop, suspend, run, balance, gesture

3 Choreographic devices you could try

a All four dancers start in the centre and follow a diagonal pathway away from the centre, doing their own new motif.

b Dancers 1 and 4 do their two motifs in unison, 1's motif is followed by 4's motif.

c Dancers 3 and 2 use Dancer 2's motif, making and losing contact, with moments of stillness.

d All four dancers do number 3's motif, making a zigzag pathway in unison.

e All four dancers do one still shape from their own motif, sharply and strongly, in canon.

d All four dancers link these actions to perform them in unison in slow motion, thus creating yet another motif!

Structure

The structure of your dance must have a sense of **unity** and move logically from beginning to end. You need to discover the different structures and styles your dance could adopt. These will depend on your dance idea, the accompaniment you have chosen, and the motifs you have created as your choreographic devices.

Your dance could be in any number and type of sections, within the time framework dictated by the exam board. A solo should be between $1^1/_2$ and 2 minutes, and a duo or group dance should be 2–3 minutes. You need to choose how many sections you will use, how long each will be, the order, and what each contributes to the dance idea.

Types of structure

Binary form

Binary form has two sections and is the simplest structure. There are sections A and B, with a short transition (bridge). Each section expresses a different part of the dance idea, but they must be linked in a sensible manner.

Ternary form

Ternary form has three sections — ABA — that act as chorus, verse, chorus. Section A returns to conclude the dance with a variation, usually on the first Section A. Section B is usually a contrasting section.

Rondo form

Rondo form has either five or seven sections: ABACA or ABACADA. Clearly, it would be boring if each Section A were identical, so variations are expected in each Section A as it appears. Many styles of dance use this structure, with the A sections being danced by an entire group, and the B, C, and D sections being performed as solos or duos.

A variation on this structure can be in theme and **variations**, with sections A1, A2, A3, A4, A5, A6 and A7. This is a more difficult structure, as Section A must have enough within it to be varied a further six times without becoming monotonous. **Pure dance** is often in this structure (see page 120).

Chance

This is a **form** used by Merce Cunningham, Richard Alston and Siobhan Davies. They might give their dancers ways of improvising movement material just before a performance. The dancers would be told the order of motifs and which areas of the stage and facings to use. Chance relationships then appear, and the dance looks different each time it is performed, even though the **movement vocabulary** is always the same essential core.

However, this method is not suitable for your GCSE final choreographic assessment, except as a way of finding movement ideas in order to structure your dance. Your dancers have to know what they are doing, where and how, at any given time, and should not be improvising in your final choreography.

Narrative form

This structure outlines a story in scenes: ABCDE. Many classical ballets have this structure. A few scenes together make up an **act**; there could be as many as three acts to a ballet. It will probably last for up to 2 hours. Remember that your dance must not exceed 3 minutes, so if you use narrative form your scenes have to be short.

Jigsaws and essays

In many ways, a dance is like a jigsaw or an essay. The idea or topic can be seen in the sections of a dance or jigsaw, or in the paragraphs in an essay. Each section of a dance has motifs made of actions, just as a jigsaw has a small scene or picture made up of pieces, or a paragraph in an essay is made of a mixture of sentences. A dance has a time framework, which is like a jigsaw's outer frame-work and an essay's introduction, middle and conclusion. The table below shows these similar structures.

Table 18 Comparing a dance with a jigsaw and an essay

Dance	Essay	Jigsaw
Actions	Words	Pieces
Motif: actions linked together	Sentence: words make sentences	Small image, such as a leaf on a tree, or the face of a person
All make a statement that expresses an idea or topic		
Section contains motifs and some variations	Paragraph has at least four sentences	Sky or an object in one area of the jigsaw
All have linked ideas that express more detail, and are based on the original statement		
Number of sections = framework	Number of paragraphs = structure	Outline of outer pieces = shape
The structure has a shape, a clear size and duration, and is logical in expressing its idea		

Choreographic styles

Details of some possible styles are given below.

Abstract dance

Abstract dance takes an idea from a source other than movement, and creates it in a non-realistic manner. There is a clear link with the original source (e.g. a poem, painting, sculpture, nature). Particular aspects of the source have been 'abstracted'

and developed through movement into a new artistic dance structure. An example is *Bird Song* (2004) by Siobhan Davies.

Comic dance

Comic dances often have a human element within them. For example, they might include realistic gestures, performed in an exaggerated manner or in an inappropriate situation, which may make us laugh. There is often mime and unusual facial expressions. Characters are portrayed in a larger-than-life manner, and can seem ridiculous. An example is the scene of 'The Marshmallow's Dance' from *Nutcracker!* by Matthew Bourne.

You should note that comic dance is not an easy style to sustain or even attempt at GCSE.

Dance drama

This style of choreography tells a story, in brief episodes or scenes. It includes characters and the situations they experience, which may have emotional and dramatic meaning. The dynamic content of such dances is high, as is the level of interaction between the dancers in order to convey particular aspects of the story. An example of this choreographic style is *Romeo and Juliet* by Kenneth MacMillan.

Dramatic dance

This style of choreography emphasises a mood or particular event without telling a story. It might be about a power struggle, for example, or someone who is sad or excited. The dance will have a tangible atmosphere. Dynamic content will be high in this style, too, and characterisation is also important. How the dancers relate to each other and to the audience is a vital feature of dramatic dances. Facial expressions and significant gestures for each character must be thought about carefully. *Perfect*, by Kevin Finnan and Motionhouse Dance Theatre, has several solos and duos that show this style.

Pure dance

This choreographic style emphasises 'dancing' and the movement itself. There is no story or characterisation, but a movement idea underpins the choreography. An example of pure dance is *Overdrive* by Richard Alston.

Dance study

Dance study is similar to pure dance but has a narrower focus, which is explored in detail. For example, a dance based on diagonals has a spatial focus. A dance study would not have characterisation or emotive moments, but would be clearly constructed to show a breadth of interpretation of one particular movement idea. It would form a demanding, possibly academic, treatment of the dance idea.

Exercises

Motifs to express an idea in a duo: a way of working for you to try

Theme: Celebration
Form: ABA

Section A

a With a partner, choose three different arm shapes that you associate with victory or celebrating. Then link them together as follows.

b Travel using the first arm shape (8 counts).

c Use jumps and canon, linked with the second arm shape (8 counts).

d Use turns with the third arm shape (8 counts).

e End this section with a transition of your choice to get back to your starting positions (8 counts).

Section B

a Together, choose two arm and body shapes that express defeat or disappointment. Create a motif that includes these shapes within the personal space of the duo (8 counts).

b Perform the motif in unison (8 counts).

c Repeat, showing a complementary relationship between you (8 counts).

d Repeat, including use of canon, a change in dynamics and a new support (8 counts).

e Repeat your original transition phrase to get back to starting positions, but in a different part of the space (8 counts).

Section A

a Repeat the whole of Section A, but vary the floor pathways and the relationships between the pair of you (4 x 8 counts).

or

b Repeat the original Section A with new accents and increased energy, leading to an ending that is a climax to the dance.

Choreography

Creating a group dance for four

Theme: this idea links with *Car*
by Lea Anderson

Form: ternary

Sit in your four with a chair each, placed like the inside of a car, facing front. The dancers are numbered:

1 = driver
2 = beside driver
3 = behind 2
4 = behind driver

Section A: the journey

Once this section is remembered, dancers can act the whole section in character.

a All dancers stand to the outside of their own chair. Open the door, get in, and shut the door (8 counts).

b Put on seatbelt (4 counts).

c All do an action of their choice (e.g. insert ignition key, switch on radio, put in a CD or tape, pull down visor) (4 counts).

d All perform Dancer 1's action in unison (4 counts).

e Dancers 1 and 2 do Dancer 2's action, and Dancers 3 and 4 do Dancer 3's action (4 counts).

f Dancers 2 and 3 do Dancer 3's action, and Dancers 1 and 4 do Dancer 4's action (4 counts).

g All open windows (4 counts).

h All lean heads out and then look ahead (4 counts).

i All sit back and look at partner (4 counts).

j All look to windscreen, and then lean well back (4 counts).

k Sit back up in canon (4 counts).

l Rear passengers undo seatbelt, get out and shut door. Front passengers repeat Dancer 2's and then Dancer 3's action (8 counts).

m Rear passengers move to front car door, lean in, pull back, open door. Front passengers move a hand to the seatbelt, lean to centre, lean back, remove seatbelt (8 counts).

n Rear passengers walk around car to opposite wing mirror. Front passengers wind all windows shut, get out and shut door (8 counts).

o All walk in formation to stand ready to enter a new **venue** (16 counts).

Transition

All enter the new venue in character (8 counts).

Section B

The new venue could be a theatre, supermarket, station, bank, club, football match etc. Possible situation ideas are: gangsters going to a bank, models going to a photo shoot, football fans going to a match, shoppers going to a mall.

All dancers must have a character who might travel in the car and go to this venue. They must move in unison

Chapter 7

Creating and using dance motifs and phrases

and canon, include a variety of group shapes, and use actions appropriate to the venue selected. The actions should be larger than those in the car.

This section must use 24 bars, and finish with each dancer back at the car doors. You would need to rehearse it thoroughly and then practise the two sections together.

Section A
Finally Section A is repeated, using the original movement material but including some of the following devices:
❖ changing the order
❖ changing spatial aspects (size, shape, direction or level)
❖ changing the dynamics
❖ building up to an unexpected ending

The dance would have a clear ending. The number of bars to be used in this section should be decided by the teacher.

You could be assessed on your performance of this work, your notes on how Section B was created, or which ideas you gave to this section. You might be asked to identify and describe the performing skills you had to use to perform this dance well.

After you have completed this exercise, you could watch excerpts of *Car* on video. Write about both your own and Lea Anderson's way of working, using one excerpt of *Car*, for homework.

Using props and a non-dance space
Aim: to create and perform a short dance in a group of three dancers
Form: rondo

Your teacher will provide both the sound and the space you will use. Your dance should last between 2 and 3 minutes, so keep the sections short (ABACA). Each dancer should use a prop of his/her choice. Relationships should be considered alongside group shapes, and unison and canon should be visible. Decide a front for the audience before choreography starts, and agree a way of working as a three to meet the deadline. You are to use the features of the space that you are given:
❖ surfaces
❖ furniture
❖ the usual function of the space
❖ the people who go there

These features will contribute to the dance idea, along with your three props. The provided sound will give a rhythmic support. Remember to give your dance a title.

CHRIS NASH

Vanessa Cook in 'Desert Faces', from *Perfect* by Kevin Finnan

CHRIS NASH

Aerial movement using slings, from *Perfect* by Kevin Finnan

Recording your choreographic progress

Throughout your course you will learn choreographic devices, allowing you to use taught movements imaginatively and to find movements of your own. You need to show that you know what an action is by making a motif; that you understand dynamics, and can change the speed, rhythm, energy and flow of your actions; that you know where all the spatial areas are, and how to vary them; that you can add a suitable ending position; and that you can find an appropriate linking movement (transition).

These are all practical skills, and you will learn some of them very early in your course. However, as well as learning them practically, you must also write about each new choreographic device you learn as you progress through the course. If you do not, you will almost certainly not use the most appropriate devices in your final choreographic assignments and you will not have enough notes to revise from for the final written paper. Keeping a record of your ideas, devices, the music you use, and ways of working with a partner or a group is vital, especially if you are aiming for grades A*–C.

A choreographic diary

To make sure you have a thorough record of your progress, keep a choreographic diary. You could use an A4 folder or one or more exercise books. It will be your personal record of what you have learnt, which your teacher can mark and/or make comments on. You could divide your first diary into the following sections:

❖ ways I found and made motifs
❖ choreographic devices I used or saw
❖ successes
❖ major problems and how I solved them

- ❖ themes/ideas we tried and my thoughts on my work
- ❖ my thoughts on themes/ideas I watched that worked well
- ❖ accompaniment we used that I might like to use again and why
- ❖ duo work I have done, and what did and didn't work
- ❖ group work I enjoyed and why
- ❖ group work I found difficult and why

For each section, include the date, what you were asked to do, the thoughts you had as you set about the task, what you actually did, what you thought about your work, any **feedback** you got, and what you might try differently next time.

Keeping your diary will give you vital practice in writing about dance, a skill most students do not have before starting this course, and one you need to learn. Dance has specialist vocabulary that describes dance positions and actions, much of which came from France. Getting used to identifying and describing movements, motifs and choreographic devices takes time and effort. You have to write in detail about the final solo or group choreography you create, so keeping an up-to-date diary will help you to gain confidence in using dance vocabulary in your written work.

Keep a special section in your diary for any full choreographic assessments you are given, which require you to make a dance with an idea, in sections with motifs and variations, and with suitable accompaniment. For these tasks, you will need to keep a log of every decision you make, from when you are set a particular task to when you have completed it. Record the reasons for the decisions you made, what worked, what didn't work, and what you changed. Note any feedback you received and how you responded to it.

It is worth taking the time to keep your diary up to date, or you will forget what you learnt at the beginning of the course. You will certainly need this information at the end.

Decision-making and reasons

The decisions you make and your reasons for them depend on how much freedom your teacher gives you. On the one hand, you might be given a list of five ideas to choose from, three pieces of music to choose from, a time limit, and a group of students to work with. You might be able to choose whether your dance will be a solo, duo or group dance, what the dance idea will be, the accompaniment and who will dance it, from within a given list of topics.

Regardless of whether you have been set a free task, or one more clearly directed by your teacher, you will have a deadline by which the dance has to be finished and assessed. You need to work out a timetable for yourself (and your dancers), stating by when key decisions will be made. For example:

* When will you have two or three motifs to include in your dance?
* When will you have chosen your accompaniment?
* What can/must you do in class to improvise/vary your motifs?
* When will you rehearse to music away from everyone else?
* When will you rehearse the dance and get feedback from a friend, parent or teacher?
* Will you take photos or film the dance before the assessment?

Whether you are choreographing a solo or a group dance, you should keep a written record of each decision, with the reason you made it. Record every problem you had and how you solved it. These evaluations of how you developed your dance will make your final choreography better, as we all learn from our mistakes. Remember, you can talk through your decisions with teachers, friends and parents, but you have to make the dance yourself.

Solo, duo or group dance

When choreographing, you will decide:

* the movements that form the motifs or transitions
* the dynamics
* the use of space
* the use of focus
* the way these relate to the accompaniment
* the sections of the dance
* when there will be an important moment, and how you will make it stand out to the audience
* when a motif appears or is repeated or varied
* the style of the dance (both performing and choreographic)
* for a solo, if you or another dancer is performing
* rehearsal times, to ensure that the dance is ready, as you want it, for the assessment

A solo moment in the style of Bharata Natyam

For a duo or group dance you will decide:

❖ how your dancers relate to each other throughout the dance
❖ the use of unison and canon
❖ the use of contact
❖ group shapes/formations

Moments inspired by *'Still Life' at the Penguin Café*

A variation on the ballroom hold   A hopping gesture by the three penguins

Duo or group dance

Preparation and expression

You may need to prepare your duo or group dancers to perform for the assessment. Keep notes on this preparation, explaining the stage you are at in teaching each dancer his/her role in your dance. They may have learnt the choreography and know the dance, but could still need help from you in expressing the subject matter as you want, with the correct use of focus, extension, projection, musicality and sensitivity to each other. Record how you go about this, and any successes or failures.

Choosing and using dancers

You might like to **evaluate** your decisions in choosing and using the dancers for your dance. **Explain** what worked and what didn't work, with reasons.

❖ Was your choice of accompaniment suitable for your dancers and the subject matter to be communicated?

- Was the style of dance you selected one that your dancers could perform appropriately to express the subject matter of the dance?
- Did you use your dancers in different relationships, with and without contact, in different areas of the space?
- Were you sensitive to your dancers and able to organise them and their roles in your dance?
- Was the number of dancers right for your dance idea? (You could use two, three, four or five.)
- Were all the dancers available for your rehearsals, performance and assessment?
- Did you need both male and female dancers?
- Did all the dancers have the relevant dance experience and expertise for your dance?
- Did they give you enough interest, time and commitment to make the dance work as you designed it?
- Did all the dancers you chose work well together for you?

Awareness of relationships

You have to make your dancers aware of the relationships in your dance:

- Do they know the dance idea and how it grows through the dance?
- Do they know what formations they should be in?
- Do they know where they are facing in the formation?
- Has the formation a feeling or mood to be felt and expressed?
- Do they know how close they are meant to be to each other?
- Do they know which area of the stage they should be in?
- Do they know where the other dancers are?
- Do they know the pathways they are travelling?
- Do they need to adjust the size of the steps to show unison?
- Are they in time with each other?
- Are they in time with the music?
- Are they using contact well?
- Is the timing of the contact right?
- Do they enter and leave the stage at the right moment and in the way you want?
- Are they aware of the rhythm of any canon?
- Are they aware of the dynamics of each move?
- Do they know when the highlights of the dance are, and their role in leading up to and away from them?

Performing skills

You could evaluate the performing skills of your dancers. These include:

❖ watching each other
❖ keeping in time with each other and the music
❖ being spatially correct in the performing space
❖ not being too close or too far away
❖ making contact sensibly
❖ using the correct focus and actions
❖ showing appropriate expression and characterisation

Solo based on three motifs from a set work

Your teacher will expect you to learn three short motifs from one of the professional works you are studying and to use these to structure a solo yourself. It should last 1–1$^{1}/_{2}$ minutes. The accompaniment may be given to you or you may be allowed to choose your own. Clearly you will need to use your knowledge of choreographic devices and the ways in which solo pieces can be structured.

The following charts may help you select a variety of devices to use. Take care that the style of dance you use stays constant throughout.

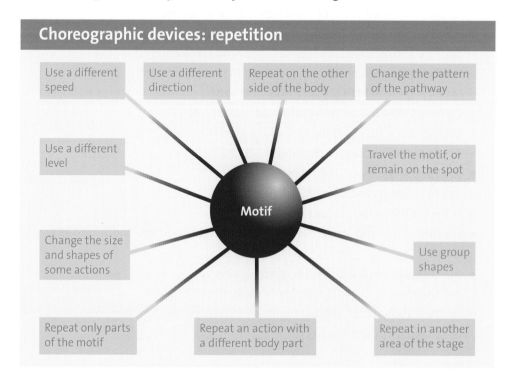

Choreographic devices: repetition

- Use a different speed
- Use a different direction
- Repeat on the other side of the body
- Change the pattern of the pathway
- Use a different level
- Travel the motif, or remain on the spot
- Change the size and shapes of some actions
- Use group shapes
- Motif
- Repeat only parts of the motif
- Repeat an action with a different body part
- Repeat in another area of the stage

Choreographic devices: variation

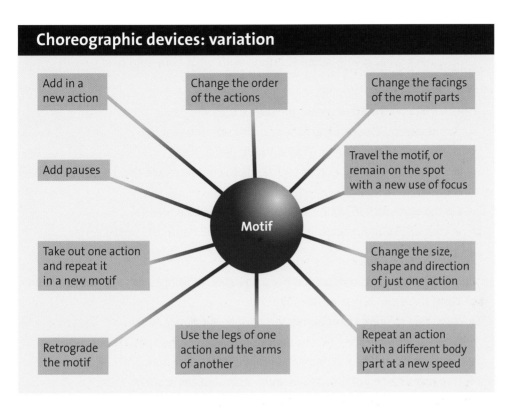

Add in a new action

Change the order of the actions

Change the facings of the motif parts

Add pauses

Travel the motif, or remain on the spot with a new use of focus

Motif

Take out one action and repeat it in a new motif

Change the size, shape and direction of just one action

Retrograde the motif

Use the legs of one action and the arms of another

Repeat an action with a different body part at a new speed

Choreographic devices: development

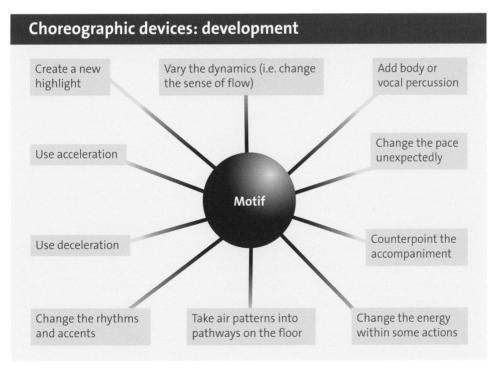

Create a new highlight

Vary the dynamics (i.e. change the sense of flow)

Add body or vocal percussion

Use acceleration

Change the pace unexpectedly

Motif

Use deceleration

Counterpoint the accompaniment

Change the rhythms and accents

Take air patterns into pathways on the floor

Change the energy within some actions

Evaluating your solo choreography

Cross-check what a solo should contain with what your solo has.

Motifs

Check that your motifs express the dance idea:

* Can the idea be seen clearly by your friends and teacher?
* Is your use of the dancer related to the dance idea?
* Are your motifs put together effectively to communicate the dance idea of each section?
* Do the dynamics in your dance express the dance idea?
* Is your use of the space clear? (It shouldn't all be on the spot!)

Action content

Check that the action content has been repeated, developed or varied in your dance:

* What have you repeated, and how?
* What has the repetition expressed about your dance idea?
* Is there an interesting mix of rhythmic, dynamic and spatial contrasts?
* Do you use contrast, climax and highlights in your dance?
* Has your dance got a sense of unity and a logical sequence?

Rehearsal

Check that you rehearsed the dance enough before the assessment:

* Did you know the dance thoroughly?
* Did you dance in time with the music?
* Did you show the highlights of your solo clearly?
* Did you get feedback on the performance of your solo as well as on the choreography?
* Did you use focus well?
* Did you use accents in the music?
* Did you have control over all your movements?
* Did you finish the dance properly, with a good ending position?

Which of these descriptions fits your solo dance?

Read the questions below and for each decide which statement best describes your dance. List these in your choreographic diary and give reasons. (Your grade will be higher if your solo fits the final statement in each category.)

Do my movements link with the dance idea?

* At times my movements link with the original dance idea.
* My movement material links with the original idea.

* My knowledge of dance vocabulary is seen clearly in relation to the dance idea.
* My movement material is manipulated effectively in relation to the dance idea.
* My dance shows an articulate, original and highly refined link with the dance idea.

Have I changed the action content in my solo?
* The use of action content has been changed in my solo.
* Dynamic content does not change.
* There is limited spatial awareness.
* Action, rhythm, dynamics and use of space are evident in the dance phrases.
* I have shown some interesting use of action, rhythm, dynamics and spatial elements.
* There is pleasing use of rhythmic, dynamic and spatial interest.
* There is sophisticated use of rhythmic and spatial design.

Does my dance have an overall structure?
* My solo has a simple overall structure.
* My solo is a well-structured whole dance.
* I use choreographic devices effectively within a unified and logical whole solo.
* My knowledge of choreographic form is clearly evident.
* My solo shows considerable understanding of choreographic form.

Which choreographic devices have I used?
* I have used a limited range of choreographic devices.
* I have included some dance phrases and I used repetition.
* Repetition and contrast are clearly evident.
* Choreographic devices, repetition with changes and contrast, and some variety, are all seen.
* I have used **development**, climax and contrast sensitively.
* I have clearly used contrast, climax and a logical sequence extremely effectively.

Do the motifs I have chosen communicate the dance idea?
* My ability to use movement to communicate is limited.
* The quality of my dance overall is uneven.
* Communication of the dance idea is erratic.
* My chosen idea is clearly communicated.
* My dance works well and communicates effectively the artistic intent.
* My dance is an exceptionally well–designed work, which communicates the artistic intent.

Evaluating your duo/group choreography

Motifs

Check that your motifs express the dance idea:

❖ Can the idea be seen clearly by your friends and teacher?

❖ Is your use of the dancers related to the dance idea?

❖ Are your motifs put together effectively to communicate the dance idea of each section?

❖ Do the dynamics in your dance express the dance idea?

❖ Is your use of the space clear? (It shouldn't all be on the spot!)

Action content

Check that the action content has been repeated, developed or varied in your dance:

❖ What have you repeated, how and by whom?

❖ What has the repetition expressed about your dance idea?

❖ Is there an interesting mix of rhythmic, dynamic and spatial contrasts between the dancers?

❖ Do you use contrast, climax and highlights in your dance?

❖ Has your dance got a sense of unity and logical sequence?

'Muybridge 1' from *Bird Song* by Siobhan Davies. Starbursts appear in this section

JOEL CHESTER FILDES

Chapter

Relationships

Check that the relationships change between the dancers so as to express the dance idea in different sections of your dance:

❖ Is your choice of duo/group formations communicating the dance idea?

❖ Do you use at least three different relationship ideas, in the most appropriate place, in your dance?

Which of these descriptions fits your duo/group dance?

Read the statements below and for each question decide which statement best describes your dance. List these in your choreographic diary and give reasons. (Your grade will be higher if your dance fits the final statement in each category.)

Do the movements link with the dance idea?

❖ At times my movements link with the original dance idea.

❖ My movement material links with the original dance idea.

❖ My knowledge of dance vocabulary is seen clearly in relation to the dance idea.

❖ My movement material is manipulated effectively in relation to the dance idea.

❖ My dance shows an articulate, original and highly refined link with the dance idea.

Does my dance have an overall structure?

❖ The structure is uneven in my dance.

❖ Choreographic form is evident in my dance.

❖ My dance has a sense of unity.

❖ My whole dance shows considerable understanding of group relationships within the choreographic form.

Which choreographic devices have been used?

❖ I have made dance phrases, which are repeated in my dance.

❖ I have used contrast and repetition.

❖ I have used repetition, changes and contrast, and some variety, effectively between my dancers.

❖ I have used development, climax and contrast effectively within a unified whole-group dance.

Does the movement material communicate the dance idea?

❖ The use of movement to communicate is limited.

❖ Communication is, at times, more or less effective.

Choreography

- ❖ The chosen idea is communicated.
- ❖ The dance works well.
- ❖ The material is effective in communicating the artistic intent.
- ❖ The dance is exceptionally well-designed, which communicates the artistic intent.

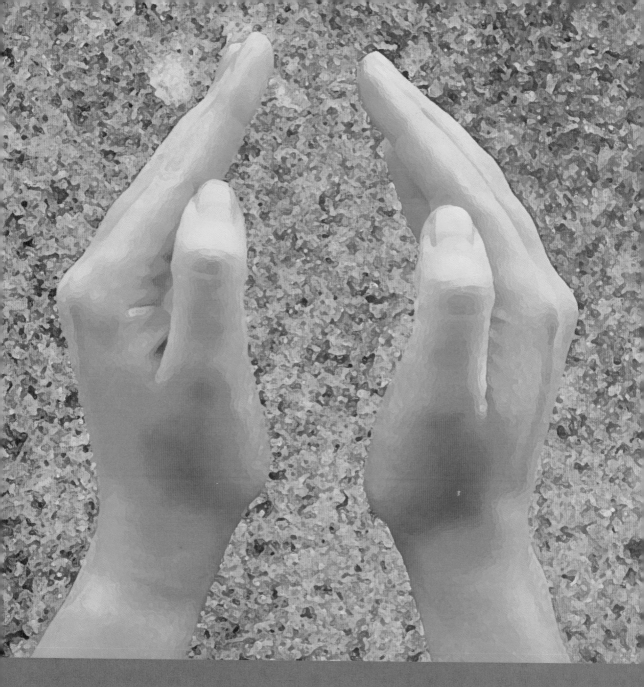

Section 3

Appreciation

Appreciation

During your course you will be shown dance on video or DVD, and you will hopefully have the chance to watch a live performance by a professional dance company. This will give you the opportunity to see what is involved in professional choreography and performance. You will learn to look for particular features of a dance work, how to talk about what you saw, and to write your observations down.

You will get to know thoroughly two set works from a list provided by the exam board, and be able to identify, describe and discuss features of both dance works. You will be expected to show your knowledge of these two works in the written paper at the end of your course, in both short answers and detailed paragraphs.

Watching dance is a complex activity, as there is often a lot going on at any one time. This section will help you to find words to describe what you have seen. You will be using the knowledge you have learnt from your practical lessons and earlier chapters in this book to show your understanding of how the idea or theme of a dance is visible through its movement content (actions, dynamics and use of space); how the dancers are used; the style of dance being performed; the accompaniment; the design of the costumes; the set design; and the lighting design. You will find examples of how you could write about part of a work, charts to list important features, and practice questions.

'Preparing for the final assessments' includes ideas for rehearsing performance pieces, stages to follow as you start choreographing your final assessment and pitfalls to avoid.

Chapter 9

Looking at professional dance works

Identifying dance styles

You need to be able to identify the style of dance being performed in any professional dance work. This chapter lists the obvious features of performance and **choreographic styles** of a dance. Look for these features in the dances you see in photographs, on videos or DVD, in live performance, and in your memory. For example, contemporary dance is most often performed in bare feet with clothing that allows freedom of movement and is appropriate for abstract or pure dance works, as seen in the photographs of *Pond Way* and *Faultline*.

Specific details are required so you can identify the style of dance and show an examiner that you really know the difference between one style and another. For instance, are the **use of contact** with others, the **use of the feet**, full body movement and props enough to identify ballet? Not really — these are also features of contemporary dance or musical theatre. Instead, look at a particular ballet and find features within it. Let's take *Romeo and Juliet*, choreographed by Kenneth MacMillan and performed by the Royal Ballet, as an example. Is there 'contact with others'?

Amy Hollingsworth and Alexander Whitely in *Pond Way* by Merce Cunningham, Rambert Dance Company

Dancers meet; Saju and Deveraj in *Faultline* by Shobana Jeyasingh

What typical example of this did you see? Perhaps a male dancer was holding a female dancer around the waist as she pirouetted or balanced.

Now think about the 'use of the feet'. In ballet, the female dancer turns, balances and travels on pointe, whereas in contemporary dance the dancers mainly perform in bare feet. The use of props and furniture is seen in narrative works, and in Act I of *Nutcracker!* by Matthew Bourne, several are used: scarves held by Matron and her orphans, and beds on which several orphans lie, fight and sit. Costume, lighting and **set design** are also important features that tell us about the choreographic and **performance styles**, as well as the subject matter of the work.

Be warned that some professional dance works have a mixture of styles, and photographs only capture one particular moment in a dance. For example, there is a morris dance in 'Section 4: Humboldt's Hog-Nosed Skunk Flea' in *'Still Life' at the Penguin Café* by David Bintley. The morris dancers are in authentic costume, while the flea jumps and flies from one to the other. The steps made by the male morris dancers derive from the folk dance style and are different to the classical ballet steps seen occasionally from the Flea and by other animals in the work. Each section of *'Still Life' at the Penguin Café* has different styles of dance; for example, there is a hint of African dance in the Southern Cape Zebra and Ballroom in 'Section 1: The Great Auk'. The styles are therefore not out of place in this ballet, but rather help the audience to identify the subject matter of the narrative.

Nine dancers in *Overdrive* by Richard Alston

CATHERINE ASHMORE

Learning how to identify dance styles and writing about your understanding and knowledge takes practice. The lists provided in this chapter will guide you on the amount of detail necessary to identify, describe and explain the relevance of the style of dance, the sound, the costumes, the set and the lighting to expressing the subject matter of the dance work to an audience. You should also look back at the style diagrams and photographs in Chapter 3 to help you.

Dance features

What the dancers do: action content

Movement: type of step, jump, travel, balance, gesture, weight transference, turn, contact with others, use of arms, eyes, feet, hands, head, hips, legs, trunk

Gestures: everyday gestures, full-body movement, isolated actions, mime, minimal movement, successive movement

Actions: using props, surfaces of dance venue (climb, slide, knock etc.), other dancers

Hand gestures towards another dancer (Paul Liburd and Didy Veldman in *Meeting Point* by Christopher Bruce, Rambert Dance Company)

How the dancers move: dynamic content

Speed: slowly, quickly, rhythmically, sudden stops, accentuated beats

Flow: fluidly, jerkily, smoothly, freely, in a controlled manner

Energy: gently, strongly, sharply, powerfully, delicately

Space: filling the space freely, carving a careful pattern, on the spot or travelling

Where the dancers move: spatial content

Level: using the floor, at medium level, with lifts and high jumps

Direction: facing downstage or any stage area, moving into different directions (sideways, backwards, diagonally etc.)

Size: small movements, large movements

Shape: symmetrical or asymmetrical body shape, linear or curved patterns (in air or floor pathways)

In unison, in character, in the air: Cupids and Clara in *Nutcracker!* by Matthew Bourne, New Adventures Dance Company

...ho the dancers ...nce with: ...elationships

- ❖ solo, partner, group work
- ❖ with/without contact
- ❖ in a large company (e.g. the Royal Ballet) or a small company (e.g. Ludus)
- ❖ in formations
- ❖ in unison or canon
- ❖ contrasting, matching or complementing others

BILL COOPER

The three penguin waiters from *'Still Life' at the Penguin Café* by David Bintley, Birmingham Royal Ballet

What the dancers wear

This could be on their feet, legs, bodies, arms, hands, faces or heads.

What props the dancers use (if any)

These might be bells, chairs, hankies, masks, poles, ribbons, scarves or sticks.

Venue or performance environment

SIMON RICHARDSON

Indoors: aircraft hangar, ballroom, cathedral, church, concert hall, corridor, gymnasium, hall, hotel, in the round, nightclub, opera house, pub, small rural theatre, sports hall, stage (e.g. school, community centre, dance centre), studio (e.g. community centre, school, professional dance centre), theatre, youth club

Outdoors: castle grounds, field, open air theatre, pub car park, seashore, ship's deck

Wave from *The Wemmick Story* by Suzannah McCreight, Springs Dance Company. Dancers: Charlotte Brown, Naomi Cook, Maggie Ho Ki Kwan

Physical setting

Staging: abstract, in the round, naturalistic, proscenium, site specific, symbolic
Set design: lighting, props, projections, use of film, cyclorama, drops, use of furniture or larger built sets with stairs, fences, rooms of a house

Dance for the camera

Special effects: layers of film, freeze frames, editing, close up and distance shots, where the cameras are placed or how they move, and the angles created

Accompaniment

Instrumental: solo, quartet, violins, guitars, keyboard, percussion, wind, brass etc.
Vocal: operatic, pop, rap, choral etc.
Spoken: story, commentary, poetry, disassociated words etc.
Sound: natural or found sounds mixed or recorded separately, synthesised sounds, electronic sounds, acoustic sounds

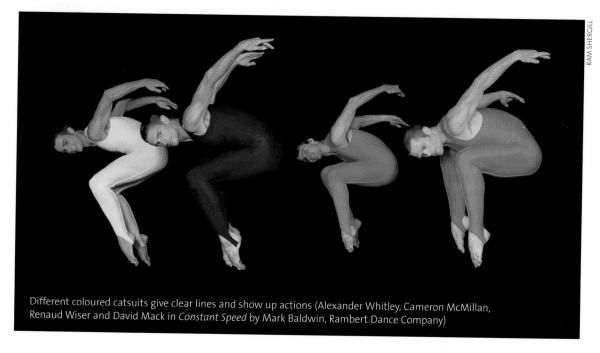

Different coloured catsuits give clear lines and show up actions (Alexander Whitley, Cameron McMillan, Renaud Wiser and David Mack in *Constant Speed* by Mark Baldwin, Rambert Dance Company)

Social, historical and cultural contexts

This is information about when, why, how, where and by whom the dance was created.

❖ When was this dance created?
❖ What are its origins?
❖ What is its style?
❖ Where was it first seen?
❖ Who can be seen performing the style professionally now?

Appreciation

Which style could it be?

- African
- Asian (**Bhangra**, **Bharata Natyam**, **Kathak**)
- ballroom
- breakdance
- capoeira
- classical ballet
- contact improvisation
- contemporary dance
- Cunningham (contemporary)
- folk dance
- Graham (contemporary)
- hip-hop
- jazz
- Latin American
- lindy hop
- minimal
- modern ballet
- modern dance
- morris
- musical theatre
- new dance
- physical theatre
- release-based (contemporary)
- rock and roll
- Russian
- Spanish
- stage dance
- street dance
- tap

SIMON RICHARDSON

Contemporary dance (Maggie (Ho Ki) Kwan and Ruth Hughes in *The Devil is Bad* by Sadie Chamberlain, Springs Dance Company)

Subject matter

Describing and explaining how these features convey to us the style and subject matter of the dance is more complex. Refer to Chapters 3 and 4 for extra details of what, how, where, and with whom the dancers might be performing to express the style and subject matter.

Design features

To describe accurately the **design features** of a dance, and how they link with the style, choreography and subject matter, you need to consider the lists below.

Costume design

What is each dancer wearing, and how it is suitable for a particular dance? Look at a dancer from head down to toe and identify what is being worn. Each item of clothing will have a colour, shape, size, style, length, material, pattern and weight.

When you have all the details of what is being worn, can you explain why that particular costume is appropriate for the dance? Does the colour match the mood of the dance, or the character the dancer is showing? Are the trousers in the style of the period in which the narrative is set? Does the material of the costume indicate the wealth or poverty of the characters?

Nutcracker! by Matthew Bourne, New Adventures. When might this be seen? The set, action and costumes should tell you

BILL COOPER

On the head

Hair: shaven, curly, gelled, in a bun, plait, loose, in a particular style

Hat: type (bowler hat, top hat, baseball cap, skullcap, beret, cowboy hat, helmet, cloth cap etc.), shape, colour, size, weight, texture, material

Mask: shape, style, colour, size, weight, texture, material, character, full/half mask, eyes only

Make-up: subtle, bold

Parts of face: cheeks, eyes, beard, moustache

As a character: style, colour, size, lines, placing

Scarf: shape, style, colour, size, weight, texture, material

Wig: shape, style, colour, size, weight, texture, material, character

Whole body

- boiler suit
- dress
- coat
- overall
- suit
- tutu
- tunic
- hemline
- neckline

Upper limbs

❖ bare arms
❖ long sleeves
❖ cap sleeves
❖ short sleeves
❖ three-quarter sleeves
❖ wrist and shoulder line (e.g. elastic, raglan, gathered, buttoned)

Hands

❖ bare
❖ with nail varnish
❖ with claws or attachments
❖ wrist fastening
❖ gloves: mitts, fingerless, long, elegant, wool, cotton, leather

Detail of costume in a duo by Kamali and Saju in *Faultline*, by Shobana Jeyasingh

Upper body

❖ blouse
❖ bolero
❖ cravat
❖ jacket
❖ leotard
❖ shawl
❖ shirt
❖ tee shirt
❖ tie
❖ waistcoat
❖ neckline

Legs

❖ bare
❖ garters
❖ leggings
❖ socks
❖ stockings
❖ tights: footless, stirrups, seamless, with seams, fishnets
❖ trouser legs: flared, skinny, elasticated
❖ hemline

Lower body

❖ belt
❖ petticoat
❖ plus fours
❖ sash
❖ shorts
❖ skirt
❖ trousers
❖ hemline

Feet

❖ bare
❖ with socks
❖ shoes: ballet shoes, boots, buckled shoes, clogs, high heels, jazz shoes, laced, pointes, sandals, slip-ons, split-soled, tap shoes
❖ sole type

Clothing sizes

- extra small
- large
- long
- loose
- maxi
- medium
- midi
- mini
- petite
- short
- small
- three-quarter
- tight

Clothing shapes

- baggy
- skinny
- flared
- full-length
- heart-shaped
- oblong
- round
- square
- thin
- V-shaped
- wide

Materials

- brocade
- card
- cotton
- denim
- feathers
- leather
- lycra
- manmade fibres
- net
- paper
- polyester
- rags
- rope
- satin
- sequins
- silk
- string
- suede
- taffeta
- towel
- velvet
- waterproof
- wool

Texture of materials

- bubbly
- coarse
- crinkly
- delicate
- flimsy
- fluid
- heavy
- jagged
- light
- rough
- sharp
- shiny
- slippery
- smooth
- thick
- thin
- transparent
- wrinkled

MAIN PHOTO: CHRIS NASH; BACKGROUND VIDEO IMAGE: PETE GAMES; DESIGN: CORPORATION POP

Faultline poster showing different textures of material and items of clothing

BILL COOPER

Models and Zebra from *'Still Life' at the Penguin Café* by David Bintley

Appreciation

Set design features

The place where a dance is performed should link with the mood, narrative and characters of the dance. You therefore need to describe the set design of a professional performance and explain its link with the subject matter of the dance.

The Wemmick Story by Suzannah McCreight, Springs Dance Company. Dancers: Ruth Hughes, Charlotte Brown, Naomi Cook, Maggie Ho Ki Kwan

SIMON RICHARDSON

Features of the set

- ❖ archway
- ❖ black box: black back curtain, floor and wings
- ❖ door
- ❖ film projected onto **cyclorama** (see below)
- ❖ flats: painted, linked to make a building
- ❖ floor surface: wood, dance mat, linoleum
- ❖ furniture, stairs or steps
- ❖ shape: apron stage, end stage, in the round, **proscenium arch**
- ❖ site-specific venue: arena, art gallery, car, ferry, museum, rooftop etc.
- ❖ size
- ❖ split-level set
- ❖ wings: where a dancer enters from side stage, defined by flats or hung curtains

Areas of stage or set

These areas are identified from the performers' view while on stage:

- ❖ downstage, downstage left, downstage right
- ❖ upstage, upstage left, upstage right
- ❖ stage right
- ❖ stage left
- ❖ centre stage
- ❖ in the wings
- ❖ offstage
- ❖ backstage

Drops

These are made of canvas or material and fly down from a batten above the stage:

- ❖ cyclorama: white drop that covers upstage wall, known as 'cyc'
- ❖ painted backcloth/**backdrop**

Drops or flags can have the following details, which you could describe:

- ❖ placing: upstage, mid-stage, down-stage
- ❖ size: column, square, covering upstage wall
- ❖ colours within the drop
- ❖ gauze curtain
- ❖ picture painted on the drop
- ❖ people within a picture
- ❖ objects within the picture
- ❖ mood of the picture
- ❖ time significance: of the day, year, century
- ❖ place significance: village, town, country

BILL COOPER

Backdrop design for the Texan Kangaroo Rat, from *'Still Life' at the Penguin Café* by David Bintley

Types of set

An example of a professional work is given for each type of set:

- ❖ abstract: *Bird Song* by Siobhan Davies, Siobhan Davies Dance
- ❖ complex: *Perfect* by Kevin Finnan, Motionhouse Dance Theatre Company
- ❖ dramatic: *Ghost Dances* and *Swansong* by Christopher Bruce
- ❖ plain: *Dance Tek Warriors* by Doug Elkins, Union Dance Company
- ❖ period: *Nutcracker!* by Matthew Bourne, New Adventures
- ❖ realistic/site specific: *Rosas Danst Rosas* by Anne Teresa De Keersmaeker
- ❖ romantic: *Romeo and Juliet* by Kenneth MacMillan
- ❖ simple: *Overdrive* by Richard Alston, Richard Alston Dance Company
- ❖ Using film: *Faultline* by Shobana Jeyasingh, Shobana Jeyasingh Dance Company

Props

General props: items placed on stage that form part of the set for the dance
Furniture: bed, chairs, freestanding mirror, park bench, table, street light etc.
Personal props: items carried and used by dancers during the dance, e.g. fan, gun, handbag, hankie, newspaper, notebook, purse, sticks, suitcase, toy, tray, umbrella, wine glass

All props have a particular shape, size, colour, weight, material and texture. They are on stage and used in a dance for a purpose. They might be important for the character or situation being expressed, and be used normally as part of an everyday scene. Or, the way they are used in the dance, and who uses them, may be significant. They might indicate a mood or aspect of a character, seem sinister or amusing, or act as a character-enhancing aid.

The victim is separated from the chair by the guards (Christopher Powney, Simon Cooper and Ted Stoffer in *Swansong* by Christopher Bruce, Rambert Dance Company)

ANTHONY CRICKMAY

Lighting design features

Lights, lamps and lanterns

- ❖ battens: rows of lights
- ❖ booms: can hold three clamped-on lanterns
- ❖ colour wheel: several rotatable colour gels
- ❖ down or top light: shines from above straight down
- ❖ flood lanterns: give a general wash
- ❖ follow spot: follows action on stage, mounted away from the stage
- ❖ footlights: up-lights from the floor, placed downstage
- ❖ gels: coloured plastic filters that fit into the frames of lanterns
- ❖ gobo: a wheel with various patterns
- ❖ overhead spot: lights a particular area on stage from directly above (Fresnel: soft-edged; profile: hard–edged)
- ❖ shutters, barn doors or gates: devices that define the shape of the light beamed onto floor

❖ shins, mids and heads: side lights that are mounted on a boom
❖ tops: side lights that shine from overhead stage right and left
❖ slide projections
❖ video projections
❖ wattage: the strength of the light shining

Ways of lighting a stage

❖ backlight: shines from upstage towards downstage
❖ beams: wide, narrow, sharp or smooth-edged
❖ **blackout**: total darkness
❖ bright: lights full up
❖ cold: created by using a blue colour state
❖ colour: made through use of gels
❖ cross-fade: as one light fades another lifts
❖ cross-light: a beam shining from the side of the stage
❖ direction: the path of a beam
❖ fade: dimming a light
❖ intensity: how bright or dim the lights are
❖ overhead: light shining down from battens directly above
❖ pool: the circular shape made on the floor by an overhead spot
❖ strobe: a flashing light
❖ warm: created by using a red and orange colour state
❖ wash: one colour covers the floor or cyc
❖ whole stage cover: everywhere is lit

Lighting decisions

We can only see what is on a stage if it is lit. A **lighting designer** works alongside the choreographer to decide which areas of the stage will be lit at any moment in the dance. The type of lantern, shape of the light, strength of the beam, and the colours to be used will all be discussed and agreed. Whether lighting changes are a gradual cross-fade or a snap cut from one lighting setting to the next, has to be suitable for the dance at that point.

Perhaps a follow spot is necessary, or side lighting is available; alongside overhead lights, this is the most common way of lighting dance. Special effects could be used at the climax of the dance, for example strobe lighting, a colour change, dry ice or smoke. The painted backdrop could be lit throughout the dance, or only lit at some points. If the stage is large, with lots of flats and

furniture, the lighting focuses the audience's attention on the important parts of the stage for each section of the dance. Blackout is often used as a device for telling the audience when a scene has ended and the next is due to start.

If the dance is not performed on stage, but on a beach, in a street or on a ship, for example, the natural light helps us see the dance. This could be at dawn and sunrise, at sunset, or at mid-day, when the sun is brightest. An outdoor evening performance will require additional lighting.

Dance on film also has particular lighting, to enable the camera to absorb the images. Most of the dance works you study for your GCSE course will be on video or DVD. They will be filmed at theatrical venues or an off-site venue. You will hopefully see at least two live performances as well, either with your school or college, or your family and friends. Questions do sometimes appear on the exam paper about the difference between a live and a recorded performance. The way we see the set, costumes, style of dance and choreography will be different. If you have seen a live performance, what is different about the experience to watching a screen performance? Can you list at least five differences?

Professional dance repertoire

'**Repertoire**' describes the dances in a company's performance schedule at any one time. Some dance works may be in the repertoire for just 1 year, others for 6 years, and then, after a 10 year gap, be brought back for another 2 years. There are numerous dance companies all over the world, each with its own repertoire and programming schedule including premières of new works and remounting old works.

A company may have one choreographer for its repertoire or perform the works of several invited or guest choreographers, as well as their resident or associate choreographers. This often depends on the size of the company, its funding, and the space it owns. Most companies depend on grants from **arts councils** and other well-known charities for their survival. Deciding who choreographs can also depend on the individual choreographer's fees, the number of dancers required to dance and be paid, the design features expenses, and any income generated before the repertoire goes on tour, which was probably bid for 2 years previously. Small and mid-scale dance companies struggle to mount new works for their repertoire if they have been unsuccessful in their bids for much-needed grants. London Contemporary Dance Theatre Company folded in 1996 after nearly 30 years for this reason.

Rambert Dance Company

Rambert Dance Company has been in existence since 1926, when Frederick Ashton's *Tragedy of Fashion* was first performed. The company has staged both classical and contemporary dance works over the years, but became focused on contemporary dance in 1967 under the directorship of Norman Morrice. The company repertoire over the past 80 years has been innovative, exciting and immensely varied. Choreographers who have contributed to the Rambert's repertoire include among others Siobhan Davies, Richard Alston, Robert North, Christopher Bruce, Trisha Brown, Lucinda Childs, Robert Cohan, Merce Cunningham, Walter Gore, Jiri Kylian, Ashley Page, Paul Taylor, Glen Tetley and Anthony Tudor.

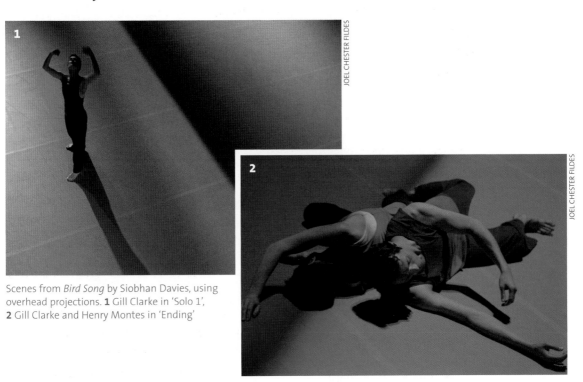

Scenes from *Bird Song* by Siobhan Davies, using overhead projections. **1** Gill Clarke in 'Solo 1', **2** Gill Clarke and Henry Montes in 'Ending'

Although photographs exist of moments in most of the ballets and dance works by these and other choreographers, there are only a few commercially available videos and DVDs (see Resource 6 in Section 4). Looking at photographs will help you learn to identify, describe and discuss all of the features of a dance moment, before you try writing about a filmed recording of a whole work.

Identifying, describing and explaining features of professional dance works

To show you how to do this, I am going to look at one scene from each of the following five dance works: *Faultline* by Shobana Jeyasingh, *Ghost Dances* by Christopher Bruce, *Nutcracker!* by Matthew Bourne, *Overdrive* by Richard Alston and *Romeo and Juliet* by Kenneth MacMillan. These works each have:

❖ a scene with a trio of dancers
❖ an identifiable style of dance performance
❖ a clear theme/dance idea/subject matter
❖ a particular type of sound accompaniment
❖ **costume design** that links with the dance idea
❖ set and lighting design that support the communication of the dance idea

All of the dances can be watched on DVD or video. Each scene is identified and described in turn followed by some tasks to **compare** and contrast their various features.

Ghost Dances by Christopher Bruce, the Houston Ballet

I have chosen the first scene, which is danced by the ghost dancers, or death figures. It lasts approximately 6 minutes and sets the scene for the dance drama that follows.

Three male dancers perform in contemporary dance style. Staring, they move stealthily and quietly, with moments of total stillness. They roll and slide across the floor, lift and move over, under and around each other. Their feet are often flexed, and their backs are rarely upright. They walk menacingly and slowly forwards, and stand aggressively in **second parallel**, holding each other's shoulders. This communicates a sense of evil, threat and power.

ANTHONY CRICKMAY

Christopher Powney, Paul Liburd and Jan de Schynkel in *Ghost Dances* by Christopher Bruce, Rambert Dance Company

At first there is silence, apart from the noise made by their bodies and breaths, followed by the sound of a drop of water landing. As they repeat the first part of their trio, a quiet melody and complex rhythm is played on pan pipes (an instrument with links to South America). The music gradually increases in volume and power, and the dancers' actions dynamically mirror the music.

The costumes are strident, violent and stark. Each dancer is wearing a skull mask, with long, greasy, dank, dark hair. Their body-hugging costumes and body make-up give them the appearance of skeletons. Fringing is tied around their lower legs, upper arms and wrists. Their scanty black loin cloths are cut into black strips. This almost-nakedness is uncomfortable and fear-inducing.

The set is basic, with a painted backcloth, which could be a scenic view of South America. There is little light, and the dimness is frightening. The dancers' faces are visible as the side-lights come up, and the overhead lights gradually pick out their entire bodies and the painted backdrop.

The subject matter for this trio is that these figures will kidnap villagers and remove them from their families forever. They have to express the role of being evil creatures searching for likely victims.

Nutcracker! by Matthew Bourne, New Adventures

I have selected a small scene from Act II, 'By Invitation Only'. It is performed by three male dancers. The scene lasts 1 minute and follows another short scene performed by five female dancers, the Marshmallow Girls. The three men are the Gobstoppers.

BILL COOPER

Act I: 'In the Orphanage', from *Nutcracker!* by Matthew Bourne, New Adventures

The complete scene has other dancers, also named as tasty sweets: Humbug, Liquorice Allsorts, and Knickerbocker Glory. Clara, a girl from Dr Dross's orphanage, has found herself in Sweetieland and wants to go to the party, but the Humbug bouncer won't let her in as she doesn't have an invitation.

The sound is provided by **orchestral music** — 'Trepak', the Russian dance from Tchaikovsky's original score. The men perform to this powerful, rhythmic and dynamic music in an energetic, threatening, bovver boys manner. Their movements have an athletic style similar to the original Russian dance, but the characters are presented in an exaggerated way. Their facial expressions, the crude, suggestive gestures of their hands and bodies, and fighting and fisticuffs are indications that

they are motorbike toughies. There is a direct correlation between the qualities of the music and the dynamics and timing of the dancers' actions.

Gobstoppers are hard, round sweets, solid all the way to the centre, and the characterisation reflects these features. The dancers' hats and the circular designs, in bold primary colours, on their T-shirts make these similarities even clearer. Bourne has selected movements, dynamics and facial expressions to convey their 'hard to the core' characters.

The dancers movements include:

❖ their necks jutting in and out quickly and aggressively
❖ punching fists and nudging elbows
❖ athletic drops to the floor and press-ups
❖ hip thrusts
❖ big jumps and hops, as if riding a motorbike
❖ flying, falling and rolling across the floor
❖ head-banging gestures, on their own and on each other!
❖ pushing and kicking each other

Clara sneaks into the party as the Humbug bouncer goes to break up the Gobstoppers' fight.

The scene is danced on a large colourful stage with a huge, brightly coloured open mouth centre stage (similar to the Rolling Stones logo), and directly in front of a candy-striped blue-and-pink backdrop with images of floating, wispy clouds across it. The floor and sidewalls of the stage are the originals from Act I, 'The Orphanage': grey, white and black.

A stark contrast can be seen between the reality of the orphanage and the fantasy world Clara is glimpsing in Sweetieland. The lighting is general and bright throughout the dance.

Act I: 'The Revolt', from *Nutcracker!* by Matthew Bourne, New Adventures

The Gobstoppers take a bow in Act II of *Nutcracker!* by Matthew Bourne, New Adventures

Romeo and Juliet by Kenneth MacMillan, the Royal Ballet

The scene I have chosen is from Scene 3 of Act I, 'Outside the Capulets' House', and lasts approximately 2 minutes. It is in classical ballet performance style and part of a narrative. The scene is a trio for three men, dancing the roles of Romeo, Mercutio and Benvolio, who decide to enter the ballroom to find Rosaline. They are Montagues, and the ballroom is in the house of a rival family, the Capulets. Their trio starts after all the other guests have entered the house.

The set is huge and on a vast stage. Flats have been constructed and painted to resemble the walls of a wealthy family's home, with, centre stage, an entrance below a raised portcullis. The men are wearing white ballet shoes, white tights, different-coloured, long-sleeved velvet jerkins with gold embroidered necklines, and masks to disguise their faces.

Romeo's two friends start the trio by travelling a circular pathway of the stage with runs, leaps and turning jumps. Romeo joins them as the central figure in a line as they dance an enchaînement, including pirouettes, developpés, **fouettés** and grande **battements en dehors**, with a sense of grandeur in their port de bras that shows they are aristocratic, romantic young men. Their steps and arm gestures are all from the classical ballet genre and performed in direct correlation with the qualities of Prokofiev's music, played by an orchestra.

DEE CONWAY

They dance in unison for this first section, which conveys that they are like-minded people who get on well with each other. Romeo then performs a short solo, demonstrating his skill with an imaginary sword, which both his friends repeat towards him and against each other. This is a sophisticated and controlled duel with fancy foot-work. As they part, Romeo again has a short solo with pirouettes, battements and quick footwork, and his friends then repeat parts of the solo.

The trio ends as Romeo walks forward and hesitates, while his friends collect cloaks and musical instruments from upstage. They swirl their cloaks elegantly around their bodies, emphasising their wealthy, aristocratic and sophisticated personalities. They all slip off stage into the Capulets' house.

Lauren Cuthbertson and Edward Watson in *Romeo and Juliet*, by Kenneth MacMillan, the Royal Ballet

Overdrive by Richard Alston, Richard Alston Dance Company

Overdrive is a pure dance work with an unusual accompaniment. The rhythms have been programmed into a sequencer by Steffen Schleiermacher, and we hear electronic samples of piano and a farfisa organ using different themes, in an interlocking method called Hocketing. The dance work is performed in contemporary style, with Cunningham-style extensions, tilts and fast footwork.

The scene I have chosen is the first part of Scene 4 and lasts just over 30 seconds. Three female dancers enter, walking from downstage right, as a male dancer is coming to the end of his solo. He joins in with their first phrase of movement and then exits stage left. This is termed 'dovetailing' by Richard Alston. The trio perform another six phrases once the male soloist has left the stage.

The three dance the same steps in unison throughout, travelling in clear pathways across the stage. There are moments of suspension, sudden cutting gestures, smooth travelling hops and curving gestures. They carve and fill the space around them with each arm and leg gesture, with great clarity in the pathways, as well as the energy and flow of these actions.

CATHERINE ASHMORE

The accompaniment, which can feel quite monotonous, is enlivened by the variety of action content and the changing accents, facings and highlights of the choreography, as it brings a visual melody layer to the sound we hear. The phrases are in bars of $7\frac{1}{2}$ counts, and the interlocking of action to sound is a joy to watch. The dancers are very aware of where they are, both in relation to the set and to each other, throughout the scene. They move harmoniously together in matching unison, until two leave the stage and one dancer remains to perform a solo. The movement phrases introduced by this trio reappear several times later in *Overdrive*, repeated and developed with a larger number of dancers.

The set is a large open space with no wings and a lit surround. The three dancers are barefoot and wearing red costumes: halter neck jerkins over fluid, loose red trousers.

Francesca Romo in *Overdrive* by Richard Alston

Faultline by Shobana Jeyasingh, Shobana Jeyasingh Dance Company

I have chosen the male trio that opens Scene 1, following the Prologue. The dance is 4 minutes long. The style of movement is quite sharp, with clear lines, and is dynamic, with extremely expressive and effective hand gestures. Some of these are natural, everyday gestures and some have origins in the Bharat Natyam style. The overall performance style is contemporary, showing a mixture of influences.

In the beginning of this scene the men dance in unison, side by side, with quickly changing arm and hand gestures, jumps, kicks and freezes. The lighting is low and dim, then changes to catch them in a frozen moment in the glare of a brightly lit box. As the light dims again they move downstage and repeat some of the original gestures and jumps, in different relationships but still in unison, and appear as a cohesive group of friends. Patches of light appear across the stage.

They split into different 2 *vs.* 1 combinations, and the energy and mood between them changes. A slow-motion section, where one dancer is lifted, carried and lowered, is followed by one dancer being kicked at, and he moves away to dance on his own. He conveys aggression, need for money and impatience through his exceptionally clear hand and arm gestures, while the pair move each other slowly from upper stage right to upper stage centre. The trio rejoin for a sequence of punching and 'why?' gestures, then show sophistication as they move slowly in unison before breaking into three simultaneous, short expressive solos, with gestures expressing individual emotions.

'Deep Dive' by Saju and Devaraj in *Faultline* by Shobana Jeyasingh

They travel together to focus offstage, stage right, as if challenging an invisible group in the audience. They revert, however, to the 2 *vs.* 1 relationships, with confrontations between each other shown through two dancers performing lots of lifts; they lower, catch and hold each other with, for example, the lifted dancer kicking at the third man. Counter-tension, with two men stretching and lifting the third, is a highlight in this section. The trio ends as they all slowly lift a pair of imaginary binoculars to their eyes, focussing towards stage right, from where two female dancers enter.

Balance with left leg kick by Yamuna Devi, from *Faultline* by Shobana Jeyasingh

The dancers perform in bare feet and are wearing identical black trousers and short-sleeved black shirts, each with a different-coloured pastel tie. The trio ends in a brightly lit area downstage from the box image. There is a clear contrast between this moment and the low, dim lighting design at the start of the trio.

The accompaniment for this trio is unusual as it seems non-metric, with, at times, many layers of human voice and electronic sounds. These include a staccato buzzing phrase and a haunting, humming undercurrent. The dance and the accompaniment coexist smoothly and harmoniously.

CHRIS NASH

Mandeep and Devaraj with a huge lift, from *Faultline* by Shobana Jeyasingh

Tasks

Now that you have the detail of each scene you can compare and contrast one scene with another. The following tasks relate to the five works described above. You should use the descriptions and your own notes from observing the scenes on film to answer the tasks. You must always:

❖ identify the name of the work, the choreographer and the particular scene to which you are referring

❖ identify relevant facts about the scene

❖ describe important detail from the scene, in order to compare facts and details that are similar or contrast facts and details that are different

Once you can do this, you can explain why certain facts and details are important to the dance and discuss methods, interpretations etc.

1 From two of these works, take the way the choreographer makes use of the three dancers, and what they do to communicate the style and subject matter. Compare the methods used by each choreographer and comment on their success in communicating the subject matter.

2 Take the design features — costume, lighting and set — and compare the choices made and how appropriate they were or were not for each dance.

3 Take the accompaniment for each scene and explain why and how they are different. (Listen to the sound on film as well as using the notes provided above.)

4 Take the subject matter of two of these dance scenes and contrast how they are expressed within the performance styles chosen.

Chapter 10

Studying two set works

For your written paper, you will study two set works chosen by your teacher from a list supplied by the exam board. However, you will probably look at other works during your 2-year course as well.

What you need to know: facts

There are basic facts about both works you will have to know and be able to spell correctly, namely:

* ❖ the full title of the dance work
* ❖ the name of the choreographer
* ❖ the name of the company dancing the work
* ❖ the name(s) of the composer/s of the accompaniment
* ❖ the title(s) of the accompaniment throughout the work
* ❖ the type(s) of accompaniment used throughout the work
* ❖ the name of the set designer
* ❖ the name of the costume designer
* ❖ the name of the lighting designer
* ❖ when the dance was first performed
* ❖ where it was performed
* ❖ how many dancers there are in the cast on the DVD/video recording

These are facts you could be asked to give in the written paper.

Appreciation

What you need to know: features

Not only do you need to know who did what, when, where and with whom, but you have to know both set works *very well*. There are many different features to any dance work, and you need to be able to write at least one paragraph on each of the following areas:

- ❖ the subject matter or idea within the whole dance and each section of the dance
- ❖ the performance and choreographic styles of the dance and each section
- ❖ the structure of the whole work (the number of sections)
- ❖ the use of choreographic devices
- ❖ how the dancers relate to each other throughout the dance (use of dancers)
- ❖ key motifs, phrases and positions in each section of the work
- ❖ the action dynamic and spatial content of the key motifs
- ❖ what the accompaniment is like throughout the work
- ❖ the set design throughout the work
- ❖ the costume design throughout the work for each dancer's costumes
- ❖ the lighting design throughout the work
- ❖ the use of camera and editing within the recordings you have seen

Figures 36–42 show the areas of knowledge you need in order to write about a dancework; its structure, how the dancers are used, its accompaniment and the design features of costumes worn.

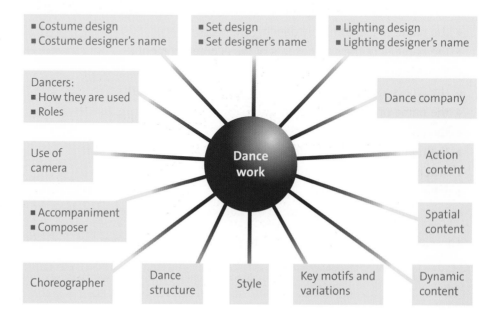

Figure 36
The constituent features of a professional dance work

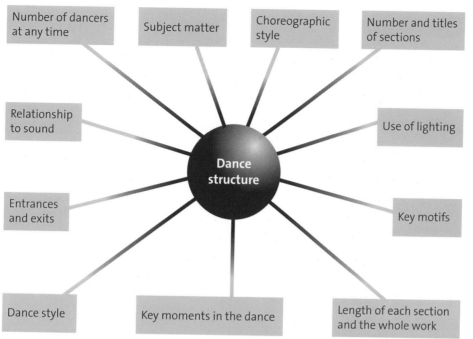

Number of dancers at any time

Subject matter

Choreographic style

Number and titles of sections

Relationship to sound

Use of lighting

Dance structure

Entrances and exits

Key motifs

Dance style

Key moments in the dance

Length of each section and the whole work

Figure 37
Dance structure

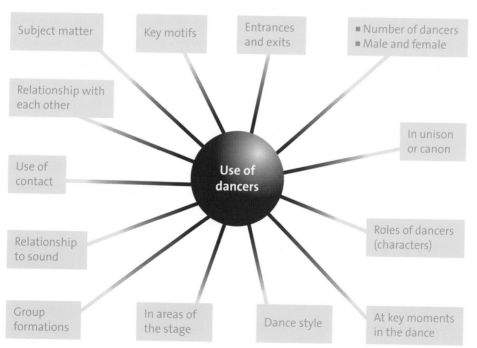

Subject matter

Key motifs

Entrances and exits

■ Number of dancers
■ Male and female

Relationship with each other

Use of contact

In unison or canon

Use of dancers

Relationship to sound

Roles of dancers (characters)

Group formations

In areas of the stage

Dance style

At key moments in the dance

Figure 38
Use of dancers

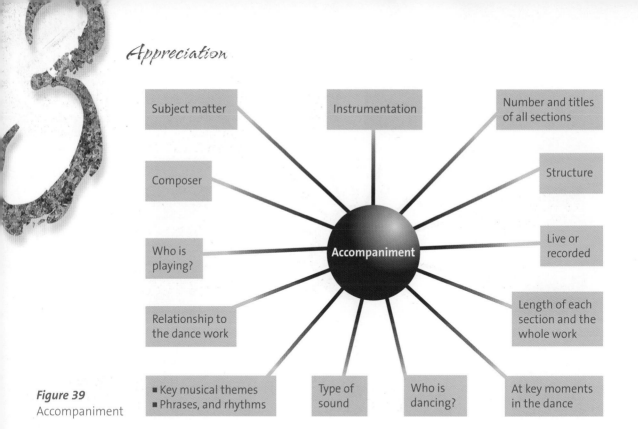

Figure 39
Accompaniment

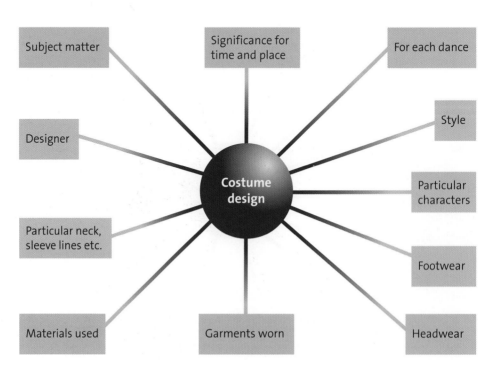

Figure 40
Costume design

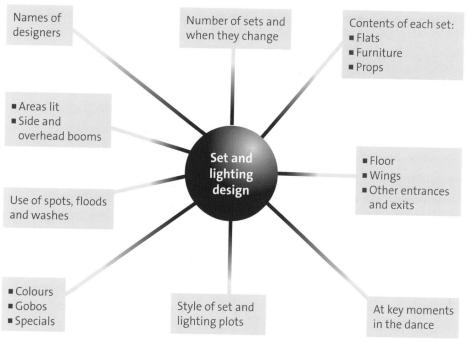

Figure 41
Set and lighting design

Figure 42
Style of the dance work

How to approach the set works

I have chosen *Swansong* by Christopher Bruce, *Dance Tek Warriors* by Doug Elkins, *Perfect* by Kevin Finnan, *Rosas Danst Rosas* by Anne Theresa De Keersmaeker and *'Still Life' at the Penguin Café* by David Bintley as examples. The facts I have gathered about these dances will give you an idea of the amount of knowledge necessary to achieve a high grade at GCSE. You will need to learn and be able to use the facts about your set work in many possible ways in the written paper.

Watch each set work several times, to be sure that you know:

❖ which bit of the dance comes first
❖ who is dancing in that part
❖ what they are doing
❖ how they are moving
❖ what they are wearing
❖ what the accompaniment is like
❖ how many sections there are
❖ what the set is like
❖ how the dance is lit

If you cannot answer most of these questions about each section of your set works, you are unlikely to achieve a grade C or above on the written paper.

With your teacher, you may be able to watch a section of each work at a time, and discuss in groups the similarities and differences between them. You could make notes to remind yourself later of the points your group made, as well as those agreed by the whole class. You will probably have the chance to try some of the movements in each section with your teacher, so you can then feel the differences and similarities in your own body. (Don't worry if the actions are not exactly the same — you are not professional dancers.)

You might like to make your own spider diagrams, copying the blank thought maps and completing the detail for each **physical setting** your teacher has chosen.

Swansong by Christopher Bruce, London Festival Ballet

Swansong was first performed by London Festival Ballet (now English National Ballet) in 1987, in Bilbao, Spain. It was premiered in the UK in Jersey, and its London premiere was at Sadler's Wells Theatre in June 1988. The original cast

for all these performances were Koen Onzia as the victim and Matz Skoog and Kevin Richmond as the interrogators. They are also the dancers in the video recording. Philip Chambon was commissioned to compose the music in 1987. It is an electric acoustic score. The designs were by Christopher Bruce, with the lighting designed by David Mohr. *Swansong* has been and is still performed live by Rambert Dance Company.

Structure

The dance is in seven sections and lasts approximately 32 minutes. The sections are:

* Introduction and Section 1: Questions and answers
* Section 2: Tea for two
* Section 3: First solo
* Section 4: Slow trio
* Section 5: Second solo — without accompaniment
* Section 6: Cane dance
* Section 7: Third and final solo with the interrogators on stage

Subject matter

The subject matter or idea within the whole dance and each section of the dance is a victim being tortured in various ways by two interrogators. These are seen as a prisoner and two guards.

Introduction and Section 1: Questions and answers

The interrogators tap questions out and no response is made by the victim. They physically pull, push and lift the victim from the chair and put him back again. They use different attacking gestures.

Section 2: Tea for two

The interrogators are humiliating the victim, who seems to panic. The chair is moved constantly and the interrogation becomes more intense and violent.

Section 3: First solo

The victim expresses his anger at his situation, his frustration and his strong desire for freedom.

Section 4: Slow trio

The chair is used by the interrogators as a weapon against the victim. It is moved so that he cannot sit on it, and pulled away from him so that he cannot reach it. He is left alone, lying crushed under the chair.

Appreciation

Section 5: Second solo — without accompaniment

The chair is used by the victim to convey the struggle of trying to let something go. He is caught within the chair, stands on it to find a way out, but is trapped by it from escaping to the unknown.

Section 6: Cane dance

The victim sits and watches the interrogators as they perform a soft shoe dance with canes. They gradually become more aggressive, using the canes as weapons, and the victim uses the chair as a shield. The victim collapses and is carried back to his chair.

The cane dance (Christopher Powney, Simon Cooper and Ted Stoffer in *Swansong* by Christopher Bruce, Rambert Dance Company)

ANTHONY CRICKMAY

Section 7: Third and final solo with the interrogators on stage

The interrogators focus on the victim's body and on the chair. The victim (or rather his spirit) travels into the light and to freedom, after glancing back to his prison.

Performance and choreographic styles

The whole dance is in narrative form and is dramatic throughout. The performance styles vary from section to section.

Introduction and Section 1: Questions and answers

- ❖ tap dance
- ❖ contemporary
- ❖ mime
- ❖ contact work

Section 2: Tea for two

- ❖ soft–shoe
- ❖ tango
- ❖ contact work
- ❖ tap dance
- ❖ contemporary
- ❖ mime

Section 3: First solo

- ❖ contemporary
- ❖ classical ballet

Section 4: Slow trio

- ❖ contemporary
- ❖ contact work

Section 5: Second solo — without accompaniment

- ❖ contemporary
- ❖ classical
- ❖ mime

Section 6: Cane dance

- ❖ upbeat soft–shoe duet (like Fred Astaire)
- ❖ contemporary and contact work

Section 7: Third and final solo with the interrogators on stage

❖ contemporary and classical steps in a lyrical style

Choreographic devices

Unison

❖ In Section 1, the interrogators dance the motif in unison.
❖ In Section 2, all three dancers perform a soft–shoe, catchy motif with a humorous feel, and the victim dances a short tango with one interrogator.

Canon

❖ In the Introduction, the interrogators enter in canon, and repeat short tapping phrases in canon in Section 1.
❖ In opening of Section 2, the victim taps out his motif as an answer to the interrogators.

Highlights

❖ In Section 2, the victim is sitting down and a red nose is slowly placed on him.
❖ In Section 3, the victim stands looking and reaching towards the light.
❖ In Section 5, the victim stands on the chair looking at the light.

Climax

❖ At the end of Section 4, the victim is held upside down on the chair by the interrogators.
❖ During the cane duo, the interrogators become more violent and hit the chair.
❖ In Section 6, the victim collapses.

Repetition

❖ The tapping motif is repeated in Sections 1 and 2.
❖ Lifting motifs are repeated in Sections 1, 4 and 6.

Motifs

These include:

❖ the tap dance motifs by interrogators
❖ manipulation of the victim motifs by all three characters
❖ arabesques, leaps and arm gestures in wing-like shapes by the victim
❖ sitting on the chair, bending forwards, leaving the chair and walking USL, by victim
❖ curled, twisted body on the floor with an arm extension, by victim

Use of the dancers

Introduction and Section 1: Questions and Answers

* The two interrogators follow each other onto the stage. The prisoner is still, sitting on a chair facing the front. They tap dance either side of him.
* Two interrogators physically grip and manipulate the victim between, below, above and around them.
* The victim has short solo phrases as answers to the questions from his 'guards'. He travels briefly away from them.

Section 2: Tea for Two

* The duet is danced by the interrogators while the victim watches from his chair.
* The victim dances with one interrogator.
* All three dance in unison.
* Two interrogators attack the victim in many ways.
* The victim is left on the stage alone.

Section 3: First solo

* The solo by the victim starts and ends on the chair, but also involves travelling to and from the chair and USL.

Section 4: Slow trio

* The two interrogators physically grip and manipulate the victim between, below, above and around them.
* The chair is a focus of the attack and defence between the three dancers.

Section 5: Second solo

* The victim dances a solo that has no accompaniment. The chair is the focus used to convey the victim's mood, place, and feelings, with his relationship to the light from USL being another important feature.

Section 6: Cane dance

* The duo by the two guards with canes is watched by the victim as he is seated on the chair.
* The guards attack the chair and the victim, who tries to defend himself with the chair.

Section 7: Third and final solo with interrogators on stage

* The victim performs a solo as the guards stand still either side of the chair.

Appreciation

Table 20 shows some key motifs, phrases and positions from each section of *Swansong*.

Table 20 Actions, dynamic and spatial content of key motifs in *Swansong*

Motifs	Actions	Dynamics	Space
Tap dance motifs	❖ Brushes ❖ Stamps ❖ Taps with feet	❖ Strong ❖ Accented ❖ Sharp ❖ Direct	Small steps travelling sideways, and forwards, towards and away from the chair
Manipulating the victim	*Guards:* ❖ Gripping ❖ Lifting ❖ Lowering ❖ Carrying ❖ Upending ❖ Pulling ❖ Pushing ❖ Supporting ❖ Holding still *Victim:* ❖ Leaning ❖ Falling ❖ Rising ❖ Balancing ❖ Swinging	*Guards:* ❖ Strong ❖ Forceful ❖ Sudden and sustained ❖ Tight energy *Victim:* ❖ Heavy ❖ Weighty ❖ Sudden and sustained ❖ Light and floating	*Guards:* ❖ Close to victim ❖ In contact ❖ Big lifting gestures ❖ In centre stage *Victim:* ❖ Between guards ❖ Over/under guards ❖ No real space of own ❖ Clear body shapes in lifts
Arabesques, leaps and arm gestures in wing-like shapes by the victim	❖ Balances ❖ Jumps ❖ Travelling ❖ Dipping and rising	❖ Smooth ❖ Loose energy ❖ Delicate ❖ Flowing ❖ Quick and fluid ❖ Slow and floating	❖ Travelling from chair to USL ❖ Direct pathways ❖ Moving around chair ❖ Large extended body shapes ❖ Use of levels and various directions
Victim's curled, twisted body on the floor with an arm extension	❖ Contracting ❖ Curling ❖ Spiralling ❖ Reaching ❖ Lying ❖ Sitting ❖ Lunge	❖ Tight energy ❖ Strong, slow ❖ Tortuous ❖ Flexible ❖ Direct, strong and slow ❖ Powerful	❖ On and near floor ❖ In a tight space ❖ Curled to extended body shape
Victim sitting on the chair bending forwards, leaving the chair and walking USL	❖ Bending with right arm and clenched fists ❖ Opening fingers out ❖ Walking and standing in parallel	❖ Slow, strong, tight energy ❖ Direct and heavy ❖ Slowly, carefully, directly	❖ Forwards body bend ❖ Arms to front and side ❖ Small extensions by fingers ❖ In straight line, from CS to USL

Accompaniment

Introduction and Section 1: Questions and answers

❖ silence broken by sounds of tapping motif by guards
❖ crashes with metallic sound
❖ metallic rhythmic sound (digitally sampled and manipulated)
❖ keyboard melody

Section 2: Tea for two

❖ 'ch–p–cha' rhythmic chant
❖ syncopated 4/4 time in tango style
❖ close link with 'tea for two' cha-cha rhythms
❖ pop-style backing group vocals
❖ crash at the end of the solo

Section 3: First solo

❖ organ sounds: lyrical fluid melody, phrases without a rhythmic structure, stately and slow
❖ human cries and sighs
❖ multi-layered metallic sounds
❖ slaps and stamps made by the dancer

Section 4: Slow trio

❖ crashes with metallic sounds and descending voices
❖ metallic rhythmic sound (digitally sampled and manipulated)
❖ multi–layered sound; slower than Section 1

Section 5: Second solo — without accompaniment

❖ silence, broken by sounds made by the chair and victim's body in contact with the floor
❖ non–metric

Section 6: Cane dance

❖ ch–p–cha rhythmic chant
❖ rhythmic drums
❖ mix of rhythmic metallic sounds
❖ canes hitting the chair and floor

Section 7: Third and final solo with the interrogators on stage

❖ reed pipe and organ sounds
❖ melodic, haunting, fluid melody

❖ sounds of the dancer's feet tapping
❖ deep drums

Set design

The setting is simple and stark. The overriding colour is black: the wings and floor are black, with a plain backcloth. A strong, wooden chair is the only item of furniture on stage. It is placed towards **SR**, downstage.

The props include a cigarette and zippo lighter, two canes, and special microphones to amplify the tapping made by the rubber soles of the split-soled jazz shoes.

Lighting design

Overhead lighting above the chair gives a cold light. This light gradually spreads across the stage and becomes warmer. Footlights show shadows on the backcloth. A diagonal shaft of light beams from USL to the chair; this light lowers at the end of Section 7, showing an extended shadow of the victim. The shaft dims, leaving only the overhead light over the chair and the two interrogators.

Costume design

The victim wears stretch blue jeans, a red T-shirt, split–soled black jazz shoes, and a clown's red nose for Section 2. The interrogators wear mid-khaki coloured trousers with pockets on the legs, leather belts, pale khaki shirts with open necks, short sleeves and breast pockets, grey split–soled jazz shoes, and baseball caps for Section 2.

Dance Tek Warriors by Doug Elkins, Union Dance Company

Dance Tek Warriors is the last choreographic section from an original, full evening's dance production. It was inspired by *Super Heroes: Teken* — a playstation game — and a poem by Rumi, a Persian poet and choreographer, originator of the Whirling Dervishes. Doug Elkins deconstructed some of the ideas Union Dance Company members had taken from these starting points and used them to choreograph this final piece.

The work has six dancers, three male and three female, and four sections of different length. The DVD recording lasts approximately 27 minutes. There are several different performance styles: **B-boying**, Capoeira, Asian martial arts and different contemporary techniques. According to Union Dance, the overall theme is: 'To become a spiritual warrior means to develop a larger vision, a special kind of courage, fearlessness and genuine heroism.'

Section 1

This is made up of six subsections:

(a) A group dance for all six dancers, with a rap accompaniment and in street performance style. Two trios in horizontal lines perform different motifs, with different speeds, energy and actions. They are all wearing yellow. The dance is very rhythmic and closely visualises the mood of the accompaniment — Man's *Final Frontier*. The set has a projection of many small squares onto a cyclorama within a yellow light. Floor and sidelights can be seen, and shadows appear over the cyclorama throughout. The lights fade as the dance finishes.

(b) A solo by Andrea Whiting to a cello accompaniment. This has a mixture of attacking and fluid gestures, performed to a smooth strings melody. It leads into a duet with two movement themes shown at the same time. The movement is sophisticated and the use of suspension is clear. The dancers occupy the same space but have no relationship between them.

(c) Two male dancers enter, each joining one of the two females. Two contrasting short contact duets take place, with no relationship between one duet and the other. One male dancer leaves and his partner follows. The remaining male dancer (Michael) walks around and past his partner (Simone), who dances earlier motifs, mainly at low level.

(d) Charmaine enters as the last duet exits with fluid movement, including curves, slow attacking gestures, street freezes and movements arising from impulses to rippling actions. There is a very relaxed, released feel to this solo. The accompaniment has changed and we hear a human voice humming or non-verbally chanting as Charmaine moves.

(e) Curtis joins her on stage, and they at first dance in unison, with the occasional moments when they are under or over each other. The US lighting changes from blue to a pinky red. Shadows appear on the cyclorama and we see a lot of contact work, with Curtis lifting, lowering and carrying Charmaine.

(f) Michael enters with a simple skipping motif, joined by Andrea, and the four dance together. In unison they perform variations of motifs seen in the earlier solos and duets. As the two off-stage dancers re-enter they move into duets briefly, leading into a six-person canon. The shadows effect is again used well, seemingly filling the stage with lots of dancers. They exit in canon as the lights lower to blackout, concluding this opening section.

The accompaniment for subsections (b), (c) (d), (e) and (f) is 'Ava' and 'Macchu Picchu', from David Byrne's album *The Forest*.

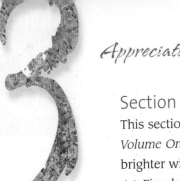

Appreciation

Section 2

This section is performed to 'Sweet Vibrations', the first track on *Jungle Massive Volume One*. The US lighting has changed back to blue but the scene is made brighter with additional white light. There are four dances within this section.

(a) Five dancers perform in a swinging, skipping, hopping, loose style of movement, with a mixture of small arm gestures and steps. The accompaniment starts with rhythmic drumming, a male voice adding a layer of rap. There are two duets and a solo. They are performed in their own area of the stage, and the dancers do not relate to anyone other than to their partner.

(b) Two duets now happen simultaneously. The pair downstage right use movements linked with capoeira, and the upstage right couple dance in street style, using rippling gestures in unison. The section ends with Andrea and Charmaine involved in a battle downstage.

(c) Six dancers perform a hand motif seen earlier in the work, in unison, very slowly and in direct contrast to the rhythms of the drumming and rap accompaniment. The music changes on 'hey, hey, hey, hey' and the dancers' movements are faster and sharper. They divide into smaller groups, leaving Charmaine performing a solo, travelling around a duet using smooth, fluid contact work.

(d) The skipping motif returns, followed by two duets using different actions in street and b-boying styles. Couples enter and exit, soloists perform separately and together in threes, before all dancers return and bring back various motifs, with pauses, gradually slowing down until the music stops and there is a blackout.

Charmaine Seet and Michael Joseph in *Dance Tek Warriors* by Doug Elkins

JEREMY MURCH

Section 3

This is a longer duet performed by Charmaine Seet and Michael Joseph. The lighting is a deep blue with a white flood, into which the dancers move. The sound is smooth, chilled, slow music, which complements the movement vocabulary.

The dancers seem to hang loosely and move in a relaxed, easy manner, in a unison duet with both contemporary and street dance styles present. This changes as they make physical contact and move one another around, under and over the other. Michael supports Charmaine in various unusual positions, from which she always moves away smoothly and calmly. 'This supportiveness and sensitivity allows the transformation to resolve their spirits,' say Union Dance. The release feel in the movement then speeds up (although the accompaniment maintains the calm atmosphere), and there is a sense of increased aggression between them before the duet concludes with an unusual balance — Michael supports Charmaine's neck as she gently sways, while the lights fade to blackout.

Section 4: the Golden Section

This last section, with its blue-lit set, starts with all six dancers walking on stage to create two lines of three. The accompaniment is different to the previous sections, and is the fifth track from the album *Devotional and Love Songs* by Nusrat Fateh Ali Khan and Party. A male voice sings Urdu lyrics and there is an Asian feel and tempo to the music. The dancers skip and walk in a relaxed manner, echoing the fluidity of the music.

There are significant hand and arm gestures used as the dancers travel in their threes. Solos repeat and vary motifs from earlier in the work, from the street, b-boying, **voguing** and contemporary styles, while duos are interspersed with walking and additional skipping motifs. As trios the dancers intermingle, travelling and using Asian hand and arm gestures in a manner that gives a spiritual feel to the street dance style. This is followed by a unison motif performed as a six, which is very fluid, with sinuous rippling through the body and arms. They skip into three duets and as identical couples bring back the various styles, including capoeira. As threes they contrast each other briefly, then move into twos again for a canon that flows from USL to DSR. They dance in a small circle before returning to capoeira-style movements, and the work ends with all lying down.

Costume

The costume designer is Ursula Bombshell. All the dancers are wearing trousers of varying styles, in shades of gold through to a dull red. Their tops are in various styles and tone in with their trousers. Some are sleeveless, others long-sleeved; some are close-fitting and others hang loosely.

Perfect by Kevin Finnan and Dancers, Motionhouse Dance Theatre

Perfect is a dance in thirteen sections. There are five dancers, three female and two male: Vanessa Cook, Junior Cunningham, Wendy Hesketh, Helen Parlor and Stuart Waters. It has an unusual and exciting set, with sand on the floor, film and giant hands (which appear in the DVD performance only), as well as slings that the

Appreciation

dancers use for aerial work. The set was designed by Simon Dormon and was one of the main starting points for the work.

The costumes, designed by Claire Armitage, are in black for the female dancers, and all differ slightly in design; the men wear black trousers and long-sleeved white shirts. The score was composed by Sophy Smith and Tim Dickinson and the film was produced by Caroline Bridges.

'Trussing Box' set design by Simon Dormon, for *Perfect* by Kevin Finnan

Features of the set: slings, sand, bench and ladder design by Simon Dormon, for *Perfect* by Kevin Finnan

The theme running through the work is the passing of time and how it shapes us as people, drawing us together and pulling us apart. We wait, are cared for, and grow in time. We can search for the silent space of time, and be frightened of ageing or changing as time passes. We may try to race against time's unstoppable force.

Section 1: Overture

A female dancer is lying DSL in front of a paper screen. Two dancers dressed in white appear in front of the screen and perform a duet using mimed hand gestures, after picking sand from the floor. Their gestures are linked with an egg timer spilling sand, showing time passing. This happens in front of a film of many different images linked with time passing. This includes night images, people bustling down a street, people sitting on a park bench and a night sky. The duet exit DSR, just before the blackout.

Section 2: Shadows

A solo dancer lies on the sand in front of the paper screen, with a bright white light shining from US towards the audience. This light is manipulated to play visual tricks on the audience, casting shadows that appear much larger than the dancer, or seem to slide from side to side. A shadow later seems threatening and the dancer appears to be suffering from a nightmare.

Both male dancers enter either in front of the screen or as a shadow behind it. The female dancer seems very disturbed, frightened and made unhappy by the different encounters. The female dancer who appears as a shadow behind

178

Chapter

the curtain reflects the main dancer's emotions. The dance finishes as the white light disappears upwards and the dancer crawls backward through the screen, tearing the bottom off it as she moves. The rest of the lower layer of the screen is gradually removed as the dance moves into the next section.

Section 3: Legs!

In this section we only see legs moving. They are visible behind the screen, in the gap between the sand and the lower edge of the screen. They move along a horizontal pathway from SR to SL and back and forth with different stepping patterns, leg and foot gestures and jumps. On the DVD recording, as they travel, we see a film above them showing similar activity, sometimes larger, moving diagonally onto the audience, or in very small images. Occasionally they seem to fly up and then drop down, this is made possible by the slings, which will appear later in the work, but are hidden from view in this section. Each pair of legs disappears up behind the screen as the section ends.

Section 4: Faces

Film is again a feature of this section, with faces appearing on the upper paper screen and the three women dancers lying, sitting and rolling on the sand below the screen. The images on the screen appear in various sizes, and one woman gradually appears distressed as she appears to be ageing, and the paper is broken up by water poured or dripping from above. The dancers on the floor move in unison for most of this section, quite quickly into a sustained gesture, and then move both along and up and down the stage in the sand. They can be seen quite clearly. They roll upstage and out of sight as the scene ends. The accompaniment is chant-like and ritualistic in style.

The downstage paper screen has almost all come down. From *Perfect* by Kevin Finnan

Section 5: Time Flies

This is a much longer section with several lighting changes. The screen is pulled down by the dancers, the paper strewn across the sand, then collected and dropped in five piles.

It is dark upstage, with a grey, speckled light playing on the torn, hanging strips of paper. The two men come into view from the slings, and travel back and forth through the screen. The three females join in and they alternate between standing, falling onto the sand and sitting on the bench like structures of the set.

The lighting becomes very bright and there are several very powerful duets with big lifts, dancers flying and being caught and lowered by a partner. Lots of different ways of meeting and parting

JAMES BELL

are clearly shown. The benches are also used. At one point two girls come down-stage and seem distressed and threatened for a while, with panicky gestures, rubbing their hands and then rubbing down the outside of their bodies and legs. The lighting changes to create a darker mood, with the upstage gauze lit from behind. The trickling sand duet material from the first section reappears occasionally. As the light brightens again there is a sense of a fight taking place, as the dancers fly over, into a partners' arms, or roll under lifted legs. It is an extremely fast, athletic and acrobatic section. The lighting changes to the darker setting once more as the rest of the torn screen is ripped and pulled down by the men. The girls rest on the bench and then fly onto the sand and back to the bench as all the paper is collected. The pace of life has been very fast in this section.

Section 6: Garden

The pace changes totally here, in terms of both the sound and the action. The paper is made into flower shapes and planted in the sand (i.e. to make a garden). A small dance just using up the paper takes place and leads into a tender duet with a flower. There is a sense of romance, shyness and teasing. The planting and clearing goes on or flowers are made by dancers sitting on the bench. Then there is a further duet, which is more intimate, but the male rejects the female; he bonds with his mate and the females support each other. The garden is planted in rows.

Section 7: Loop

Two female dancers water the sand and plants with watering cans and the men use wooden rakes to rake each row between the flowers. The white slings are untied and all the dancers use them to either hover high up or to walk along the rows. The girls pick up sand and let it trickle through their hands as they walk. All walk floor patterns across, down and round the plants and each other. They flick and lie in the sand then rub

Use of props in rehearsal of *Perfect* by Kevin Finnan

WWW.WITHALITTLEHELP.CO.UK

it off their clothes. All are clearly enjoying playing with and on the sand. The females then pick up the plants as the men indulge in a playful fight. They watch from the benches but then join in, starting playful fights with each other. One female is left on her own.

On the DVD there are two screens shown at times, one large and one small, placed either side by side or one higher than the other. One shows a close-up and the other a distance shot.

Section 8: Interlude 1: Longing

As we see the solo start the lighting dims almost to blackout. The gauze from upstage is moved smoothly as the dancer continues her emotional solo. The curtain billows as the music rises, and she sinks to roll under and behind the curtain. Behind the now blue pattern on the gauze (seen in Overture), she continues her solo, and we see it again on two screens. We see her in close up before other dancers join her in the space.

Section 9: Hands of time

On the DVD performance, the lighting changes quite often in this section. The dancers are controlled by a giant hand, which prods, pushes and pulls them across and around the stage. The film overlay is interesting as a device and coordinated with the dancers' actions. They move in many different numerical and gender combinations. The giant hand controls when they are in unison and the stage is split from upstage to downstage in lighting zones, with two clear squares of light that break up the dimmer setting. The hand also deals with each dancer in canon at various moments. They use the benches to fly from and sit on, and after all being squashed by the hand they argue. The music is rhythmic and the sound and music complement each other. More hands and arms prod, squeeze, pick up, push or nudge the dancers along, and they become more frantic as the music builds. The two couples sink to the floor and as the solo female watches from the bench SL, they embrace and then split from each other. The section ends with series of blackouts as different pairings meet and change.

CHRIS NASH

The DVD recording of *Perfect* by Kevin Finnan has giant hands that manipulate the dancers

Section 10: Pregnant Pause

This scene is a complete contrast with what has come before. It shows several different film sequences of the bumps of pregnant women. Two men climb ladders upstage and two women are lying downstage, considering the time factor of labour and birth. The trickling sand motif appears. The men do not relate to the women until the final part of this section, when they perform a fluid duet in unison behind the gauze, reaching out to the women. The accompaniment is calm and smooth and fills out the mood of the action well.

Section 11: Rakes

The title of this section says it all. The two men use the rakes in duets with two of the women. They lift, turn, carry and support their partners with the rakes. One duet is quite tenderly performed, whereas the other becomes aggressive and at times disturbing. Upstage left, the third female dancer creates people from sand behind the two duets. The accompaniment continues from the previous section, with both fluid melodies and dynamic rhythmic phrases that coexist with the dance. The aggressive man rakes

Flying over raked circles, from *Perfect* by Kevin Finnan

the sand in circles, discards his rake, and lies on his left side. The third female brings him a sand person as the light changes from bright to an intimate glow. She then steps onto his right hip to reach for the sling above.

Section 12: Interlude 2: Time in Limbo

The lights are low with a hint of blue. The other four dancers move from the floor to reach the slings, climbing the frames and untying them. They hang and either walk on the air, or walk in a circle, or sway and then let the slings go. They grab another for the next section and hang with the slings under their armpits facing stage left.

Flying in unison in 'Arc of Time', from *Perfect* by Kevin Finnan

Section 13: Slings: Arc of Time

This climax of the work is different and physically challenging. It echoes the movements of pendulums, which swing rhythmically in arcs as seconds pass. The dancers move in matching unison at first and then split into all sorts of combinations, varying the speed, direction and pathways of their actions. We see arcs going in many directions both consecutively and simultaneously. The dancers have a sense of weightlessness and flow that is a joy to watch.

Their work in twos and a three is both complex and fluid. The slings and dancers wrap around each other, or they walk slowly and heavily as others swing. Sometimes their feet do not touch the ground; at others they draw lines in the sand as they swing to and fro. The flying becomes more and more energetic and faster as they swing their bodies up and away from the floor. They turn in the sling

so that at times it is across the front of the body rather than the back. The dancers link elbows in twos at the middle of a swing. It is adventure playground fun, with shadows lighting the back wall as the section draws to a close. They each leave their sling to swing gently, in canon, and go and sit on the bench stage right. The light dims and they reach towards the empty slings.

Perfect has many interesting features: the structure of the set itself, with the raised floor covered in at least 2–3 cm of sand, and the different surfaces on which we see film projections — paper downstage and gauze both down- and upstage. The space is changed throughout the dance by the way the lights, gauze, sand, paper and, most importantly, film sequences are used. It is a non-linear narrative work lasting 70 minutes, and both emotional and emotive.

Costume design

Claire Armitage designed the costumes. The female dancers' dresses are made in black polyester jersey material. Each has a different neckline and upper-body back design.

Lighting and set design

Mark Parry designed the lighting and Simon Dormon designed the set.

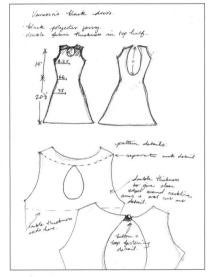

Costume design sketch for Vanessa's dress by Claire Armitage, for *Perfect* by Kevin Finnan

Rosas Danst Rosas by Anne Teresa De Keersmaeker

This work has been performed both on stage and filmed on a specific site. In these notes I refer to the film. The setting is an old school building in Belgium, built in 1936. It has a U-shape structure, with buildings around a central playground, long corridors and many classrooms, some of which are divided by transparent partitions. There are several walls of glass and natural internal shafts of light, which are used as dancers travel and guide specific camera shots. How the camera is used and the editing techniques of the film are clearly important features in this work. The music and movement are minimalist. The film was made in 1997 and directed by Thierry de Mey, but the dance was first performed in 1983 as De Keersmaeker's first work with her own company of four female dancers at a festival in Brussels. The dance lasts 57 minutes. The music is by Thierry de Mey and Peter Vermeersch, and includes industrial sounds, the human voice, rhythmic clapping, silence, music called *Habanera* and a percussive score.

There are five sections or movements in this dance, with short transitions from one to the next. The principal dancers in the film are Cynthia Loemij, Sarah Ludi, Anne Mousselet and Samantha Van Wissen. Another eleven appear in the latter sections, including the choreographer. The work is created around four basic movements: lying, standing, sitting and walking. The costumes include socks over black tights or leggings, a grey thigh-length skirt and different styled tops, loose but with different necklines and sleeve lengths. The dancers wear black lace-up shoes for all sections, apart from those when they are lying down.

Moving in

We hear water falling and shoes scraping the floor as one dancer is seen moving a chair, then turning and pausing repeatedly. The camera pans from that classroom to another, along a corridor, as we hear running footsteps. Chairs have been moved and dancers are seen walking at different speeds, from lit to dark areas, through rain as if crossing an open-air space, and along distant corridors. They place chairs ready for the second section and lean as if tired against a classroom wall. The many windows and glass roof allow the camera to film easily, zooming in or out on the dancers as they move into the environment of the school and its classrooms and corridors. The dancers finally meet in a line facing a glass partition, standing with their backs to the camera. They take a deep breath and fall suddenly to the floor, lying on their left sides.

Floor (first movement)

All four dancers stay close to the floor throughout this section. There is a phrase of everyday gestures, performed very quickly with dramatic pauses, intakes of breath and unexpected rolls. These everyday actions reappear throughout the work. The repeat of the phrase is then performed very slowly and in perfect unison. We see the clean wooden panelled floor and hear the actions of the dancers' hands and bodies as they slide along or drop onto it. The camera allows us to see isolated gestures made by one dancer and long shots of all four, moving slowly, their intake and exhalation of breath audible. They finish lying once again on their left sides, just as they started the section. They depict tired, exhausted women.

Chairs (second movement)

This image continues in this section. The film cuts to a shot of a sole dancer lying across three chairs on her left side. All four dancers are involved in this scene, using the chairs, which are in a diagonal relationship, one row of chairs per dancer. They are in a different classroom, bigger than the last, and are now wearing shoes as well as socks. The three tiers to the right of the screen have three chairs, and that furthest to the left of the screen only has two.

The dancers sit on, lie on, fall off, climb back on and roll from one chair to another at different points in this section. Many gestures are repeated (some from the lying section) and some are new, e.g. hands running through hair, arms wrapped around the stomach, adjusting the neck of clothing,

HERMAN SORGELOOS

Chairs from *Rosas Danst Rosas* by Anne Teresa De Keersmaeker

hands clasped and either thrust deep down in front of the body or flung outstretched strongly away from the body. Other gestures include: a sudden turn of the head to look behind; flopping forwards; extending the right arm to the side; having the hands on the lap with the back straight and looking up.

The dancers perform in matching unison, contrasting unison and complementary unison. Similarly, various types of canon can be seen as the phrases and short motifs interlock, pause and change speed. The accompaniment is very rhythmical and has few accents, but the dancers' panting and breaths, along with the noise of their shoes and hand slaps on the chairs, provide interesting accents. The camera gives us long shots that show all four dancers as well as the detail of the venue: the tiled floor, tiled walls, pillars, doors leading off and huge windows. There are also close-ups of actions and faces, and panning from one dancer to another, as well as seeing the actions from behind the dancers. The section ends with all the dancers facing away from the camera towards the various open doors, which were originally behind them.

Building (third movement)

The film edit shows dancers appearing in several different parts of the building. More dancers seem to be involved, as three use corridors and two use a doorway, stairs and a large open space. The 'pulling the neckline down, baring one or both shoulders' gesture is especially explored, possibly as a provocative or experimental seductive gesture. The two dancers seem to be trying to outdo each other with the size of their actions, added dynamic changes and particular glances at each other. One of them joins two others to form a trio moving through a dilapidated, yellow painted door, into a corridor where at least three other dancers seem to be waiting. They pass them and travel behind another soloist absorbed in playing with her neckline. The trio ignore the soloist, who glances over her shoulder as they turn, gesture and walk away down the corridor back to those waiting. Another soloist

repeats the neckline motif and is similarly ignored. In yet another corridor, off a T-junction, a trio travel to and fro as the last soloist hesitates, repeats a variation of the neckline motif, then charges towards the trio, as one of them runs towards the camera. We then see different trios dancing the turning gesture and stepping motif in various parts of the building, with one dancer running between the spaces. We watch through the windows of the outside walls from afar as they all move across the inside of each classroom or corridor. A dancer sitting on the bench outside signals the move to the next section. The accompaniment includes a theme played on a clarinet.

Travelling in unison, from *Rosas Danst Rosas* by Anne Teresa De Keersmaeker

Glass interiors

A soloist travels along a corridor, in a lit reflection on the floor, and appears to look through panes of glass whichever way she turns. As she turns she swings her long hair around and later smoothes it back and down. She passes a seated dancer, who ignores both her and the trio, who then repeat parts of her solo material. The film moves to a much bigger space with a large group of dancers near a glass wall, all facing different directions and some with their necklines askew. They use the neckline or turning motifs and travel simultaneously along pathways or on the spot. We see at least three glass-panelled corridors, each with dancers performing variations of the same motifs. The camera follows a soloist walking along and through corridors as others turn, tilt and walk back in front of her. She introduces a bouncy, skippy motif, and the neckline motif reappears again. The camera then pans back along the soloist's journey until the viewpoint is outside the building, looking at innumerable panes of broken glass. It continues to pan to the right at first floor level, when a dancer exits and walks across the roof towards the camera, poses provocatively while performing the hair and neckline motifs, pauses and then turns and runs noisily back across the roof to end the section.

Lying down

This is a short reprise of the first section by four different dancers. The movement material is similar, but in a different order. The dancers face a different direction and the accents, pauses and speed changes are varied.

Inner court (fourth movement)

This court is in fact the central playground. Four dancers perform outside to a jazzy and at times blues accompaniment, which includes melodies played on saxophones and a clarinet. The music becomes multi-layered as the section develops, with the sound of the dancers' feet and the intakes of their breath becoming increasingly obvious. There appears to be three parts to this section, divided by two long pauses made by the dancers. The lighting in the third part resembles the breaking of day, so it feels as if they have danced all night.

The dancers start with their backs to the glass windows and are easily visible as they walk, turn and gesture. As the camera shifts and they dance against a brick wall, the light seems dusk-like. They move to the centre of this huge playground as the music changes. Motifs are shared between them, with **accumulation**, **fragmentation** and simpler uses of canon. It is a fading light environment, and the different explorations of the use of four dancers is extremely complex and fascinating. Quite basic gestural and travelling move-ments are performed with dynamic variations and accents. The dancers are no longer wearing black leggings. We see different pathways and straight, circular and diagonal lines, as the lights seem to fade more and more.

After the dancers pause for the second time, the light changes as they travel together. The hair gesture returns, the hugging gesture has shifted from stomach to chest level, and we see the dancers from both long and close-up shots. The section builds to a climax in speed and energy as one dancer falls (possibly exhausted) onto the concrete playground and another looks down on her almost scathingly.

Coda

Each dancer shows exhaustion, either leaning on an outside wall of the school; moving slowly and repeating the hair motif heavily; putting a chair on the end of a row inside a lit classroom and lying down on her left side; or repeating mono-tonously her last motif, ending with a clenched fist behind her back in the corner of a yard, only to be passed by a crowd of dancers running from a far door through the opening next to her and towards the camera. The work finishes with a close up of her clenched fist, which slowly opens and drops heavily to her side as she sighs. Blackout.

Filming

This includes long moving shots, fast cuts, aggressive angle changes, edited film, and one camera filming the dance while a second records close-ups and panning shots.

Appreciation

'Still Life' at the Penguin Café by David Bintley, the Royal Ballet

This lovely ballet was created in 1988 for the Royal Ballet. It is now in the repertoire of the Birmingham Royal Ballet. There are seven scenes, each linking with the overall theme: Bintley's concern for endangered species, including man. The original idea came from the music and pictures of half-human half-penguin creatures in a sophisicated café setting, used on the album cover of Simon Jeffes's *Penguin Café Orchestra*.

The Great Auk penguin species became extinct in 1844 due to being thoughtless killed by humans. The ballet has scenes about the characteristics of many different endangered species, and 'Still Life' is the name of the cabaret held in the café. The penguins are a link running through the work. The music is orchestral, and its qualities inspired Bintley's choice of animal for each separate piece of music and scene. The set for each scene is different and acts as an appropriate setting for each animal or place. The costumes are realistic, with complex masks or make-up and appropriate clothing, to leave no doubt in the audience's mind as to which animals are being represented. The style of dance in each scene differs from one to another, ranging from American hoedown, modern ballet, English Morris dance, ballroom, and stage to minimalist mime. I have described the content of the first five scenes, which refer to the threat to the animal kingdom. These were the scenes recommended by AQA when this work was previously on the GCSE specification.

Scene 1

There are two parts to this scene: the penguin waiters and the café.

(a) The penguin waiters

This scene has a painted backdrop, centrally placed, just forward of upstage. It depicts icebergs, the sea and the sky, and has the authentic feel of the penguins' natural environment. A male voice tells us, in a very serious manner, about the fate of the Great Auk and possible problems ahead for mankind, as a camera pans over the backdrop and rests on a dancer dressed in a long-tailed black suit, a realistic penguin mask, yellow leg warmers, black ballet shoes, a white bow tie and waistcoat, and black gloves. The dancer is carrying a tray holding three pink glasses in his right hand and is pointing his left index finger upwards as if to say, 'Now, listen hard.'

Three dancers arrive in canon and travel through the space with waddling steps, in turnout, with hops, jumps and polka steps in various motifs. It is a rhythmic,

BILL COOPER

light-hearted dance, with solo phrases and group work seen as they trace a figure of eight around and between each other, as if serving drinks in a crowded place. White circular follow spots are focused on each penguin throughout this short trio. This part ends as the backdrop flies up to reveal the setting for part (b). The downstage area is in blackout as the penguins move upstage.

Dancing in style in the Penguin Café. Section 1: *'Still Life' at the Penguin Café* by David Bintley, Birmingham Royal Ballet

BILL COOPER

(b) The café

A much larger backdrop upstage sets the scene of an upmarket, elegant tearoom or café, with pictures of big windows, tables and chairs, plants and drapes. There is a warm glow to the lights and the floor is decorated by a gobo design of lacy green patterns. Standing centre upstage are a couple, the lady wearing a long evening dress and her partner a dinner suit and a penguin mask, in a ballroom hold. This is almost a dream environment with a close relationship between an animal and a human.

The scene involves a large corps de ballet who dance ballroom-style steps in pairs as the waiters intermingle with their trays. The music is similar to that in part (a), but fuller, more fluid and rhythmic, as they swoop, dip, swing and turn in pairs. They leave the dance floor to take their seats in a filmed set of tables and chairs, awaiting the 'Still Life' cabaret.

Appreciation

Scene 2: Utah Longhorn Ram

This is a scene for a solo female and five male dancers. The soloist wears a full mask, resembling a ram, and a long, cream evening dress and satin-heeled shoes; the men are in evening suits. They all move in a style of dance associated with Fred Astaire and Ginger Rogers, and extravagant American musicals of the 1930s and 40s. Her male escorts line up behind her and take it in turns to swing her and lift her horizontally as a group. As she spins forward her skirt is peeled off and she is seen in a frilled leotard and flesh-coloured tights. Downstage becomes dark as she and her partner dance together in a follow spot, and the backdrop changes to a huge, rust-coloured rock. The duet takes prominence as the four men skip in pairs and travel upstage before exiting. The music has a lilt and flow to which the duet continues with lively steps, skips and elegant ballroom moves, until she is lifted and lowered to end the dance at her partner's feet, lying along his left leg.

They then move towards the filmed café scene to a round of applause, and all the penguin waiters stand to welcome them back. The film clip ends as the camera focuses on a sole figure centre stage.

Final position of a duet. 'The Utah Longhorn Ram' from *'Still Life' at the Penguin Café* by David Bintley, Birmingham Royal Ballet

Scene 3: the Texan Kangaroo Rat

The black curtains open to reveal a new setting — a full-width backdrop of magnified cacti, which make the rat seem very small. The backdrop does not extend higher than halfway up the back curtain. Twitching is a characteristic action of rats and is a prominent motif in this solo. After awakening in a shaft of light with a series of foot and head twitches, the dancer travels with hops and skips. He is wearing a short-sleeved T-shirt and denim dungarees, with soft pink dance shoes and a full head mask with whiskers. It is a lively, quick-moving solo with a sense of American hoedown actions and style, with slapping knee gestures as the dancer hops around and a side shuffle with digging elbows. It is a fun solo with some gymnastic, even street-like movements, as the dancer takes his weight on all fours and scurries, leaps and turns, staying close to the floor.

Slapping motif by the Texan Kangaroo Rat, from *'Still Life' at the Penguin Café* by David Bintley, Birmingham Royal Ballet

The filming of this solo is interesting as there are top shots looking down on the animal and moments filmed from behind, as the rat appears to be close to the dancers in the café. The lighting is bright on the stage and the dancer is within a follow spot at all times. The solo has a false ending, as the dancer lies and twitches as if going to sleep, but suddenly gets up, scratching furiously as if he is bothered by a flea, and travels towards and exits USL to applause from the café, seen again as a film clip.

Scene 4: the Hog-Nosed Skunk Flea

This scene has one female dancer as the flea, dressed in a bright orange catsuit with black or gold circular designs around the body and limbs, pointe shoes, and a half mask with antennae. She follows five male dancers onstage, who are dressed in complex Morris dance costumes, with black shoes, white leggings, black breeches with coloured braces, long-sleeved white shirts and fancy hats with ribbons in similar colours to the braids hanging behind their heads. She is mischievous and jumps from one to another, leads them into a tangled heap, and is quite clearly frightened as she squeals when they try to swat her with their sticks. The male dancers seem clumsy, awkward and heavy-footed by comparison to her delicate, lively, quick actions.

Jumping in unison: the Hog-nosed Skunk Flea from 'Still Life' at the Penguin Café by David Bintley, Birmingham Royal Ballet

BILL COOPER

The set is another large backdrop, this time of animal fur, which is where one might find a flea. The stage floor has a plain, light brown wash, and the flea is within a spotlight throughout the dance. The music is rhythmic and orchestral,

Appreciation

and the steps clearly match the timing and speed of the music. She is lifted and passed backwards over their heads before following them as they exit, only to jump on the back of the rear dancer, and exits with them to USR as they skip, turn and hit each others' sticks. Blackout heralds the end of the scene.

Scene Five: the Southern Cape Zebra

The back curtains open to reveal an African landscape at sunset, with a striped pattern projected on the floor and a dancer dressed in an all-in-one black-and-white striped catsuit, a headdress with the design of a zebra face, and a white tassel in each hand, which look a bit like short tails. He has a mane running from the top of his head to the base of his spine. The eight models enter, each wearing a white or black-and-white stole over a black sleeveless velvet top, full striped skirts, long elegant black gloves, high-heeled black shoes, and skull headdresses perched on top of slick dark wigs.

BILL COOPER

The dance has three styles which, with the music, convey the place, the animal and the clothing that might have been made from that animal. The Zebra shows a sense of African dance in his travelling jig steps, and contemporary dance in his balances, turns and extended shapes. The models move in sophisticated measured walks,

The Southern Cape Zebra poses in front of the models in *'Still Life'* at *the Penguin Café* by David Bintley, Birmingham Royal Ballet

using hand and facial minimal **pedestrian gestures** and some flexed foot, high-leg poses, which could be contemporary in style. They group together, a bit like a herd, and look nervously one to another, just before the zebra is killed. A red light picks him out spinning and falling to the floor. The camera switches to the models, who appear to be looking in hand mirrors and absorbed in themselves and their make-up. As they exit, the camera picks out the Great Auk hovering over the dead Zebra, then returns to the models departing, and back again to the Great Auk beside a blood-red patch. We see him turn sadly away from the sight. The stage goes into blackout.

Tasks

Use the information on *Swansong* and *'Still Life' at the Penguin Café* to answer the following questions.

Swansong: general facts

Copy out these statements and fill in the gaps.

1 Swansong is a dance in ___ sections.

2 It was choreographed by C_ _ _ _ _ _ _ _ _ _ _ B_ _ _ _ _.

3 There are ___ dancers: ___ men and ___ women.

4 The whole dance lasts approximately ___ minutes.

5 The composer of the music is P_ _ _ _ _ C_ _ _ _ _ _.

6 It is an e_ _ _ _ _ _ _ acoustic score.

7 Four different sounds you can hear are: _____, _____, _____ and _____.

8 An item of furniture on stage is placed _ _ . It can be described as _____.

9 The lighting designer is D_ _ _ _ M_ _ _.

10 The costume designer is C_ _ _ _ _ _ _ _ _ _ B_ _ _ _ _.

11 The dance was originally performed in S_ _ _ _ _ in 198___.

12 It was performed by London F_ _ _ _ _ _ _ B_ _ _ _ _ Company.

13 Two other companies that have performed *Swansong* are _ _ _ _ _ _ _ _ _ and _.

14 It was first performed in London in 19_ _ at _ _ _ _ _ _ _ _ _ _ _ _ _ _ Theatre.

15 Identify one moment in *Swansong* when lighting is important.

_____

16 Describe what the interrogators are wearing.

_____

_____

Swansong: set and placings

1 Mark an X to show where the chair is on stage.

2 Draw the pathway of the special light feature seen in Sections 3 and 7.

3 The interrogators enter the stage one after the other. Show where they enter and go to.

4 How does the movement in Section 3 end?

'Still Life' at the Penguin Café: general facts

Copy out these statements and fill in the gaps.

1 *'Still Life' at the Penguin Café* is a dance in _____ sections.
2 It was choreographed by D_ _ _ _ _ B_ _ _ _ _ _ _.
3 There are _____ dancers in the Utah Longhorn Ram.
4 The whole work lasts approximately _____ minutes.
5 The composer of the music is S_ _ _ _ _ J_ _ _ _ _ _.
6 The music is played by an _____.
7 What do we hear before the first dance starts?
8 The lighting designer is John B _ _ _ _.
9 The costume designer is _ _ _ _ _ _n G_ _ _ _ _ _ _.
10 The dance was originally performed by The _ _ _ _ _ _ _ _ _ _ _ _ _ in 19 _ _.
11 Name the dancer who danced the Texan Kangaroo Rat.
12 There are _____ dancers in the the Hog-nosed Skunk Flea: _____ male and _____ female.
13 It was first performed at _____ in London.
14 Describe the backdrop in the Southern Cape Zebra.
15 The floor lighting colour in Section 2: the Café is _____.

'Still Life' at the Penguin Café: music

1 Can you name the music for the three sections?
2 Describe the qualities of one piece of music you named in question (1).
3 Identify two dance actions performed to this piece of music and say how they relate to it.

'Still Life' at the Penguin Café: costume design

1 Choose one animal seen in *'Still Life' at the Penguin Café* and describe what the dancer is wearing.
2 Many of the dancers wear masks in this work. Name a different animal from that you chose in question (1) and describe the mask in detail.
3 The Morris dancers do not wear masks. How do their costumes tell us they are Morris dancers?
4 Descibe briefly the costumes worn by the ladies in the café.

'Still Life' at the Penguin Café: set and placings

1 Using an X, show where the first dancer starts on the diagram below.

2 There is a backdrop depicting an icy place. Write B on the diagram to show where this is on stage.

3 The first motif of the first dancer travels from DSL. Draw an arrow on the diagram to show the direction and pathway on the stage.

Essay

Using the information provided, compare Section 3: First Solo of *Swansong* with Section 3: the Texan Kangaroo Rat of *'Still Life' at The Penguin Café*. Write your answer as an essay, with an introduction, paragraphs and a conclusion. It should be personal, with examples taken from each work to prove you know them both.

Dance tables

The facts in the following tables outline how old a dance work is, the company that first performed it and where it was performed. You could create similar tables including the facts of each dance work you have seen.

Four of the dances detailed in Table 21 have been on the AQA written paper as possible set works. There are resource packs produced by the dance companies and NRCD, as well as CD-ROMs from Arts Pool and Sound Moves Music Company available on most of these works.

Dance work	Choreographer	Company	Number of dancers	Composer	Accompaniment	Set designer	Lighting designer	Costume designer
Bird Song	Siobhan Davies	Siobhan Davies Dance	8	Andy Pink	Eclectic mix	David Ward Sam Collins	Adrian Plaut	Genevieve Bennett
Dance Tek Warriors	Doug Elkins	Union Dance	6	David Byrne Nusrat Fateh Ali Khan	Eclectic mix		Bill Deverson	Ursula Bombshell
Faultline	Shobana Jeyasingh	Shobana Jeyasingh Dance	8	Scanner Errollyn Wallen Singer: Patricia Rozario	Eclectic mix	Dick Straker	Lucy Carter Film: Peter Gomes	Ursula Bombshell
Ghost Dances	Christopher Bruce	Houston Ballet	11	Inti Illimani	South American folk	Christopher Bruce	Nick Chelton	Belinda Scarlett
Nutcracker!	Matthew Bourne	New Adventures	18 4 actors	Tchaikovsky	Classical	Anthony Ward	Howard Harrison	Anthony Ward
Overdrive	Richard Alston	Richard Alston Dance	11	Terry Riley	Electronic hocketing		Charles Balfour	Jeanne Spaziani
Perfect	Kevin Finnan	Motionhouse Dance Theatre	5	Sophy Smith Tim Dickinson	Eclectic mix	Simon Dormon	Mark Parry Film: Caroline Bridges	Claire Armitage
Romeo and Juliet	Kenneth MacMillan	The Royal Ballet	20+	Prokofiev	Classical	Nicholas Georgiadis		Nicholas Georgiadis
Rosas Danst Rosas	Anne Theresa De Keersmaeker	Rosas	18	Peter Vermeersch Thierry De Mey	Minimalist	Thierry De Mey	Thierry De Mey	Rosas
'Still Life' at the Penguin Café	David Bintley	The Royal Ballet	20+	Simon Jeffes	Penguin Café Orchestra	Hayden Griffiths	John B. Read	Hayden Griffiths
Swansong	Christopher Bruce	English National Ballet	3	Phillip Chambon	Eclectic mix	Christopher Bruce	David Mohr	Christopher Bruce

Table 21 Details of eleven dance works set by AQA

Carlos Acosta, José Martin, Yohei Sasaki as the trio in Act I of *Romeo and Juliet* by Kenneth MacMillan, March 2008, the Royal Ballet

Act II: 'The Wedding Pose', from *Nutcracker!* by Matthew Bourne, New Adventures

Structure and content: *Bird Song*

Bird Song is structured around a central solo, which is based on the song of the Australian pied butcher bird. The dance work is divided into 16 sections, with the 7 that follow the 'Bird Song solo' echoing, reflecting and developing ideas conveyed in the first 8 sections. There are eight dancers, who perform 'in the round'. Tables 22–24 indicate some of the movement features you can see in *Bird Song*.

'Beginning' is a driven, chaotic group section. Dancers shift suddenly between directions, levels and areas of the space. They perform short, repeated actions.

Appreciation

Table 22 'Beginning', *Bird Song* (2004) by Siobhan Davies

'Beginning'	Use of dancers	Action content	Dynamics	Use of space
	Eight as ensemble			
1st	All different	Small gestures and steps	Rhythmic	Cluster, on spot
2nd	All different	Swinging and swaying	Smooth	Sideways on
3rd	All different	Travel, then sink to floor	Rhythmic	As cluster
4th	All the same	Crawl on hands and knees	Slow, steady	All in same direction, near floor
5th	All different	Get up, travel and hold still	At different times	Dancers move to their left
6th	All different	Small gestures	Rhythmic	On spot, right side to camera
7th	All different	Travel	Rhythmic	In, away, around each other
8th	Back together	Travel	Rhythmic	Backwards
9th	Gestures	On spot	Slow motion	Close to each other
10th	One behind the other	Standing, arms signal in extended lines	Moving slowly	Diagonal line, arms at different levels
11th	All different	Leg and hip actions	Rhythmic	In and out from body
12th	All the same	Crawling backwards	Slowly, smoothly	Backwards
13th	All different	Lying to kneeling, rocking	Changing	Low-level, different directions
14th	All become the same	Walking, ending in a circle	Rhythmic, smooth	General to end in circle
15th	In pairs	Moving each other, lift and lower	Smooth	To edge of space
16th	Passing through each other	Running	Racing	All in the same direction
17th	All different	Upper body and arm gestures	Rhythmic	In cluster
18th	All the same	Looking up	Still	In cluster
19th	All the same	Crawling	Slowly at first	New direction
20th	All different	Hands and feet, lollop, travel with padding feet	Rhythmic, quick, lively	All going same way
21st	All slightly different	Travelling steps, jumping two feet to two feet	Rhythmic, quick, lively	Going backwards, tiny jumps
22nd	All slightly different	Twisting spine, arm and leg gestures	Jerky, quick	In cluster
		All stand, walk in dim light to new zones		

Music: *Infinite Monkeys* by Mannlicher Carcano (4 min 30 sec)

Table 23 Section 6a: '4 Corners 1'

'4 Corners 1'	Use of dancers	Action content	Dynamics	Use of space
Duet A (1 min 20 sec)	❖ Eight dancers are on stage ❖ Two duets (A and B) — A: one male and one female (Henry Montes and Gill Clarke) dance in unison and canon, matching and contrasting arm pathways	Lying on backs, arms move from sides, up behind head, and back to sides	❖ Slowly, then with varying speeds ❖ Cool, calm, gentle In silence, except for sounds their arms make on the floor	❖ Near camera, arm pathways varied ❖ Moving in own quartile only
Duet B (2 min)	❖ Two females stand facing each other (Sarah Warsop and Sasha Roubicek) ❖ Duet A in close contact ❖ Duet B link arms only	❖ Use of retiré ❖ Outward circling from low to high ❖ One dancer kneels ❖ Codes of movement ❖ Linear gestures	❖ In silence ❖ Smooth, careful, delicate	❖ High and low levels ❖ In separate quartile to Duet A ❖ Signals, angles, use of square
Quartet: Tammy Arjona, Pari Naderi, Laurent Cavanna, Marius Raczynskj (2 min)	Four move into quartile: in pairs and solos	❖ Walking and turning ❖ Use of arm gestures from duet A	❖ Sound rhythms used ❖ Measured phrases	❖ In own zone ❖ Straight pathways measuring territory across quartile
Duet B			Slow and smooth	Two levels
Duet A tableaux		In close contact with head jerks and hand gestures	Quick and sharp	❖ Near floor ❖ Tiny actions
Duets A and B		❖ A in contact, use of arm gestures ❖ B uses arm gestures from Duet A ❖ Stand and change places ❖ Travel within quartile ❖ Use arm and leg gestures ❖ Reverse Duet A's arm motif ❖ Restarts sense of competition for territory	❖ Slow and smooth ❖ Start and stop, still smooth ❖ Quick	❖ Near floor ❖ Change levels, larger actions
Quartet		Travelling into pairs and lifts with extended arm gesture	Rhythmic	
Duet A		Rocks in contact	Slowly	Near floor
Duet B		Stepping new relationship	Rhythmic	New floor pattern
Quartet (1 min 40 sec)		Travels	Rhythmic	Out of quartile, new spacing
Duet B		Curved arm gestures		Large
7 minutes: Quiet music. Echoing piano-like notes.				
Design: two thin white lines divide space into quartiles				

Appreciation

Table 24 Section 5a: 'Diagonal'

'Diagonal'	Use of dancers	Action content	Dynamics	Use of space
2 min 15 sec	❖ All eight dancers perform solos ❖ All do different actions at different speeds at same time ❖ Eight short motifs ❖ All finish on knees ❖ All still for a while at end	❖ Different supports, swaying, rocking ❖ Arms to second and to sides or body centre ❖ Varying air patterns ❖ All gradually stand ❖ Swing, sway, step turn with occasional odd jumps ❖ Stepping sideways	❖ Use varying speeds and energy ❖ Moments of stillness and silence ❖ Chaotic climax as volume increases	❖ All facing same direction, at low level, in linear pattern ❖ Moving sideways ❖ Diagonal lines across floor from overhead projection ❖ Dancers seem pulled towards and away from a central diagonal line ❖ Lighting change to dots which pulsate

Sound: starts quietly and builds in volume — industrial mechanical sounds with rhythmic phrases

JOEL CHESTER FILDES

Section 4a: 'Snake 1', *Bird Song* by Siobhan Davies, Siobhan Davies Dance

200

Table 25 Section 4a: 'Snake 1'

'Snake 1'	Use of dancers	Action content	Dynamics	Use of space
Collage of found sounds: mechanical, whistling, knocking, non-metric (2 min 30 sec)	❖ Follow the leader into formations ❖ Four dancers exit splitting arcs of action into separate positions ❖ Four dancers exit and four dancers stay on set	❖ Stillness ❖ Running and stillness, using many different body shapes ❖ All lying on floor in new, undulating shape ❖ Unison moment in a horizontal line, near floor	❖ Rhythmic, accented ❖ Short pauses ❖ Fast travelling rippling effect	❖ Spotted, lit floor design ❖ Travelling in and out of linear and circular formations ❖ Spiralling outwards ❖ Individual body designs make a picture

Table 26 Section 3a: 'Muybridge 1'

'Muybridge 1'	Use of dancers	Action content	Dynamics	Use of space
Series of rattling sounds (3 min)	❖ Quartet move in unison and canon (various combinations) ❖ Three are in contact, leaving 1 isolated, to 4, to new trio, to 4 ❖ Dance phrase split across quartet	❖ Finger tips almost touching in arm gestures in front of body ❖ Travelling on feet with arm gestures from Section 1 ❖ Lying on backs ❖ Solo uses arm gesture ❖ Trio joins solo, all four walk, hands in contact ❖ Stop, then exit	❖ Stop motion film ❖ Stop and start ❖ Sense of fluidity between stops ❖ Delicate, curved gestures ❖ Strong contact work	❖ Different levels ❖ A new environment ❖ Dark starbursts leave after-images

Table 27 Section 2a: 'Solo 1'

'Solo'	Use of dancers	Action content	Dynamics	Use of space
Music: *Scratch* by W. Mark Sutherland Looped series of clicks (3 min)	❖ Female soloist: Gill Clarke ❖ A detailed sputtering solo	❖ Walks to white spot ❖ Gestures ❖ Travels with swinging steps and elbow gestures ❖ Quirky sidestepping with tiny jerky arm gestures	❖ Jerky, rhythmic to popping sounds ❖ Smoother ❖ Quick, sharp	❖ Straight path-way ❖ Tiny ❖ To edge and around the space ❖ Small ❖ Moves into yellow light

Appreciation

Table 28 Section 1a: '4 Musical Lines 1'

'4 Musical Lines 1'	Use of dancers	Action content	Dynamics	Use of space
Pari Naderi and Sasha Roubicek (2 min 20 sec)	❖ Two female dancers duet — one follows the other ❖ Contrasting material performed together	❖ Steps on tiptoes ❖ Arm gestures ❖ Bouncing ❖ Four themes from an original phrase	Variety: each dancer is different	❖ Blue floor with white speckles like the surface of the moon ❖ Small ❖ Larger
Marius Raczynskj and Sarah Warsop (1 min 20 sec)	❖ Two more dancers enter ❖ Female solo, others close together			
Sasha Roubicek, Henry Montes and Laurent Cavanna (40 sec)	Male enters followed by another		One is slow	
Music: *Language Universal* by audio.nl (4 min 20 sec)				

Table 29 'Improvisation 1'

'Improvisation 1'	Use of dancers	Action content	Dynamics	Use of space
Silent — tunes in head (4 min 20 sec)	❖ All eight dance in solo ❖ Four still centrally, four solos, as lit line extends across stage	Many different motifs	Keeping rhythm of own tune in each motif	Dancers occupy different areas of lit design
	All get involved successively	One female travels, the others more static		Small for some, extensive for others
	Duet A	On spot, gestures		
	Duet B		Focus: move then still	
	New male and female duet	Action and reaction Catching up, development of new duet (links to quartet in Section 6)		Long, curved, lit lines slash across the floor like comet trails
	Trio: male joins the new duet			Echoes and traces of earlier actions and use of space
	Rhythms and material improvised	All exit except two men still on floor		

Table 30 'Bird Song solo'

'Bird Song solo'	Use of dancers	Action content	Dynamics	Use of space
Music: *The Pied Butchers of Storey Creek* by David Lumsdaine (4 min)	Male solo Henry Montes	Hands and arms 'dabbling down'	❖ Loose, hanging ❖ Jerky actions	Downwards
		❖ Arms extend high parallel ❖ Movement coming from lungs and thorax ❖ Spine arches		Towards high back, large action
		Arms curve down (as in Duet A, Section 1) as weight lifts up and down to ball then whole foot	❖ Arms smooth ❖ **Weight transference** rhythmic ❖ Gentle jerking action	Small actions
		Arms extend again but descend differently: curving, small swinging action		Large followed by small
		Little jerky arm gestures to high extension		Small to large
		Repeats, bringing elbows around and arms out		Face new direction
		Swinging	Quick	Made larger
		❖ Instinctive reflexes ❖ Spasms, ripples and jerks in trunk, shoulder girdle	Spattering rhythm and long pauses	Tiny isolated actions
		❖ Arms high, swing backwards to lunge ❖ Still (turn, stop, look)		
		Elbows pulling back repeatedly	Jerky, sharp, fast	Quite small actions
		Shivering action	Rippling quickly	
		Focus changes, stillness in lower half of body		
		Travel (skittering) and stopping	Very quick to slowing down	
		Elbow pull-back motif		Larger
		Travel ending in starting position		Kneeling on floor
		Swinging arms	Getting faster and stops	
		❖ Head gestures ❖ Focus changes as standing	❖ Smooth ❖ Jerky	Stands
		❖ Swinging alternate arms, turns, moving lunge sideways, pause with left arm forwards ❖ Focus changes ❖ Swinging bent arms, slows down	❖ Smooth ❖ Feet jerky then still ❖ Powerful ❖ Decelerates	Close to body
	As the female enters, he exits			

Appreciation

Table 31 'Improvisation 2'

'Improvisation 2'	Use of dancers	Action content	Dynamics	Use of space
Silence and whipping sounds (3 min 50 sec)	Female brings on two females, Tammy Arjona, Pari Naderi and Gill Clarke	❖ Female 1 travels then stops ❖ Sasha Roubicek enters	❖ Female 1 is quick and rhythmic ❖ Female 2 is slow	❖ Around circle (spot), then to corner ❖ Around edge of space to a corner
	❖ 4 dancers on stage ❖ Short duets	❖ Female 1 travels then stops ❖ Female, Sarah Warsop, enters and a male, Laurent Cavanna, follows ❖ Female and male chase to join others, Sasha Roubicek and Laurent Cavanna	❖ Both quick, rhythmic ❖ Fast	❖ The lit black and red circles appear and fade ❖ Sense of changing environment
	❖ Other four enter ❖ Some exit as link to '4 Musical Lines 2'	❖ Contact work near floor ❖ Repetitions from earlier in work	Slow	❖ Low level ❖ Some small gestures on spot, others travel

Pari Naderi in 'Improvisation 2', *Bird Song*, Siobhan Davies Dance

JOEL CHESTER FILDES

Table 33 Section 1b: '4 Musical Lines 2'

'4 Musical Lines 2'	Use of dancers	Action content	Dynamics	Use of space
Whipping sounds overlay the rhythmic, percussive beat (1 min 30 sec)	❖ Four dancers ❖ One still, one solo and in trio — Pari Naderi, Marius Raczynskj, Sarah Warsop and Sasha Roubicek ❖ Links with '4 Musical Lines 1'	❖ One solo with small gestures ❖ Soloist in white travels, swinging, reaching, with full body action	❖ Slow ❖ Fluid ❖ Quick	❖ Trio in a corner ❖ One solo in another corner ❖ Ends with blackout

Table 34 Section 2b: 'Solo 2'

'Solo 2'	Use of dancers	Action content	Dynamics	Use of space
Piano and voice: *When I'm 84* by Walter Zimmerman (3 min)	Female solo, Gill Clarke	❖ She stands ❖ Arms curving ❖ Moves into blue light	❖ Slower than 'Solo 1', softer, calmer ❖ A reflective memory of 'Solo 1'	❖ Small white triangle of light enlarges to an oblong then covers half the space ❖ Ends in corner

Table 35 Section 3b: 'Muybridge 2'

'Muybridge 2'	Use of dancers	Action content	Dynamics	Use of space
Strings music: *Canon BWV 1073*, J. S. Bach Silence (2 min)	Quartet: two male and two female — Tammy Arjona, Henry Montes, Marius Raczynskj, Gill Clarke	❖ All run on ❖ Swinging, swaying, reaching pausing ❖ 'Dancey'	❖ Delicate ❖ Fluid ❖ Liquid ❖ Ongoing	❖ Large actions ❖ Square floor pattern
	Two others join in: Sarah Warsop and Laurent Cavanna	Unison and canon explored		Blackout

Table 36 Section 4b: 'Snake 2'

'Snake 2'	Use of dancers	Action content	Dynamics	Use of space
Industrial sounding rhythms (2 min)	❖ Eight dancers as two groups of four ❖ Changing formations	❖ Running ❖ Solos ❖ Walking ❖ Lying down	❖ Builds in energy ❖ Decreases ❖ Slows down	❖ Linear group changes ❖ Curving pathways ❖ Changing levels ❖ Low level ❖ Two lines ❖ Red floor projection slashed by curving comet lines

Table 36 Section 6b: '4 Corners 2'

'4 Corners 2'	Use of dancers	Action content	Dynamics	Use of space
Rhythmic Metallic and voices collage (30 sec)	Four dancers: Duets A and B	As in Section 6a		
Musical fragments from '4 Corners 1' (30 sec)	Quartet enter	Travel actions from 'Beginning'		Across space diagonally and exit
	Duet B	One standing, the other near floor	Slow, fluid	Two levels, big gestures
(2 min)	Duet A	In contact	Very slow	Each duet in own zone around partner
(2 min 30 sec)	Duets B and A	❖ Travels and stops ❖ Counter-tension: female stands in close contact	❖ Fast and fluid with pauses, accelerates ❖ Contrasts visible in use of time	Two diagonal zones seen on a blue floor
(30 sec)	Duet A link to 'Ending'	Lifting and lowering in close contact	Very careful, slow, weighted actions	

Table 37 'Ending'

Ending	Use of dancers	Action content	Dynamics	Use of space
Piano music 'The Three *Träumerei* Variations' by John Rea (3 min)	Male solo: Laurent Cavanna Duet A: Henry Montes and Gill Clarke	❖ Male: big fluid gestures, uses space ❖ Duet moves slowly in contact ❖ Solo walks, extends second arm	Contrasting between solo and duet	❖ Duet on spot on floor: enclosed environment ❖ Solo uses general space ❖ Grey floor with white dots which appear and fade ❖ Blackout at end

Snake 2 from
Bird Song by
Siobhan Davies

JOEL CHESTER FILDES

Chapter 11

Preparing for the final assessments

Performance assessments

You could have three or four performance assessments at the end of your course, each of which will demand different rehearsal schedules and things to practice. These assessments are the set dance, the **performance in a duo/group dance**, the solo composition based on a set work, your own solo that you have choreographed, and you may be dancing another candidate's group dance, which he/she has choreographed.

The set dance

This is a dance that the exam board has set as a solo for every candidate in the country to perform for the final external assessment. It counts for 20% of your overall grade. The set study lasts just over 1 minute, has a musical accompaniment, and several different phrases of varying degrees of difficulty. Ideally, you should be able to dance the set study on your own.

The assessment will be a formal occasion. You will be filmed, as the exam board will need to see a recording of your performance for the external assessment.

Learning the set dance

To learn the set dance, you must attend every lesson when your teacher is teaching it. Look interested and ready to start, and concentrate on the movements you have to learn. Work with as much energy as is required; you should be fit enough to perform without getting too breathless.

You need to remember what to do, in the right order, in the right rhythm, and in the correct place. If you do not understand how to do a particular movement, then you must ask for help. Other students could be struggling in the same way as you. At any particular point in the dance, ask to see a movement repeated more slowly, or for the teacher to explain how to do it again. Check which way

you should be facing, where a limb should be, how strongly or quickly you should do a movement, and what the rhythm is. These are all important factors that will help you perform a movement accurately.

Practising the set dance

You can only remember the dance from beginning to end if you have practised it many times. There will be parts you find easier and others you may find more difficult. You are expected to perform the dance as if it is part of you. You must:

❖ extend fully
❖ dance in time with the accompaniment
❖ dance with the appropriate dynamics
❖ focus in certain directions
❖ perform in the style of the dance
❖ project your interpretation of the study
❖ enjoy dancing it!

You can practise dancing on your own or with others. You could do it full out in the dance space at your school/college, or mark it in a small place, such as at home or in a corner of the dance space. Think it through while sitting on your own, maybe listening to the music as you do so. If you cannot think the dance through on your own, you cannot make your body do it.

Only you can improve your grade; no one else can do it for you. You are the one who rehearses, asks questions, gets feedback from the teacher, cross-checks with the video recording, uses mirrors if your dance space has some, and then improves. It will be a shame if you do not make the effort to enjoy dancing a dance that you have not had to choreograph, and which you know every dance GCSE candidate in the country has to dance.

Performance in a duo/group dance

This is a dance the exam board asks your teacher to organise. Like the set dance, it counts for 20% of your final grade. The piece could be a duo, a trio, or have four or five dancers. It will have a clear subject matter, theme or dance idea. It will be in a particular performance and choreographic style. You might have a particular role to play in this dance. It will be clearly linked in three ways to one of the set works listed by the AQA exam board.

Your teacher will either choreograph the dance for your class; invite a dance artist to choreograph it; choreograph most of the dance but give the class the opportunity to vary some motifs themselves; or use dance phrases a dance artist has introduced in a workshop, and together with the class create a dance for assessment. Your teacher will probably choose who will dance with whom, how many dancers there will be, how long the dance will last (between 3 and $3^1/_2$ minutes), the accompaniment, whether props, sets or costumes are needed, and how the dance links with a professional work in three different ways.

You may learn some performance pieces in Year 10, in different styles and based on different set works and their ideas. You may therefore already have some styles of dance you prefer. If you have performed in several group pieces your teacher will suggest which one to submit as your final assessment. These will differ from one person to another in your class.

Style

There are certain styles of dance that come under the category of popular and social dance rather than that of performing arts. These are not so suitable for your GCSE dance assessment. So, however much you might want to be assessed on your ability in funky styles of dance (e.g. hip-hop, street, breakdance, body popping, folk, disco, ballroom, Latin American), you can only use movements in these styles if they are part of an assessment and linked with a set work that is performed by professional dancers in one of these styles.

Styles of dance that are regarded as a performing art use physical and visual contact to express an idea. Dance styles that could be used in your group dance are those seen in any of the set works prescribed by AQA and which in particular are seen in the work chosen by your teacher for this assessment.

Assessment

There are no marks available for choreography in the group dance. Instead, you are marked on your:

* ability to express the dance idea clearly
* technical skill
* sensitivity to other dancers in a variety of dance relationships
* response to the accompaniment
* awareness of the space around you
* accuracy in using the performance style
* accuracy in your use of dynamics
* use of focus
* ability to demonstrate your skill as an artist
* safe practice as a performer in a group dance, in the way you perform and what you wear
* use of visual contact with other dancers and the audience

In your group dance, you will be expected to show that you know:

❖ the dance idea and how it grows through the dance
❖ all the movements you are expected to dance
❖ the formations you are all in
❖ where you are facing in the formation
❖ a feeling or mood to be felt and expressed
❖ how close you are meant to be to the others
❖ which area of the stage you should be in
❖ where the other dancers are
❖ the pathways you are travelling
❖ whether you should adjust the size of steps to show unison
❖ whether you are in time with each other
❖ whether you are in time with the music
❖ whether you are using physical and visual contact well
❖ whether you have the timing of contact right
❖ when to enter and leave stage at the right moment and in the way the teacher wants
❖ the rhythm of any canon
❖ the dynamics of each movement
❖ when the highlights of the dance are
❖ your role leading up to and away from any highlights or to the end of the dance
❖ how to project your role in the dance clearly and expressively to an audience
❖ what is suitable clothing, footwear, hairstyle and jewellery (if at all) for your role

Practising the group dance

Practising with the other dancers will often be crucial to you getting the best mark you can. You must work as a team and help each other to get the right movements at the right time so you can project the dance idea clearly as a group. Give feedback to each other, in a pleasant manner, if any elements are not working. Show your work to your teacher so that he/she can give you feedback.

Have a video made of your group dancing and use it to improve your own skills, spacing and timing. Watching yourself on film can help you to spot your mistakes and work at getting the dance right.

Remember, on the assessment days you must concentrate, watch, remember, give your best physical effort and perform your role with commitment and expression as best you can.

Dancing in another candidate's group choreography

You might be asked to dance in a duo, trio, quartet or quintet choreographed by a member of your class. Your input to the piece is as a dancer, not a choreographer; your role is to perform the movements your fellow candidate has chosen to express his/her dance idea. Although you will not be graded for your performance, it is important that you know the answers to the points listed under 'Assessment' for the group dance above (see pages 209–10). You must also dance in the style the candidate wants.

Practising another candidate's group choreography

You are expected to be reliable and supportive to the candidate who invited you to be in his/her choreography. You must turn up to every rehearsal you are required for, ready and willing to learn new movements, which you must remember from one rehearsal to the next. The dance will last between $2^1/_2$ and 3 minutes, so your fitness, movement memory, and dance skills must be good.

Timetabling

You will have to calculate how much time to allocate to working on your own choreography and be fair in the amount of time you give to the other candidate's choreography. Once committed to another candidate's choreography you cannot back out, as he/she will have considered how you move when choosing the movements for his/her dance.

From January to March of Year 11, how you use your time in class, at lunchtime and after school has to be planned and agreed. As a priority, make a timetable for yourself, from when you receive the tasks up to the assessment. It can be in a diary, with comments on when and how things are working. This will help your teacher if you have a problem you cannot solve.

Your teacher needs to know and support your timetable to make sure you are ready for the final assessment. Members of your family can remind you of rehearsal times if they know your proposed schedule, and might even give feedback you could use.

Your solo composition task

When you study the professional work, as guided by your teacher, remember that you are creating a short solo. It must contain links to three motifs seen in the work — choosing the motifs that are right for you is vital. You will be expected to show the original motifs before you show your solo, which should have repetitions,

variations and developments of the motifs within it. The motifs have to be linked together, so think carefully about transitions between them and between each section of your solo and meeting the time limits of 1–1½ minutes.

Your solo should have a clear structure. If it is a character role, you will need to consider the moods, age and intent of the character. A Ghost Dancer from *Ghost Dances* by Christopher Bruce will perform very differently to a Cupid from Matthew Bourne's *Nutcracker!*. Take care that your choice of music and its length are suitable for the motifs you have selected.

Watching the DVD/video of the professional work often and making notes on which motifs you like or you think you can adapt for your skill will help you score a better mark. Work on your own and stay focussed on the motifs you chose, and don't be concerned about anyone else's work. Enjoy dancing your final composition. It counts for 15% of your final grade and is marked on the choreography, not the performance skills you show. Your evaluation of your progress as a choreographer will also be assessed.

Your solo choreography

When you perform your solo choreography, there no marks available for your performance skills. But it is through the way you dance that your choreography is expressed to your teacher or the external moderator. How you dance your solo is therefore vitally important, as the performance is the only way your dance idea and the choreographic devices you have chosen to use can be seen, appreciated and assessed.

What makes your solo different to the set dance and the group dance is that you have to choose the movements. In the set dance the exam board did the choosing, and in the group dance it was your teacher. The movements you choose must link with your dance idea, which has to be linked with a starting point from the list provided by AQA, as well as being ones your body can do. You will also choose the accompaniment, and will have to dance using its rhythms, themes, dynamics and **instrumentation**. This choice has to meet the exam board's recommendations: it must not be a popular vocal song or music that has no changes of rhythm or contrasts. You should be able to hear the musical phrases and dance with them or in counterpoint to them. It should last between 1½ and 2 minutes (see pages 125–29 for more information).

Practising your solo choreography
You have to be a confident dancer to perform a solo, and you need to be sure that you can perform well a dance you have created on your own. You can rehearse at

home or in the dance space, without worrying about other people not arriving for rehearsals. However, this means you will be working on your own a lot and will need to be disciplined about the way you use your rehearsal time. You should ask for feedback from your teacher or friends, or use a mirror, photographs or video to crosscheck that you are performing in such a way that the moderator will be able to understand your dance idea.

Your group choreography

This can be for two to five dancers who are chosen by you or your teacher. You need to check that the dancers are prepared to meet and rehearse with you whenever you have planned to teach them your choreography.

Ideally, you should not be in your group choreography yourself, as you need to be able to see how the group is dancing your choreography — if the dancers are in the right place, doing the right actions at the right time with correct dynamics, expressing their roles as you have planned.

You will need to prepare your ideas and motifs thoroughly before rehearsals with your dancers. They will not want to wait around while you spend 10 minutes working out what you want them to do.

You will be able to use more choreographic devices in a dance for two to five people than in a solo, using, for example, different group shapes, relationships, unison, canon, contrast, mirroring and use of contact. This is an exciting and dynamic challenge, which your dancers should enjoy dancing for you.

Your dancers will need to know what the overall theme of your dance is, and the idea behind each section, their movements to dance and the role they are showing, as well as what the sound is and how their actions relate to it (they might each like a recording of the music to rehearse with).

The movements you choose must link with your dance idea, which has to be linked with a starting point from the list provided by AQA, as well as being movements your dancers can do.

You therefore need to teach and rehearse your dancers so that they know the dance well in time for the assessments, first by your teacher, then for a film, and then maybe by the external moderator. You should work out a schedule first for you to choreograph the motifs, and then a timetable of when you will teach sections to each dancer. The dancers should have a copy of the timetable so that they know when you need them. You may have to check there is a space where you can rehearse and list that on your schedule.

You could ask your teacher to film sections of your dance once they have been learnt, so that you and your dancers can see where changes might need to be made. You will therefore act as a choreographer and rehearsal director in preparing and finalising your group dance. Being a performer in your own group dance is an additional pressure you do not need, and I strongly advise you to avoid this if at all possible.

If you are choreographing your own solo you will have to rely on using a mirror, film or a feedback (opinion) from a friend, parent or teacher, to know how it looks. If you are choreographing a duo or group dance you will be able to see and give feedback (opinion) on your dancers at any rehearsal if you are not dancing yourself.

Choreography checklist for a solo or group choreography

Make sure you:

- ❖ read the list of ideas you could use provided by your teacher
- ❖ make thought maps on at least two of these
- ❖ start to consider the style of dance and type of accompaniment you would like to use
- ❖ decide whether you are choreographing a solo, duo, or group dance
- ❖ decide who will dance in it and check they are willing to give up their time for you
- ❖ start to improvise actions that might make up motifs to go in your choreography
- ❖ note down when the internal assessment will happen and how many weeks you have until then
- ❖ work out an outline timetable of jobs to do by particular dates
- ❖ find out what other commitments you have to fulfil during this period
- ❖ note down in your choreographic diary all your ideas and deadlines, and check you are keeping to schedule
- ❖ listen to several types of accompaniment, and narrow yourself down to three possible ones to use
- ❖ discuss your idea with your teacher or produce written work that is commented upon, stating how you want your dance to grow and the accompaniments you like
- ❖ check that the sound lasts no more than 2 minutes for a solo and no more than 3 minutes for a duo or group dance
- ❖ choose at least two motifs that link with the dance idea, and see what they look like performed by another dancer
- ❖ decide if the motifs are what you want, refine them where necessary, and consider when they might appear in your dance — if you do this in class, you will have to concentrate hard so as not to be distracted by other people

Accompaniment

The next vital step is to know your accompaniment's structure, which means listening to it many times. Make a timeline or graphic score of your accompaniment. Decide which sections of your dance idea will go with the sections you can hear in the sound. You need to try these out yourself, altering the timing of your motif if necessary, so that the motifs relate clearly to the sound. Ask someone to watch you, or, even better, use one of your dancers, to see for yourself.

Make sure your dancers know the dance idea and the sound. They may like a copy of the sound for rehearsing the dance and getting to know the accompaniment. Give your teacher the original recording for safe-keeping and use a copy for rehearsals.

Revising and practising your group dance choreography

At this stage, your practical timetable is vital. You have to continue choreographing the dance while your dancers learn and rehearse the parts you have already taught them. Continually ask for feedback on how your dance is growing. To get a grade C or above, your dance's structure, idea and your use of the dancers all have to fit together well.

When you reach the point where you can picture the whole dance in your mind, you need to consider how it can be performed in order to gain the best grade. Your relationship with your dancers is important at this stage. You need to become a bit like a teacher and advise them on how you want a motif danced, where they should look, and how strongly or gently you want to see the movement done.

If your dancers are in your own dance exam group, they will have their own dances to work on as well, so cooperation between you will be vital. Do not have a dancer in your dance, or appear in their dance, if they are using the same starting point, dance idea or sound as you. It can be very confusing!

Once your dance is finished and your dancers know the dance, rehearse in the assessment space. Check that your use of the space is clear and relevant to the idea. Make sure you are happy with the way they are dancing, the entrances, exits, style, characters, musicality and use of focus. Get the dance filmed and watch it together, so you can point out any changes you want.

Make sure your choreographic diary is up to date, from one rehearsal to another. You will have to prepare a brief programme note giving the title of your dance, the starting point you selected from the list, and details of the accompaniment you use. This note will inform your teacher and moderator about your dance.

Appreciation

Written examination

The written examination is marked by an external examiner, not by your teacher. It lasts 1 hour and counts for 20% of your final grade. It is marked out of 50. You are expected to answer all the questions; for some you must write short answers in a box, while others questions require a paragraph of information as an answer. You will therefore need to remember many facts from your GCSE course and be able to supply your knowledge of the features of two professional dance works from the AQA precribed list, as well as being able to write about your own performance and choreographic skills.

All the notes you have made throughout the course on the features of dances will help you revise for the exam. It is therefore important that you always make your own notes, right from the start of the course. Keep them safe and up to date, and make sure they are clear so you can read them in the month prior to the written exam.

Structure of the paper

The paper takes the form of a series of questions. At the very beginning of the paper you have to name the two professional dance works you have studied, giving both the title of the dance and the name of the choreographer. As your answers, you may be required to write short sentences or a paragraph or two, to make a drawing and label it, to use a floor plan, or to fill in the missing gaps in words or sentences. Your questions could be on the following areas:

❖ **Areas of knowledge linked with performance skills a dancer needs and uses:** good studio practice; health and safety; technical skills (physical and interpret-ative); action, dynamic and spatial features; dancing with others, in a set dance or a group dance.

❖ **Choreographic knowledge and skills involved in making dances:** ways of finding movement ideas; ideas for dance and suitable actions, dynamics and spatial content; making motifs; varying, repeating and developing motifs; structuring dances; using accompaniment; working with other dancers.

❖ **Critical appreciation and knowledge of two professional dance works:** costume designs; lighting designs; physical settings; accompaniments (sound used); dance relationships; the theme of each dance; motifs you have learnt; structure of the work; styles of dance; use of camera; the roles of people involved in producing dances.

The information in this book will help you revise these areas, alongside the notes you make after each practical lesson. You will also need to learn specialist dance vocabulary, so that you can understand the questions and use the terms, spelled correctly, in your written answers.

Revision tasks to help you write about your own skills

1 List five different actions you could do that would make you travel across the dance space.

2 Draw a floor plan of a stage. Add two contrasting pathways you could take across the space.

3 **a** Describe the dynamics and actions you would use if you were to cross the space as a terrified person.

 b Explain your choices.

4 Imagine you will cross the space to meet someone you have not seen for a long time and have missed greatly. Describe a simple motif you might perform as you meet each other that expresses your pleasure in meeting again.

5 How is a dancer expected to stay healthy? List six points a dancer should consider.

6 Name four points on safety in relation to a dancer's clothing and environment that he/she can follow easily.

7 **a** Identify why dancers need to cool down at the end of class.

 b Describe two ways a dancer might cool down.

8 List four different types of accompaniment your choreography could use.

9 Look at the two photographs, from *Overdrive* by Richard Alston and *Perfect* by Kevin Finnan, and both describe and compare the actions, dynamics and use of space made by the dancers.

Maria Nikoloulea leaping in *Overdrive*, by Richard Alston

Arching backwards: Helen Parlor in *Perfect*, by Kevin Finnan

10 Name three ways in which a dancer could improve his/her performance skills.

11 a Create a motif using these action words: gesture, turn and fall.

b Choose one of these actions and describe four ways you could develop its spatial and dynamic content.

12 What are the advantages of not dancing in a duo or group dance you have choreographed?

Revision tasks to help you write about the two set works

Some questions will expect you to identify and describe moments in the dances. The revision tasks below might help you to test your knowledge on the set works you have been studying with your teacher for this written paper.

1 How does the set work start?

2 How does the set work end?

3 Describe briefly one solo within each set work. Give details of the subject matter and the key actions performed to express this.

4 a Describe the set used in one scene from one set work.

b Compare this with a very different set in the other work.

c Name that work and the choreographer.

5 Using the same two works, comment on the costumes worn and how they link with the subject matter of each work.

6 a Identify the type of sound used in one set work.

b Describe the type of sound heard in your other set work.

c Explain why the accompaniment is different for each work.

You must know at least three scenes from each of the two works thoroughly. Ideally you will know and be able to write fully about the whole of the two set works if you are aiming for grades A*– C.

You are expected to be able to quote specific examples of features from each work, and maybe to compare them. It is important that you can visualise in your imagination particular scenes from the two set works. This will mean that you include enough facts in your essay. Make sure that the facts you use are to do with the focus of each question, and remember not to just tell the story of the dances. This will not score you marks unless the storyline is asked for in the question.

So, read every question carefully and be sure you write down the details and facts that are relevant to the question and to the two set works you have studied.

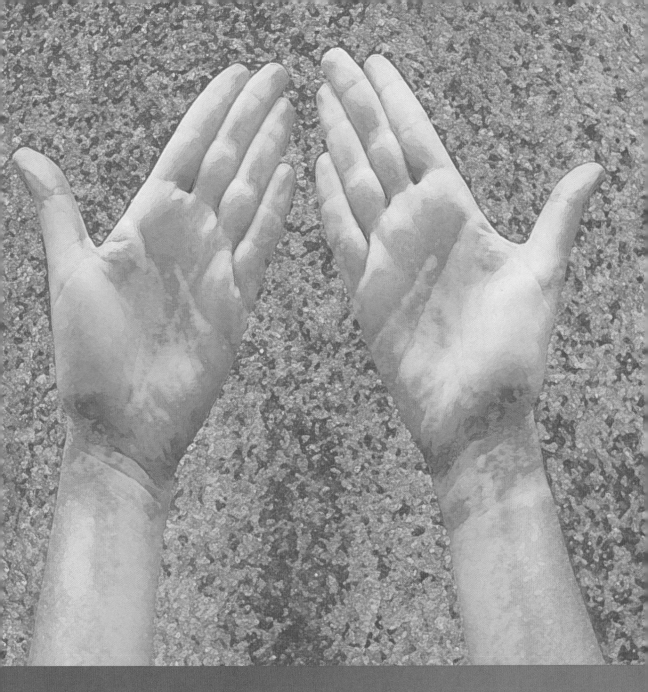

Section 4

Resources

Resources

If you would like to know more about dance than you have time to learn during your GCSE course, then this section contains vital information. It is particularly useful if you are aiming to pursue a career in dance. It provides details of:

- ❖ national and regional dance agencies
- ❖ theatres where you can watch live dance performances
- ❖ national organisations that provide workshops or special courses for young people
- ❖ dance companies
- ❖ music for dance
- ❖ dance DVDs and videos
- ❖ further reading

This information will encourage you to try other styles of dance outside school time, to consider asking for a particular dance DVD or CD as a birthday present, and to check which dance companies might be performing near you, and get tickets to see them. If you are aiming for a Grade A*–C, then extra workshops, theatre visits and watching dance DVDs are a must.

Dance agencies

Dance agencies provide a range of services, and they can be of use to you and your teachers in various ways. You just have to contact them and be specific in what you hope to find out.

If you want to try a new style of dance, a national dance agency (NDA) or a regional dance agency (RDA) will be able to tell you when and where classes for young people and adults are held in, for instance, Asian dance, Bhangra, hip-hop, Irish dancing, Krump or release-based techniques. If you want to perform more often, there are youth performance groups and companies all around the country. You may have to audition for some, whereas you will be able to join others straight away and be given the chance to perform when you are considered ready. Both the NDAs and RDAs should be able to help you with this.

Many county, district and town councils have youth dance classes and companies too, so a telephone call or look at their websites will give you further local information.

National and regional dance agencies

England

The North

Cheshire Dance

1st Floor
Winsford Library
High Street
Winsford
Cheshire
CW7 2AS
Tel: 01606 861770
Fax: 01606 550629
info@cheshiredance.org
www.cheshiredance.org
Cheshire Dance is the development agency for dance in the county and beyond. It supports artists, educators and communities of interest by encouraging, fostering and providing resources for their activities and by creating links between them. Cheshire Dance Workshop offers increased access to the arts.

Dance City

Temple Street
Newcastle-upon-Tyne
NE1 4BR
Tel: 0191 2610505
Fax: 0191 2300486
info@dancecity.co.uk
www.dancecity.co.uk
(Serves Tyneside, Northumberland, County Durham, Teeside and Cumbria.)
Offers artistic support, education, dance performances, participation and regional development.

Dance Initiative Greater Manchester

Zion Arts Centre
Stretford Road
Manchester
M15 5ZA
Tel: 0161 2327179
Fax: 0161 2327483
info@digm.org.uk
www.digm.org
Delivers projects, classes, workshops and performance opportunities. Also provides grants, training advice and information opportunities for people of all ages to enjoy dance.

Dance Northwest

Dance Northwest
www.dancenorthwest.org.uk
A national dance agency partnership.
Contact the individual Regional Agency Partners: Cheshire Dance, DIGM, Ludus Dance and MDI.

Merseyside Dance Initiative

24 Hope Street
Liverpool
L1 9BX
Tel: 0151 708 8810
Fax: 0151 707 0600
info@mdi.org.uk
www.merseysidedance.co.uk
Merseyside Dance Initiative works with community centres, schools, colleges and housing associations to bring dance to the community. It provides opportunities to participate in, create and see all kinds of dance. Each year holds a 2-week contemporary dance festival, which sees professional dance artists and companies from across the world arriving in Liverpool to participate in venues across the city.

Yorkshire Dance

3 St Peter's Buildings
St Peter's Square
Leeds
LS9 8AH
Tel: 0113 2439867
admin@yorkshiredance.com
www.everybodydances.com
Runs courses, classes and workshops, with regular performances both in the centre and various venues in Yorkshire. A focus for artists to meet, dance, choreograph and make contact with new audiences.

The Midlands

Dance 4

3–9 Hockley
Nottingham
NG1 1FH
Tel: 01159 410773
info@dance4.co.uk
www.dance4.co.uk
Serves Nottingham, Lincolnshire, Leicestershire, Northamptonshire and the East Midlands.
Offers professional training advice and support for dance artists. Provides an outreach participation programme in Nottinghamshire. Has special programme for youth dance.

DanceXchange

DanceXchange Administration
Birmingham Hippodrome
Thorp Street
Birmingham
B5 4TB
Tel: 0121 6893170
Fax: 0121 6893179
info@dancexchange.org.uk
www.dancexchange.org.uk
Dedicated to the production and distribution of high-quality dance. Offers opportunities for people of all walks of life to participate in dance as a performer or audience member.

Derby Dance Centre

Dance House
Chapel Street
Derby
DE1 3GU
Tel: 01332 370911
Fax: 01332 370788
n.cawkwell@deda.uk.com
www.deda.uk.com
Deda provides young people aged under 16 with a year-round programme of creative activities, including drop-in classes and performance groups. It also has a wide range of adult dance classes.

Oxford City Council

Arts Officer (Dance and Theatre)
Oxford City Council, Leisure and Culture
c/o OVADA
21 Gloucester Green
OX1 2AQ
Tel: 01865 247164
dance@oxford.gov.uk
www.oxford.gov.uk
Oxford City Council's dance development programme aims to increase participation in dance, to enhance the dance activity in the city, and to support dance-based projects and local professional dance artists. There are numerous classes running in Oxford (covering a wide variety of styles) for young people.

The East

Cambsdance

6 The Old Maltings
135 Ditton Walk
Cambridge
CB5 8PY
Tel: 01223 245254
info@cambsdance.org.uk
www.cambsdance.org.uk
A new collective, formed in 2006, creating programmes for dancers of all ages and experience.

Dance East

Northgate Arts Centre
Sidegate Lane West
Ipswich
Suffolk
IP4 3DF
Tel: 01473 639230
Fax: 01473 639236
info@danceeast.co.uk
www.danceeast.co.uk
Serves Suffolk, Norfolk, Bedfordshire,
Cambridgeshire, Hertfordshire, Essex,
Peterborough, Southend and Thurrock.

Dance Digital

2 Bond Street
Chelmsford
Essex
CM1 1GH
Tel: 01245 346036
Fax: 01245 354223
admin@dancedigital.org.uk
www.essexdance.co.uk
Dance Digital (the new name of Dance in Herts
and Essexdance) offers a range of dance events
in professional and educational/community
contexts. It also focuses on the development
of dance work using emerging technologies.

Lincolnshire Dance

The Stables
Wellingore Hall
Wellingore
Lincolnshire
LN5 0HX
Tel: 08712 200398
Fax: 01522 811846
info@lincolnshiredance.com
www.lincolnshiredance.com
The Dance Development Agency for the county
of Lincolnshire, coordinating dance programmes
for young people, professionals and older dancers.

Norfolk Dance

The Garage
Chapel Field North
Norwich
NR2 1NY
Tel: 01603 283399
info@norfolkdance.co.uk
www.norfolkdance.co.uk
Provides imaginative and challenging
opportunities for people of all ages and abilities
to become involved in dance. Offers classes,
workshops, performances and professional
development in Norwich and across the county.

The South
East London Dance

Stratford Circus
Theatre Square
London
E15 1BX
Tel: 0208 2791050
Fax: 0208 2791054
office@eastlondondance.org
www.eastlondondance.org
East London Dance is the regional dance
development agency for East London. It offers
an extensive education programme, which includes
professional development for dance and non-dance
specialist teachers, as well as participatory projects
for schools in East London, with a focus on pupils
working with professional dance artists and
companies.

Greenwich Dance Agency

The Borough Hall
Royal Hill
London
SE10 8RE
Tel: 0208 2939741
Fax: 0208 8582497
info@greenwichdance.org.uk
www.greenwichdance.org.uk
Greenwich Dance Agency offers a range of
activities, including classes, workshops and
events, enabling local people to participate in
and experience dance. It provides opportunities
for professional artists to develop their skills
and extend their practice.

Hampshire Dance

14 Leigh Road
Eastleigh
Hampshire
SO50 9DE
Tel: 023 80652712
Fax: 023 80652713
info@hampshiredance.org.uk
www.hampshiredance.org.uk
Promotes the experience and understanding
of dance. Focus on youth dance, dance in
education, dance and disability, and professional
development for dancers.

Laban

Creekside
London
SE8 3DZ
Tel: 0208 6918600
Fax: 0208 6918400
info@laban.org
www.laban.org
Laban provides undergraduate and postgraduate
courses, evening classes and short courses for
adults and children. Its building houses a
300-seat purpose-built dance theatre in which
there are regular performances. It has a huge
library and archive and its own publications.

South East Dance

28 Kensington Street
Brighton
BN1 4AJ
Tel: 01273 696844
Fax: 01273 697212
info@southeastdance.org.uk
www.southeastdance.org.uk
The leading organisation in the UK for screen
dance. Has produced and commissioned dance
films, offers dance film and video training for
artists. Specialises in working with 'at risk' children
and young people.

Surrey County Arts Dance

Westfield School
Bonsey Lane
Woking
GU22 9PR
Tel: 01483 519282
sa.dance@surreycc.gov.uk
www.surreycountyarts.org.uk
Surrey County Arts Dance supports youth dance
initiatives, professional development, creative and
academic mentoring or coaching, educational
outreach, and inset delivery.

The Place

17 Duke's Road
London
WC1H 9PY
Tel: 0207 1211000
Fax: 0207 1211142
info@theplace.org.uk
www.theplace.org.uk
The Place offers dance training, creation and
performance. It has an extensive video archive
and library. The space includes London
Contemporary Dance School, Richard Alston
Dance Company and the Robin Howard Dance
Theatre. Runs many professional projects and
pioneering education and outreach.

The Southwest

Activate Dance and Theatre Performance Agency

27 West Borough
Wimbourne
Dorset
BH21 1LT
Tel: 01202 884340
Fax: 01208 886304
info@activateperformingarts.org.uk
www.activateperfomingarts.org.uk
Promotes and sustains dance opportunities for people in Dorset and the southwest. Special focus on artists working towards encouraging more performances and new audiences.

Bath Dance

info@bathdance.org.uk
www.bathdance.org.uk
A new location for information on news, opportunities and events for all forms of dance in Bath and beyond.

Dance in Devon

Bradninch Place
Gandy Street
Exeter
EX4 3LS
Tel: 01392 667050
info@danceindevon.org.uk
www.danceindevon.org.uk
A new organisation offering classes, workshops, specialist projects, support for artists and opportunities for young people.

Dance Southwest

PO Box 5457
Bournemouth
BH1 1WU
Tel: 01202 554131
Fax: 01202 554131
office@dancesouthwest.org.uk
www.dancesouthwest.org.uk
The regional strategic agency for dance.

Gloucestershire Dance

Colwell Centre Arts Centre
Derby Road
Gloucester
GL1 4AD
Tel: 01452 550431/07917 796959
admin@gloucestershiredance.org.uk
www.dancesouthwest.org.uk/gloucestershire
Gloucestershire Dance initiates dance opportunities throughout the county. It works in schools, after school clubs, holiday schools, with aspiring young dancers, and with people who have learning and mobility difficulties. It also promotes professional contemporary dance performance.

Swindon Dance

Regent Circus
Swindon
SN1 1QF
Tel: 01793 601700
info@swindondance.org.uk
www.swindondance.org.uk
Serves Wiltshire and the south.
This is a centre for advanced training with dance classes for all ages. Organises professional performances and productions.

Take Art

The Mill
Flaxdrayton Farm
South Petherton
Somerset
TA13 5LR
Tel: 01460 249450
Fax: 01460 249455
art@takeart.org
www.takeart.org
'Dance is for everyone and everyone can dance.'
Offers a range of dance opportunites for Somerset.

The Works

Crusader House
Newham Quay
Truro
Cornwall
TR1 2DP
Tel: 01872 261770
info@dtcworks.co.uk
www.dancesouthwest.org.uk/network/
    the-works-cornwall
The Works is the development agency for
dance and theatre in Cornwall. It works with
artists, companies, venues, cultural development
organisations, educational establishments and
community groups.

Wiltshire Dancing

Arc Theatre Trowbridge
College Road
Trowbridge
BA14 0ES
Tel: 0845 2990476 (option 8)
info@wiltshiredancing.co.uk
www.dancesouthwest.org.uk/network/
    wiltshire-dancing
A consortium who support the strategic
development of dance in Wiltshire.

Scotland

Citymoves Dancespace

c/o Aberdeen Art Gallery
Schoolhill
Aberdeen
AB10 1FQ
Tel: 01224 611486
citymoves@aberdeencity.co.uk
www.aberdeencity.gov.uk
The regional dance agency for northeast Scotland.

Dance Base National Centre for Dance

14–16 Grassmarket
Edinburgh
EH1 2JU
Tel: 0131 2255525
Fax: 0131 2255234
dance@dancebase.co.uk
www.dancebase.co.uk
The centre offers professional dancers'
programmes, outreach, community dancers'
programme, and contributes to the Edinburgh
Festival Fringe and the International Festival.

Dance House

20 St Andrews Street
Glasgow
G1 5PD
Tel: 0141 552 2442
info@dancehouse.org
www.dancehouse.org
Dance House offers a diverse range of dance
classes for all abilities, education outreach,
a professional workshop programme, teacher
training courses and large-scale performance
projects.

The Space

Dundee College
Kingsway Campus
Old Glamis Road
Dundee
DD3 8LE
Tel: 01382 834834
Fax: 01382 858117
enquiry@dundeecollege.ac.uk
www.dundeecoll.ac.uk/?the_scottish_school_
    of_contemporary_dance.xml
Offers the only full time 3-year training in
contemporary dance to professional level.
Strong links with the profession, particularly
Scottish Dance Theatre.

Wales

Community Dance Wales

Sbectrwm
The Old School
Bwlch Road
Fairwater
Cardiff
CF5 3EF
Tel: 02920 575075
Fax: 02920 575073
www.communitydancewales.com
Community Dance Wales offers continual
professional development (CPD) for teachers
and dance practitioners in schools, working with
sports council and PE and school sport initiatives.
It has a network of organisations across Wales,
which work with these school-aged groups.

Welsh Independent Dance (WID)

Chapter
Market Road
Cardiff
CF5 1QE
Tel: 02920 387314
info@welshindance.co.uk
www.welshindance.co.uk
The national artist-led umbrella organisation for
professional dance artists working independently
in Wales.

BILL COOPER

Brazilian Woolly Monkey from *'Still Life' at the Penguin Café* by David Bintley, Birmingham Royal Ballet

Theatres where you can see dance

Every GCSE dance student should ideally watch two live dance performances each year. Watching professional performances is a wonderful way of getting ideas. You could also attend the extra workshops dance companies might provide through their education department. Dance companies have mailing lists, which you can join, that provide information on when they are performing in your area. Theatres will have useful leaflets and programmes with dance photographs that you could use for inspiration.

The list below of theatres offering dance performances is organised by area. There will hopefully be a theatre near to your school or home that you can visit. You may have to pay to go to the theatre or attend a workshop, but it will be worth it. There are grants available to support you if you need help financially.

England

The North

Bradford

The Alhambra Theatre
Morley Street
Bradford
West Yorkshire
BD7 1AJ
Tel: 01274 432375
administration@bradford-theatres.co.uk
www.bradford-theatres.co.uk/alhambra_2.asp

The Lamproom Theatre
Westgate
Barnsley
S70 2DX
Tel: 01226 200075
enquiries@barnsleylampoon.com
www.barnsleylampoon.com

Theatre in the Mill
Shearbridge Road
University of Bradford
West Yorkshire
BD7 1DP
Tel: 01274 233200
theatre@bradford.ac.uk

Gateshead

Baltic Centre for Contemporary Art
Gateshead Quays
South Shore Road
Gateshead
NE8 3BA
Tel: 01914 78 1810
Fax: 01914 78 1922
Textphone: 0191 4404944
info@balticmill.com
www.balticmill.com

Caedmon Hall
Prince Consort Road
Gateshead
Tyne and Wear
NE8 4LN
Tel: 01914 338420

Halifax

Square Chapel Arts Centre
10 Square Road
Halifax
West Yorkshire
HX1 1QG
Tel: 01422 349422
Fax:01422 347928
info@squarechapel.co.uk
www.squarechapel.co.uk

Huddersfield

The Lawrence Batley Theatre
Queen's Square
Queen Street
Huddersfield
West Yorkshire
HD1 2SP
Tel: 01484 430528
Fax: 01484 425336
theatre@ibt-uk.org
www.ibt-uk.org

Hull

Hull New Theatre
Kingston Square
Hull
North Humberside
HU1 3HF
Tel: 01482 226655

Leeds

The Carriageworks
3 Millennium Square
Leeds
LS2 3AD
Tel: 0113 2243801
carriageworks@leeds.gov.uk
www.carriageworkstheatre.org.uk

The Gallery and Studio Theatre
Leeds Metropolitan University
Civic Quarter
Leeds
LS1 3HE
Tel: 0113 8125998
gallerytheatre@leedsmet.ac.uk
www.leedsmet.ac.uk/arts

The Grand Theatre
46 New Briggate
Leeds
LS1 6NZ
Tel: 0844 848 2706
boxoffice@leedsgrandtheatre.com
www.leedsgrandtheatre.com

The Riley (based at Northern School of Contemporary Dance)
98 Chapeltown Road
Leeds
LS7 4BH
Tel: 0113 2193018
www.nscd.ac.uk

West Yorkshire Playhouse
Playhouse Square
Quarry Hill
Leeds
LS2 7UP
Tel: 0113 2137700
Fax: 0113 2137250
info@wyp.org.uk
www.wyplayhouse.com

Manchester

The Lowry
Pier 8
Salford Quays
M50 3AZ
Tel: 0870 7875780
Fax: 0161 8762001
info@thelowry.com
www.thelowry.com

Newcastle

Dance City
Temple Street
Newcastle-upon-Tyne
NE1 4BR
Tel: 0191 2610505
Fax: 0191 230 0486
info@dancecity.co.uk
www.dancecity.co.uk

Theatre Royal
100 Grey Street
Newcastle-upon-Tyne
NE1 6BR
Tel: 08448 112121
boxoffice@theatreroyal.co.uk
www.theatreroyal.co.uk

Sheffield

The Crucible Theatre and The Lyceum
55 Norfolk Street
Sheffield
South Yorkshire
S1 1DA
Tel: 0114 2496000
info@sheffieldtheatres.co.uk
www.sheffieldtheatres.co.uk

York

Grand Opera House York
Cumberland Street
York
YO1 9SW
Tel: 0844 847 2322
www.grandoperahouseyork.org.uk

York Theatre Royal
St Leonard's Place
York
YO1 7HD
Tel: 01904 623568
Fax: 01904 550164
boxoffice@yorktheatreroyal.co.uk
www.yorktheatre.co.uk

The East

Bury St Edmunds

Theatre Royal
Westgate Street
Bury St Edmunds
Suffolk
IP33 1QR
Tel: 01284 769505
admin@theatreroyal.org
www.theatreroyal.org

Colchester

Mercury Theatre
Balkerne Gate
Colchester
CO1 1PT
Tel: 01206 573948
boxoffice@mercurytheatre.co.uk
www.mercurytheatre.co.uk

Felixstowe

The Spa Pavilion Theatre
Undercliff Road West
Seafront
Felixstowe
IP11 2DX
Tel: 01394 282126
www.thespapavilion.org

Halesworth

New Cut Arts
The Cut
New Cut
Halesworth
Suffolk
IP19 8BY
Tel: 01986 873285
info@newcut.org
www.newcut.org

Ipswich

The New Wolsey Theatre
Civic Drive
Ipswich
IP1 2AS
Tel: 01473 295900
tickets@wolseytheatre.co.uk
www.wolseytheatre.co.uk

Lowestoft

The Marina Theatre
The Marina
Lowestoft
Suffolk
NR32 1HH
Tel: 01502 533200
info@marinatheatre.co.uk
www.marinatheatre.co.uk

The Midlands

Birmingham

The Drum
144 Potters Lane
Aston
Birmingham
B6 4UU
Tel: 0121 3332400
Fax: 0121 3332440
info@the-drum.org.uk
www.the-drum.org.uk

Birmingham Hippodrome and The Patrick Centre
Birmingham Hippodrome Theatre Trust Limited
Hurst Street
Birmingham
B5 4TB
Tel: 0844 338 5000
Fax: 0844 338 5030
tickets@birminghamhippodrome.com
www.birminghamhippodrome.com

Midlands Arts Centre (MAC)
Cannon Hill Park
Birmingham
B12 9QH
Tel: 0121 4403838
info@macarts.co.uk
www.macarts.co.uk

Cannock

Prince of Wales Centre
Church Street
Cannock
Staffs
WS11 1DE
Tel: 01543 578762
Fax: 01543 574439
princeofwales@cannockchasedc.gov.uk
www.cannockchasedc.gov.uk/princeofwales

Leicester

De Montfort Hall
Granville Road
Leicester
LE17RU
Tel: 0116 2333111
Fax: 0116 2333182
dmh.tickets@leicester.gov.uk
www.demontforthall.co.uk

Lichfield

Lichfield Garrick
Castle Dyke
Lichfield
WS13 6HR
Tel: 01543 412121
Fax: 01543 412120
garrick@lichfielddc.gov.uk
www.lichfieldgarrick.com

Malvern

Malvern Theatres
Grange Road
Malvern
Worcestershire
WR14 3HB
Tel: 01684 892277
Fax: 01684 893300
boxoffice@malvern-theatres.co.uk
www.malvern-theatres.co.uk

Newcastle-under-Lyme

New Vic Theatre
Newcastle-under-Lyme
Staffordshire
ST5 0JG
Tel: 01782 717962
Fax: 01782 712885
tickets@newvictheatre.org.uk
www.newvictheatre.org.uk

Northampton

The Derngate Theatre
Royal and Derngate
Guildhall Road
Northampton
NN1 1DP
Tel: 01604 624811
Fax: 01604 250901
box.office@royalandderngate.co.uk
www.royalandderngate.co.uk

Nottingham

Lakeside Arts Centre
University Park
Nottingham
NG7 2RD
Tel: 0115 8467777
www.lakesidearts.org.uk

Nottingham Playhouse
Wellington Circus
Nottingham
NG1 5AF
Tel: 0115 9419419
Fax: 0115 9241484
Minicom: 0115 9476100
www.nottinghamplayhouse.co.uk

Oxford

Pegasus Theatre
Magdalen Road
Oxford
OX4 1RE
Tel: 01865 722851
Fax: 01865 204976
info@pegasustheatre.org.uk
www.pegasustheatre.org.uk

Stafford

Stafford Gatehouse Theatre
Eastgate Street
Stafford
ST16 2LT
Tel: 01785 254653
Fax: 01785 225622
gatehouse@staffordbc.gov.uk
www.staffordgatehousetheatre.co.uk

Stoke-on-Trent

The Regent Theatre
Piccadilly
Stoke-on-Trent
ST1 1AP
Tel: 0870 0606649
Fax: 01782 214738
www.theambassadors.com/regent

Repertory Theatre
Leek Road
Stoke-on-Trent
ST4 2TR
Tel: 01782 209784
www.stokerep.org.uk

Victoria Hall
Bagnall Street
Stoke-on-Trent
ST1 3AD
Tel: 0870 0606649
Fax: 01782 214738
www.theambassadors.com/victoriahall

Wellingborough

The Castle Theatre
Castle Way
Wellingborough
NN8 1XA
Tel: 01933 270007
Fax: 01933 229888
info@thecastle.org.uk
www.thecastle.org.uk

Wolverhampton

The Grand Theatre Wolverhampton
Lichfield Street
Wolverhampton
WV1 1DE
Tel: 01902 429212
Fax: 01902 573301
www.grandtheatre.info

Wolves Civic
North Street
Wolverhampton
West Midlands
WV1 1RQ
Tel: 0870 320 7000
boxoffice@wolvescivic.co.uk
www.wolvescivic.co.uk

The South

Brighton

Brighton Dome
29 New Road
Brighton
BN1 1UG
Tel: 01273 709709
tickets@brightondome.org
www.brightondome.org

Theatre Royal
New Road
Brighton
BN1 1SD
Tel: 0870 0606650
Fax: 01273 764407
www.theambassadors.com/theatreroyal

Dartford

The Mick Jagger Centre
Shepherds Lane
Dartford
Kent
DA1 2JZ
Tel: 01322 291100
www.themickjaggercentre.com

The Orchard Theatre
Home Gardens
Dartford
Kent
DA1 1ED
Tel: 01322 220000
orchard.theatre@dartford.gov.uk
www.orchardtheatre.co.uk

Eastleigh

The Point
Leigh Road
Eastleigh
Hampshire
SO50 9DE
Tel: 0238 0652333
thepointboxoffice@eastleigh.gov.uk
www.thepointeastleigh.co.uk

Guildford

The PATS Theatre
University Box Office
Senate House
University of Surrey
Guildford
Surrey
GU2 7XH
Tel: 01483 686876
www.surrey.ac.uk/dance/events/performances.html

Canterbury

Gulbenkian Theatre
University of Kent at Canterbury
Canterbury
Kent
CT2 7NB
Tel: 01227 769075
gulbenkian@kent.ac.uk
www.kent.ac.uk/gulbenkian

The Marlowe Theatre
The Friars
Canterbury
Kent
CT1 2AS
Tel: 01227 787787
Fax: 01227 479662
marlowetheatre@canterbury.gov.uk
www.marlowtheatre.com

Swanley

Hextable Dance
39 Egerton Avenue
Hextable
Swanley
Kent
BR8 7LG
Tel: 01322 618618
Fax: 01322 618600
info@hextabledance.com
www.hextabledance.com

London

Barbican Theatre Department
Barbican Centre
Silk Street
London
EC2Y 8DS
Tel: 0207 6388891
info@barbican.org.uk
www.barbican.org.uk

Bonnie Bird Theatre
Laban
Creekside
London
SE8 3DZ
Tel: 0208 691 8600
info@laban.org
www.laban.org

Coliseum Theatre
8 St Martin's Lane
London
WC2N 4ES
Tel: 0207 632 8300

Peacock Theatre
Portugal Street
Holborn
London
WC2A 2HT
Tel: 0844 4124322
www.peacock-theatre.com

Robin Howard Dance Theatre
The Place
17 Duke's Road
London
WC1H 9PY
Tel: 0207 1211100
Fax: 0207 1211142
www.theplace.org.uk

The Round House
Chalk Farm Road
London
NW1 8EH
Tel: 0844 482 8008
Fax: 0207 424 9992
boxoffice@roundhouse.org.uk
www.roundhouse.org.uk

Royal Albert Hall
Kensington Gore
London
SW7 2AP
Tel: 0207 589 8212
www.royalalberthall.com

Royal Festival Hall
Southbank Centre
Belvedere Road
London
SE1 8XX
Tel: 0871 663 2500
Fax: 0871 663 2594
www.rfh.org.uk

Royal Opera House/Linbury Studios
Bow Street
Covent Garden
London
WC2E 9DD
Tel: 0207 304 4000
www.roh.org.uk

Sadler's Wells/Lilian Baylis Studio
Rosebery Avenue
London
EC1R 4TN
Tel: 0844 412 4300
ticket.office@sadlerswells.com
www.sadlerswells.com

The South West

Frome

The Merlin Theatre
Bath Road
Frome
Somerset
BA11 2HG
Tel: 01373 465949
www.merlintheatre.co.uk

Gloucester

Gloucester Guildhall
23 Eastgate Street
Gloucester
GL1 1NS
Tel: 01452 503050
guildhall.boxoffice@gloucester.gov.uk

Street

Strode Theatre
Church Road
Street
Somerset
BA16 0AB
Tel: 01458 442846
theatre@strode-college.ac.uk
www.strodetheatre.co.uk

Yeovil

Octagon Theatre
Hendford
Yeovil
Somerset
BA20 1UX
Tel: 01935 422884
Fax: 01935 845945
www.octagon-theatre.co.uk

Scotland

Aberdeen

His Majesty's Theatre
Rosemount Viaduct
Aberdeen
AB25 1GL
Tel: 01224 641122
www.hmtaberdeen.com

Lemon Tree
5 West North Street
Aberdeen
AB24 5AT
Tel: 01224 641122
www.boxofficeaberdeen.com

Edinburgh

Edinburgh Festival Theatre
13/29 Nicolson Street
Edinburgh
EH8 9FT
Tel: 0131 5296000
Fax: 0131 6621199
bookings@eft.co.uk
www.eft.co.uk

King's Theatre
2 Leven Street
Edinburgh
EH3 9LQ
Tel: 0131 5296000
Fax: 0131 6621199
bookings@eft.co.uk
www.eft.co.uk

Glasgow

King's Theatre
297 Bath Street
Glasgow
G2 4JN
Tel: 0870 060 6648
www.theambassadors.com/kings

Tramway
25 Albert Drive
Glasgow
G41 2PE
Tel: 0845 330 3501
Fax: 0141 2760954
info@tramway.org
www.tramway.org

Inverness

Eden Court Theatre
Bishops Road
Inverness
IV3 5SA
Tel: 01463 234234
www.eden-court.co.uk

Melrose

The Wynd Theatre
The Wynd
Melrose
TD6 9PA
Tel: 01896 820028
drama@thewynd.com
www.thewynd.com

Musselburgh

Brunton Theatre
Ladywell Way
Musselburgh
EH21 6AA
Tel: 0131 6652240
info@bruntontheatre.co.uk
www.bruntontheatre.co.uk

Peebles

Eastgate Theatre and Arts Centre
Eastgate
Peebles
EH45 8AD
Tel: 01721 725785
Fax: 01721 725775
mail@eastgatearts.com
www.eastgatearts.com

Pitlochry

Pitlochry Festival Theatre
Port-Na-Craig
Pitlochry
PH16 5DR
Tel: 01796 484626
Fax: 01796 484616
www.pitlochry.org.uk

Northern Ireland

Belfast

The Grand Opera House
Great Victoria Street
Belfast
BT2 7HR
Tel:0289 0240411
Fax: 0289 0236842
info@goh.co.uk
www.goh.co.uk

Old Museum Arts Centre
7 College Square North
Belfast
BT1 6AR
Tel: 0289 0233332
www.oldmuseumartscentre.org

Londonderry

The Millennium Forum Theatre
Newmarket Street
Londonderry
BT48 6EB
Tel: 0287 1264455
boxoffice@millenniumforum.co.uk
info@millenniumforum.co.uk
www.millenniumforum.co.uk

The Playhouse
5–7 Artillery Street
Londonderry
BT48 6RG
Tel: 0287 1268027
info@derryplayhouse.co.uk
www.derryplayhouse.co.uk

Wales

Aberdare

The Coliseum
Mount Pleasant Street
Trecynon
Aberdare
Rhondda Cynon Taff
CF44 8NG
Tel: 01685 881188
Fax: 01685 883000
info@coliseum-aberdare.co.uk
www.rct.arts.org

Cardiff

Wales Millennium Centre
Bute Place
Cardiff
CF10 5AL
Tel: 08700 402000
Fax: 02920 636401
enquires@wmc.org.uk
www.wmc.org.uk

Carmarthen

Lyric Theatre
King Street
Carmarthen
Carmarthenshire
SA31 1BD
Tel: 0845 226 3510
www.carmarthenshireonline.co.uk/lyric

Llandudno

Venue Cymru
The Promenade
Llandudno
LL30 1BB
Tel: 01492 872000
info@venuecymru.co.uk
www.venuecymru.co.uk

Mold

Clwyd Theatr Cymru
Mold
Flintshire
CH7 1YA
Tel: 01352 756331
Fax:01352 701558
admin@clwyd-theatr-cymru.co.uk
www.clwyd-theatr-cymru.co.uk

Narberth

The Queens Hall
High Street
Narberth
SA67 7AS
Tel: 01834 861212
Fax: 01834 861989
ask@thequeenshall.org.uk
www.thequeenshall.org.uk

Porthcawl

The Grand Pavilion
The Esplanade
Porthcawl
CF36 3YW
Tel: 01656 815995
pavilion@bridgend.gov.uk
www.grandpavilion.co.uk

Swansea

Swansea Grand Theatre
Singleton Street
Swansea
SA1 3QJ
Tel: 01792 475715
www.swanseagrand.co.uk

BILL COOPER

Ballroom scene from *Romeo and Juliet* by Kenneth MacMillan

National dance organisations

Bedford Interactive Research

11a Woodlands Road
Lepton
Huddersfield
West Yorkshire
HD8 0HX
Tel: 01484 609354
www.dance-interactive.com
Creates and sells ICT of first class quality,
e.g. Wild Child, Choreographic Outcomes, Motifs
for a Solo Dancer and Graham Technique resource
packs with interactive CDs and CD-Rom, plus
accompanying booklets.

Dance Books Ltd

Dance Books Ltd
The Old Bakery
4 Lenten Street
Alton
Hampshire
GU34 1HG
Tel: 01420 86138
Fax: 01420 86142
www.dancebooks.co.uk
Sells the largest range of dance books, CDs,
videos, DVDs, magazines etc. An excellent mail
order service.

Dance UK

The Urdang
The Old Finsbury Town Hall
Rosebery Avenue
London
EC1R 4QT
Tel: 0207 7130730
Fax: 0207 8332363
info@danceuk.org
www.danceuk.org
Provides information for public and professionals.
Encourages career development, develops dance
networks, puts the case for healthier dancers,
raises profile of dance in UK and lobbies politicians
and funders.

Dancing Times

45–47 Clerkenwell Green
London
EC1R 0EB
Tel: 0207 2503006
Fax: 0207 2536679
dt@dancing-times.co.uk
www.dancing-times.co.uk
A monthly magazine with excellent
reviews and information, and sells books,
videos and DVDs.

Foundation for Community Dance

LCB Depot
31 Rutland Street
Leicester
LE1 1RE
Tel: 0116 2533453
Fax: 0116 2616801
info@communitydance.org.uk
www.communitydance.org.uk
Supports community dance and is concerned to provide access to, participation in, and progression in dance experiences. Campaigns for community dance, providing information, advice and guidance to dance artists and organisations about issues to be faced. Supports development of networks and the strategic development of community dance for new audiences and under-represented communities.

Movement Unlimited

91 Highbury New Park
London
N5 2EU
Tel: 07956 953734
info@movementunlimited.co.uk
www.movementunlimited.co.uk

National Dance Teachers' Association (NDTA)

PO Box 4099
Lichfield
WS13 6WX
Tel: 01543 308618
office@ndta.org.uk
www.ndta.org.uk
Runs courses for teachers, produces the termly publication *Dance Matters*, and fights the cause for dance in education.

National Resource Centre for Dance (NRCD)

University of Surrey
Guildford
Surrey
GU2 7XH
Tel: 01483 689316
nrcd@surrey.ac.uk
www.surrey.ac.uk/NRCD
Sells resource packs on set works, videos of past A-level set solos, and other videos and publications. Runs courses for teachers as part of its education service and has an archive that aims to preserve the nation's dance heritage.

Royal Opera House Bookshop

The Royal Opera House
Bow Street
Covent Garden
London
WC2E 9DD
Tel: 0207 2129331
shop@roh.org.uk
www.rohshop.org
Sells videos, DVDs, CDs, books and magazines of operas, ballets, modern dance works. Many gifts also available.

Sadler's Wells Theatre Bookshop

Sadler's Wells Theatre
Rosebery Avenue
London
EC1R 4TN
www.sadlerswells.com/page/shop
Sells videos, DVDs, books on dance, items of clothing and other resources linked with a company performing there.

Royal Academy of Dance Shop

Royal Academy of Dance Enterprises Ltd
36 Battersea Square
London
SW11 3RA
Tel: 0207 3268080
www.radenterprises.co.uk
Sells ballet clothing, and books, CDs and DVDs
for ballet and contemporary dance.

Royal Academy of Dance

36 Battersea Square
London
SW11 3RA
Tel: 0207 3268000
Fax: 0207 9243129
info@rad.org.uk
www.rad.org.uk
Provides training and courses for children
and young people, students and teachers
and examinations to reward achievement.
One of the largest dance education and training
providers in the world.

Youth Dance England

Unit 7G2
The Leathermarket
Weston street
London
SE1 3ER
Tel: 0207 9409800
info@yde.org.uk
www.yde.org.uk
Works to raise the profile of youth dance and
promotes strategic projects for young people.
Coordinates events for youth dance groups to
attend nationally and regionally.

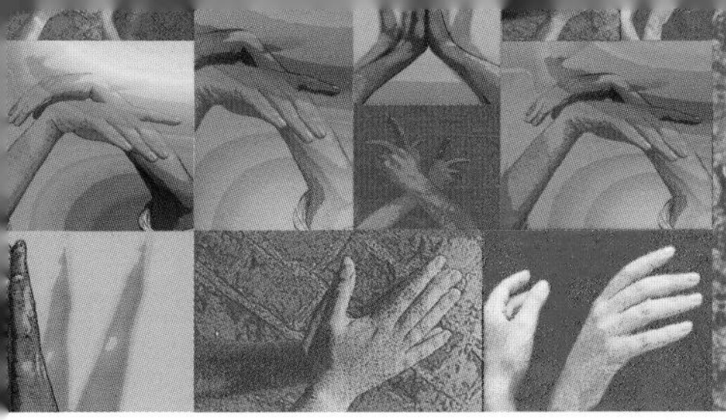

Dance companies

Akram Khan Company

Unit 232A
35 Britannia Row
London
N1 8QH
Tel: 0207 3544333
Fax: 0207 3545554
office@akramkhancompany.net
www.akramkhancompany.net

Bare Bones Dance Company

DanceXchange
Birmingham Hippodrome
Thorp Street
Birmingham
B1 5TB
Tel: 0121 6893170
Fax: 0121 6893179
info@dancexchange.org.uk
www.barebonesdance.co.uk

Birmingham Royal Ballet

Thorp Street
Birmingham
B5 4AU
Tel: 0121 2453500
Fax: 0121 2453570
info@brb.org.uk
www.brb.org.uk
Has well-established education department
and small shop.

CandoCo Dance Company

2T Leroy House
436 Essex Road
London
N1 3QP
Tel: 0207 7046845
info@candoco.co.uk
www.candoco.co.uk
Has an education officer.

The Cholmondeleys and The Featherstonehaughs

LF1.1 Lafone House
The Leathermarket
11–13 Leathermarket Street
London
SE1 3HN
Tel: 0207 3788800
admin@thecholmondeleys.org
www.thecholmondeleys.org
Has an education department.

Cork City Ballet

Firkin Crane Theatre
Shandon
Cork City
Co. Cork
Ireland
Tel: 00 353 (0)21 4375155
corkcityballet@yahoo.com
www.corkcityballet.com

Dance Theatre of Ireland

Bloomfields
Lower Georges Street
Dun Laoghaire
Co. Dublin
Ireland
Tel: 00 353 (0)1280 3455
Fax: 00 353 (0)1280 3466
info@dancetheatreireland.com
www.dancetheatreireland.com

Diversions — The Dance Company of Wales

Dance House
Wales Millennium Centre
Pierhead Street
Cardiff Bay
CF10 4PH
Tel: 0292 0635600
Fax: 0292 0635601
diversions@diversionsdance.co.uk
www.diversionsdance.co.uk
'Dance explorer' is its education
department. It runs a range of courses
for young people.

EDge

The Place
17 Duke's Road
London
WC1H 9PY
Tel: 0207 1211000
The postgraduate performance company
of London Contemporary Dance School.

English National Ballet

Education and Community Unit
Markova House
39 Jay Mews
SW7 2ES
Tel: 0207 5811245
Fax: 0207 2250827
learning@ballet.org.uk
www.ballet.org.uk
Has high-quality education department.

Green Candle Dance Company

Oxford House
Derbyshire Street
Bethnal Green
London
E2 6HG
Tel: 0207 7397722
info@greencandledance.com
www.greencandledance.com
Has established education department.

Henri Oguike Dance Company

Office No. 2
The Cottages
Laban Centre
Creekside
London
SE8 3DZ
Tel: 0208 6947444
Fax: 0208 6943669
info@henrioguikedance.co.uk
www.henrioguikedance.co.uk
Has an education team.

Independent Ballet Wales

30 Glasllwch Crescent
Newport
South Wales
NP20 3SE
www.welshballet.co.uk
Runs workshops at performance theatres.

IRIE! Dance Theatre

The Moonshot Centre
Fordham Park
Angus Street
New cross
London
SE14 6LU
Tel: 0208 6916099
info@iriedancetheatre.org
www.iriedancetheatre.org
Promotes African peoples' dance.

Jiving Lindy Hoppers

Tel: 0208 9928128
jivinglindyhoppers@yahoo.com
www.jivinglindyhoppers.com
Has education team.

Jonzi D Productions

Sadler's Wells Theatre
Rosebery Avenue
London
EC1R 4TN
Tel: 0207 8410308
Fax: 0871 2531814
mail@jonzi-d.co.uk
www.jonzi-d.co.uk
Original Hip Hop theatre. Runs an education
programme.

Loop Dance Company

The Brook Theatre
Old Town Hall
Chatham
Kent
ME4 4SE
Tel: 01634 831531
info@loopdancecompany.co.uk
www.loopdancecompany.co.uk
Runs education workshops.

Ludus Dance

Assembly Rooms
King Street
Lancaster
LA1 1RE
Tel: 01524 35936
www.ludusdance.org
A dance in education company. Runs dance
classes for young people, courses for teachers
and has visual and audio resources for sale.

Motionhouse Dance Theatre

Spencer Yard
Leamington Spa
CV31 3SY
Tel: 01926 887052
info@motionhouse.co.uk
www.motionhouse.co.uk
Has an education department.

New Adventures Dance Company

Sadler's Wells
Rosebery Avenue
London
EC1R 4TN
Tel: 0207 7136766
info@new-adventures.net
www.new-adventures.net
Runs education programmes.

Northern Ballet Theatre

West Park Centre
Spen Lane
Leeds
LS16 5BE
Tel: 0113 2745355
Fax: 0113 2745381
learningandaccess@northernballettheatre.co.uk
www.nbt.co.uk
Has learning and access department. Runs school
workshops and projects and has a youth dance
programme.

Phoenix Dance Theatre Company

3 St Peter's Buildings
St Peter's Square
Leeds
LS9 8AH
Tel: 0113 2423486
Fax: 0113 2444736
www.phoenixdancetheatre.co.uk
Has education department offering good
workshops at primary and secondary level.

Rambert Dance Company

94 Chiswick High Road
London
W4 1SH
Tel: 0208 6300600
Fax: 0208 7478323
rdc@rambert.org.uk
www.rambert.org.uk
Has very well-established education department.
Tel: 020 8630 0615 education@rambert.org.uk
Excellent archive and shop. Runs workshops in
contemporary style on present and past rep.
Highly recommended.

Richard Alston Dance Company

The Place
17 Duke's Road
WC1H 9PY
Tel: 0207 1211010
radc@theplace.org.uk
www.theplace.org.uk
Has education department which leads
workshops, Inset and provides resources.

Rosas Dance Company

Rosas
Van Volxemlaan 164
1190 Brussels
Belgium
www.rosas.be

The Royal Ballet

Royal Opera House
Covent Garden
London
WC2E 9DD
Tel: 0207 2401200,
0207 2129410 (Education Dept)
education@roh.org.uk
www.roh.org.uk
www.royalballet.org.uk
Has a very well-established education
department.

Scottish Ballet

261 West Princes Street
Glasgow
Scotland
G4 9EE
Tel: 0141 3312931
www.scottishballet.co.uk
Has education department that runs
community dance companies, school
workshops and 'drop-in' classes.

Shobana Jeyasingh Dance Company

Moving Arts Base
Syracusae
134 Liverpool Road
Islington
London
N1 1LA
Tel: 0207 6974444
admin@shobanajeyasingh.co.uk
www.shobanajeyasingh.co.uk
A national and international touring
company with movement vocabulary
based in contemporary dance with
influences of Bharata Natyam, Kalari
and Chan. Runs education workshops
for primary through to university students.

Siobhan Davies Dance

Siobhan Davies Studios
85 St George's Road
London
SE1 6ER
Tel: 0207 0919650
info@siobhandavies.com
www.siobhandavies.com
Runs limited but focused education
programme and has very useful CD-Roms
and DVDs for sale.

Resource

Springs Dance Company

99 Tressillian Road
London
SE4 1XZ
Tel: 01634 817523
Mob: 07775 628442
info@springsdancecompany.org.uk
www.springsdancecompany.org.uk
Has education programme that provides
classes and workshops in schools and various
community venues.

Union Dance Company

Top Floor
6 Charing Cross Road
London
WC2H OHG
Tel: 0207 8367837
www.uniondance.co.uk

Transitions Dance Company

Laban
Creekside
London
SE8 3DZ
Tel: 0208 6918600
l.scott@laban.org
www.laban.org/transitions_dance_company.phtml

DAVID BUCKLAND

Characteristic movements of Siobhan Davies as seen in *Winsboro Cotton Mill Blues*, Rambert Dance Company

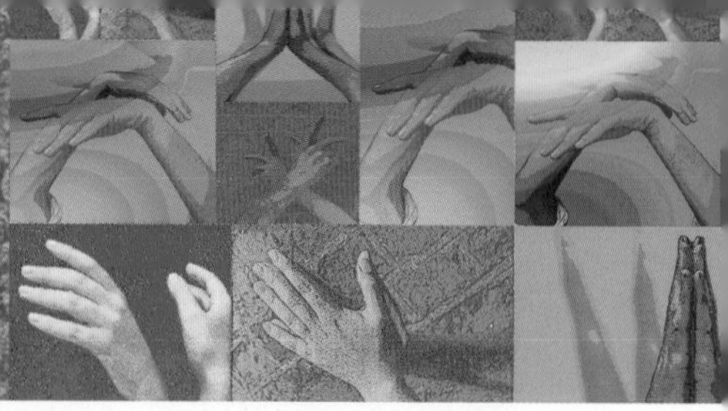

Music composed for dance

Title	Composer	Where to buy
'a bird in the hand...two in the bush'	Paul Pavey	Dance Books Ltd The Old Bakery 4 Lenten Street Alton Hampshire GU34 1HG **www.dancebooks.co.uk**
A-level Choreography Music	Andrew Kristy	Sound Moves Music Co Ltd PO Box 14 Worcester WR3 8XH Tel: 01905 755421 **www.sound-moves-music.co.uk**
'blood is thicker...than water' (Music for Modern and Contemporary Dance Classes)	Paul Pavey	Dance Books Ltd — see above
'Clash'. Ludus Dance Company	Martin Hughes, Adrian Burford, Mark Burford	Dance Books Ltd — see above
Contemporary Dance Music Vols 1–8	Michael Price	Dance Books Ltd — see above
Cross Channel	Steve Blake	The Cholmondeleys LF 1.1 Lafone House The Leathermarket 11–13 Leathermarket Street London SE1 3HN Tel: 0207 3788800 **www.thecholmondeleys.org**
Dancesounds Vols 1–11	Paul A. Jackson	Dancesounds PO Box 134 Tunbridge Wells Kent TN2 4YB Tel: 01892 823089 **www.dancesounds.co.uk** Dance Books Ltd — see above

Title	Composer	Where to buy
Dance works on CD *Double Take/Flesh and Blood*	Steve Blake	Dance Books Ltd — see above The Cholmondeleys — see above
Driven	Sophie Smith Tim Dickinson	Motionhouse Dance Theatre Spencer Yard Leamington Spa CV31 3SY Tel: 01926 887052 **www.motionhouse.co.uk**
Hobson's Choice	Paul Reade	Royal Opera House Bookshop
Perfect	Sophie Smith Tim Dickinson	Motionhouse Dance Theatre — see above
Play Without Words	Terry Davies	Dance Books Ltd — see above
Romeo and Juliet	London Symphony Orchestra	Royal Opera House Bookshop
Sergeant Early's Dream and *Ghost Dances*	Sergeant Early's Band Incantation	Dance Books Ltd — see above Rambert Dance Company — see above
Swansong	Philip Chambon	Rambert Dance Company — see above
The Ballets — The Nutcracker, Sleeping Beauty, Swan Lake	London Symphony Orchestra	Dance Books Ltd — see above
Tales of Beatrix Potter	Royal Opera House Orchestra	Royal Opera House Bookshop Dance Books Ltd — see above
The Car Man	Terry Davies	Dance Books Ltd — see above
The Rite of Spring, Petrushka, Pulcinella, The Firebird Suite	Philadelphia Orchestra	Dance Books Ltd — see above
White Man Sleeps	Keith Volans	Dance Books Ltd — see above
GCSE Dance: *Choreography Music for Solos and Group Dances*	Andrew Kristy	Sound Moves Music Co Ltd — see above
Music for Contemporary Class 1–2	Philip Taylor	Dance Books Ltd — see above
Music for Dance 4–6	Chris Benstead	Dance Books Ltd — see above Rambert Dance Company 94 Chiswick High Road London W4 1SH Tel: 0208 6300600 **www.rambert.org.uk**
Perfecting Eugene	Hughes, Burford, Hughes	Dance Books Ltd — see above
Primary Dance Activities 1, 2, 3 and 4	Andrew Kristy	Sound Moves Music Co Ltd — see above
Weightless	Bell and Brown	Rambert Dance Company — see above

Resource 6

Dance videos and DVDs

Choreographer	Dance work	Title of DVD/video Dance company	Style	Available from
Alvin Ailey	Revelations	Alvin Ailey: an evening with the Alvin Ailey American Dance Theatre	Jazz, pure, narrative	❖ Royal Opera House ❖ Rad Enterprises
Richard Alston	Overdrive	Alston in Overdrive Richard Alston Dance Company		Dance Books Ltd
	Pulcinella	Pulcinella; Soldat Rambert Dance Company	Contemporary with narrative. Both have humour	❖ Dance Books Ltd ❖ Royal Opera House ❖ Dancing Times
	Rumours, Visions, Okho, Light Flooding into Darkened Rooms, Brisk Singing	DVD Essential Alston	Contemporary. Several excerpts of different works	Dance Books Ltd
	Wildlife	Different Steps	Abstract, Cunningham	Rambert Dance Company
Lea Anderson	Double Take Flesh and Blood	The Cholmondeleys and The Featherstonehaughs	Dramatic, realistic, minimal, new dance	❖ Dance Books Ltd ❖ The Cholmondeleys
	Car	The Cholmondeleys	Dramatic, realistic, minimal, everyday gestures. Site specific	The Cholmondeleys
	Cross Channel	The Cholmondeleys and The Featherstonehaughs	Dramatic, realistic, minimal, everyday gestures. Site specific	MJW Productions Ltd www.mjwproductions.com
Sir Frederick Ashton	The Dream	American Ballet Theatre	Classical, narrative, comic sections	❖ Royal Opera House Bookshop ❖ Dance Books Ltd ❖ Rad Enterprises
	Cinderella	The Royal Ballet		
	La Fille mal gardée	The Royal Ballet	Narrative, comic ballet, folk, mime, morris	❖ BRB ❖ Dancing Times
	The Tales of Beatrix Potter	The Royal Ballet	Classical, narrative	Dance Books Ltd
Mark Baldwin	Constant Speed	Rambert Dance Company	Abstract, contemporary	Rambert Dance Company
David Bintley	Hobson's Choice	Birmingham Royal Ballet	Narrative ballet, clog	❖ BRB ❖ Dancing Times

Choreographer	Dance work	Title of DVD/video Dance company	Style	Available from
David Bintley	'Still Life' at The Penguin Café	The Royal Ballet	Dramatic ballet and other styles	❖ Dance Books Ltd ❖ BRB ❖ Royal Opera House Bookshop ❖ Rad Enterprises ❖ Dancing Times
Matthew Bourne	Nutcracker!	New Adventures Dance Company	Narrative, modern ballet, dramatic and humorous	❖ Dance Books Ltd ❖ Dancing Times ❖ Rad Enterprises ❖ Royal Opera House Bookshop
	An in-depth insight to Matthew Bourne's Nutcracker!	Andrew Kristy Gareth Griffiths	Teachers Resource DVD and CD	❖ Dance Books Ltd ❖ Sound Moves Music
	Swan Lake	Adventures in Motion Pictures	Narrative, contemporary	❖ Dance Books Ltd ❖ Dancing Times ❖ Rad Enterprises ❖ Royal Opera House Bookshop
	The Car Man	Adventures in Motion Pictures	Narrative, contemporary	❖ Dance Books Ltd ❖ Dancing Times ❖ Royal Opera House Bookshop
Christopher Bruce	Sergeant Early's Dream	Three By Rambert Rambert Dance	Dramatic, comic, contemporary	❖ Dance Books Ltd ❖ Rambert Dance Company ❖ Royal Opera House
	Rooster; Swansong	Christopher Bruce's Triple Bill	Contemporary, dramatic	❖ Dance Books Ltd ❖ Rambert Dance Company ❖ Royal Opera House
Emily Burns	Perfecting Eugene	Ludus Dance	Dance drama, contemporary	Dance Books Ltd
Robert Cohan	Forest	Video and resource pack Phoenix Dance Theatre Company	Abstract, contemporary, Graham	Phoenix Dance Theatre Company
Merce Cunningham	Beach Birds for Camera	Merce Cunningham Dance Company	Abstract, Cunningham	❖ Dance Books Ltd ❖ Dancing Times
Siobhan Davies	Bird Song	Siobhan Davies Dance	Abstract, release, Cunningham	Siobhan Davies Dance
	Wyoming	Siobhan Davies Dance	Abstract, release, Cunningham	Siobhan Davies Dance
Anne Theresa De Keersmaeker	Rosas Danst Rosas	Rosas	Off site: minimalist	Dance Books Ltd
Doug Elkins	Dance Tek Warriors	Union Dance Company	Contemporary, Capoeira, street	www.uniondance.co.uk
Kevin Finnan	Perfect Driven	Motionhouse Dance Theatre	Contemporary, aerial, site-specific	www.motionhouse.co.uk
Mikhail Fokine	Petrushka	Paris Opera Ballet	Narrative Ballet, folk, mime	❖ Dance Books Ltd ❖ Royal Opera House

Choreographer	Dance work	Title of DVD/video Dance company	Style	Available from
T. C. Howard	*Clash*	Ludus Dance	Dramatic, contemporary	Dance Books Ltd
Shobana Jeyasingh	*Surface Tension*	Shobana Jeyasingh Dance Company	Pure, Bharata Natyam, contemporary	Dance Books Ltd
	Faultline		Eclectic styles	Dance Books Ltd
Jiri Kylian		*Peter and the Wolf* Royal Ballet School	Narrative, modern ballet	❖ Dance Books Ltd ❖ Royal Opera House Bookshop ❖ Dancing Times ❖ Rad Enterprises
	L'Enfant et les sortilèges	Nederlands Dans Theatre	Narrative, modern ballet	
	L'Histoire du soldat	Nederlands Dans Theatre	Narrative, modern ballet	❖ Dance Books Ltd ❖ Dancing Times ❖ Rad Enterprises ❖ Royal Opera House Bookshop
	Sinfonietta/Symphony in D/Stamping Ground	Nederlands Dans Theatre	Three contrasting popular ballets	❖ Dance Books Ltd ❖ Dancing Times ❖ Royal Opera House
Gillian Lynne	*A Simple Man*	Northern Ballet Theatre	Dance drama, ballet, clog, modern	❖ Dance Books Ltd ❖ Dancing Times ❖ Rad Enterprises ❖ Royal Opera House
Kenneth Macmillan	*Romeo and Juliet*	The Royal Ballet	Classical, dramatic narrative	❖ Dance Books Ltd ❖ Dancing Times ❖ Royal Opera House Bookshop
Bronislava Nijinska	*Les Noces*	*The Firebird/Les Noces* The Royal Ballet	Classical, dramatic, narrative	❖ Dance Books Ltd ❖ Royal Opera House Bookshop ❖ Dancing Times
Robert North	*Lonely Town, Lonely Street*	*Three By Rambert* Rambert Dance Company	Dance drama, jazz, contemporary	❖ Dance Books Ltd ❖ Rambert Dance Company
	Troy Game	Dance Theater of Harlem	Contemporary, Capoeira, all-male cast	❖ Dance Books Ltd ❖ Dancing Times ❖ RAD Enterprises ❖ Royal Opera House Bookshop
Henri Oguike	*Signal*	Video Phoenix Dance Theatre Company	Abstract, contemporary	Phoenix Dance Theatre Company
Ashley Page	*Soldat*	Rambert Dance Company	Narrative, Cunningham, ballet	Dance Books Ltd
Jane Scott-Barrett	*Wild Child*	Ludus Dance Company	Modern, dramatic	Dance Books Ltd

Further reading

Ashley, Linda (2002) *Essential Guide to Dance*, Hodder Arnold.

Ashley, Linda (2005 2nd edn) *Dance Sense Theory and Practice for GCSE Dance Students*, Northcote House.

Bremser, Martha (1999) *Fifty Contemporary Choreographers*, Routledge.

Jordan, Stephanie (1992) *Striding Out: Aspects of Contemporary and New Dance in Britain*, Dance Books Ltd.

Jordan, Stephanie and Allen, Dave (eds) (1993) *Parallel Lines: Media Representations of Dance*, John Libbey.

Macaulay, Alistair (2000) *Matthew Bourne and his Adventures in Motion Pictures*, Faber and Faber.

Mackrell, Judith (1992) *Out of Line: the Story of British New Dance*, Dance Books Ltd.

Pritchard, Jane (1996) *Rambert: A Celebration*, Rambert Dance Company.

Roy, Sanjoy (1999) White Man Sleeps: *Creative Insights*, Dance Books Ltd.

Sanders, Lorna (2004) *Akram Khan's* Rush: *Creative Insights*, Dance Books Ltd.

Sanders, Lorna (2004) *Henri Oguike's* Front Line: *Creative Insights*, Dance Books Ltd.

Resource packs and interactive CD-Roms

Bird Song (Davies 2004)

- ❖ Interactive CD-Rom and flash cards — Arts Pool
- ❖ Resource pack by L. Sanders — NRCD
- ❖ 'Creative insight' section on Siobhan Davies Dance website
- ❖ Biography of Siobhan Davies — Rambert Dance Company
- ❖ *Choreographer Fact Card: Siobhan Davies* by S. Preston — NRCD
- ❖ *Siobhan Davies: The Development of a Choreographic Style* by L. Sanders — NRCD

Dance Tek Warriors (Elkins 1998)

❖ Interactive CD-Rom and flash cards — Arts Pool
❖ Resource pack by Union Dance

Faultline (Jeyasingh 2007)

❖ Interactive CD-Rom and flash cards — Arts Pool
❖ Resource Pack by Shobana Jeyasingh Dance Company
❖ *Choreographer Fact Card: Shobana Jeyasingh* by L. Sanders — NRCD
❖ Resource packs on earlier works — NRCD

Ghost Dances (Bruce 1981)

❖ Interactive CD-Rom and flash cards — Arts Pool
❖ *Teacher Notes* and *Study Notes* — Rambert Dance Company
❖ *Choreographer Fact Card: Christopher Bruce* by L. Sanders — NRCD
❖ *Christopher Bruce — Approaches to Choreography: A Resource Pack for Teachers* by L. Sanders — NRCD
❖ Biography of Christopher Bruce —Rambert Dance Company

Nutcracker! (Bourne 1992 and 2002)

❖ Interactive CD-Rom and flash cards — Arts Pool
❖ Interactive CD and DVD by A. Kristy and G. Griffiths — Dance Books Ltd and Sound Moves Music
❖ Resource pack by L. Sanders — NRCD

Overdrive (Alston 2003)

❖ Interactive CD-Rom and flash cards — Arts Pool
❖ Resource pack — Richard Alston Dance Company
❖ Biography of Richard Alston —Rambert Dance Company

Perfect (Finnan 2005)

❖ Interactive CD-Rom and flash cards — Arts Pool
❖ Resource pack — Motionhouse Dance Theatre Company

Romeo and Juliet (MacMillan 1965)

❖ Interactive CD-Rom and flash cards — Arts Pool
❖ Resource Pack — the Royal Opera House Education

Rosas Danst Rosas (De Keersmaeker 1997)

❖ Interactive CD-Rom and flash cards — Arts Pool

'Still Life' at the Penguin Café (Bintley 1988)

❖ Interactive CD-Rom and flash cards — Arts Pool
❖ Resource pack from Birmingham Royal Ballet
❖ Resource pack by L. Sanders — NRCD

Swansong (Bruce 1987)

❖ Interactive CD-Rom and flash cards — Arts Pool
❖ *Teacher Notes* and *Study Notes* — Rambert dance Company
❖ *Choreographer Fact Card: Christopher Bruce* by L. Sanders — NRCD
❖ *Christopher Bruce — Approaches to Choreography: A Resource Pack for Teachers* by L. Sanders — NRCD
❖ Biography of Christopher Bruce —Rambert Dance Company

Glossary

abstract: choreographic dance style based on an idea developed from a stimulus.

acceleration: increase of speed.

accompaniment: sound heard while dance is happening.

accumulation: a motif is established as dancers join in, in canon.

act: section of a ballet. It is subdivided into scenes.

action: something a dancer does, e.g. travel, turn, gesture, fall.

adagio: slow, controlled movement sequence.

air pattern: shapes left in the air by a sequence of gestures.

allegro: quick, lively movement sequence.

arabesque: movement in which one leg is extended straight behind in the air while standing on the other leg.

arm positions:

> *first position* Arms at medium level, forwards from the body.
>
> *second position* Arms at medium level, sideways from the body.
>
> *third position* One arm in first and the other in second.
>
> *fourth position* One arm above head and one in second.
>
> *fifth position* Both arms in a curved shape above head.

armada: movement in capoeira: step back and turn, with reverse half-moon kick.

arms high parallel: arms above head and straight.

artistry: performing as a dancer with technical and interpretive skills.

arts council: organisation that funds choreographers, dancers and dance companies, and has policies to influence dance development.

assemblé: movement in which support is changed from one foot to two with a jump.

asymmetric: uneven or imbalanced, e.g. as regards shape, time, structure.

aú: movement in capoeira: a cartwheel.

backdrop: canvas that hangs upstage, often with painted or designed images on it.

balance: holding still with control and poise.

ball heel position: standing in wide second, with weight on one ball and one heel. Used in *Front Line*.

ballet: formal style of classical dance (danse d'école).

battlements en dehors: circular leg gesture going out from the body.

B-boying: a style of street dance.

BD: backwards and deep.

bênção: movement in capoeira meaning blessing: a front, straight kick.

BH: backwards and high.

Bhangra: a social, lively form of Asian dance.

Bharata Natyam: a classical style of Asian dance.

binary form: dance or piece of music in two sections: AB.

blackout: lighting term for a completely dark stage/performance area.

brush: movement where foot strokes the floor with the ball and toes.

canon: dancers start a phrase one after the other.

capoeira: African-Brazilian movement style.

chance: choreographic method in which movements are organised randomly.

changing the order: altering the sequence in which actions appear in a motif.

character: role expressed by a dancer in a narrative dance work.

chassé or slide: whole foot glides across the floor, on bent legs, to then take weight.

choreograph: to create, arrange or design dance motifs and dances.

choreographic devices: ways motifs can be repeated, developed and varied.

choreographic styles: ways in which a choreographed dance conveys its subject matter, e.g. narrative, abstract, dramatic, comic, pure.

climax: high point in a dance. It stands out clearly as a statement.

cocorinha: movement in capoeira: an escape or dodge through crouching.

compare: to look at similarities and differences between two or more things.

complement: to fill out a movement; showing the same action simultaneously, for example at different levels.

complementary canon: dancers move one after the other, showing the same actions at different levels or in different sizes.

complementary unison: dancers move at the same time, showing the same shapes but at different levels or in different directions.

composer: person who creates music.

contemporary dance: form of dance originated by Martha Graham. Uses contractions, release, spiral, flexed joints and parallel. Cunningham, new, postmodern and contact improvisation are also forms of contemporary dance.

continuous canon: dancers start a motif at different moments and continue until the last dancer has finished.

contracted (limb): the leg bends from an extended shape at the knee joint, or the arm bends at the elbow.

contraction: extension of the back and curling/tightening of the centre of the body.

contrast: demonstrate the differences between two things.

contrasting canon: dancers move one after the other, performing different actions.

contrasting unison: dancers move in time with each other, all doing different actions.

control: managing the body weight smoothly, accurately and appropriately when performing an action.

cooling down: stretching and moving slowly at the end of a class to calm the heartbeat.

coordination: ability to perform complex actions, using the arms and legs simultaneously.

correlation: close relationship, e.g. between music and dance.

costume design: planning clothing to suit a particular dance's idea and style.

counterpoint: interlocking sounds between music and dance, of rhythms and themes, filling in the silent moments in a bar of music.

counter-tension: when dancers take each other's weight with contact and powerful energy.

cyclorama: plain white canvas/cloth hung upstage.

dance drama: choreographic style of dance with dramatic incidents.

dance idea: theme, subject matter or topic of a dance.

dance style: performance style, e.g. ballet, contemporary, jazz, folk, capoeira.

dance work: a professional dance.

deceleration: slowing down.

demi-pointe: standing on the balls of the feet.

describe: in a GCSE exam question, give detail.

design plan: costumes, lighting and set. These are relevant to the dance idea.

design features: details of costumes, lighting and set seen in a dance work.

développé: movement in ballet: unfolding of the leg.

development: changing the features of a motif, e.g. dynamics, order, space.

dig: tap the floor sharply with the ball of the foot taking the weight.

direction: pathway a movement takes — forwards, backwards etc.

disassociation: when dance and accompaniment happen at the same time but are unrelated.

DL: deep, to the left.

DLB: deep, to the left and backwards.

DLF: deep, to the left and forwards.

DR: deep to the right.

dramatic: with dynamic contrasts, moods and feelings.

DRB: deep, to the right and backwards.

DRF: deep, to the right and forwards.

drop: lower weight towards floor.

DSL: downstage left.

DSR: downstage right.

dynamics: qualities of any movement; how it is done, e.g. quickly, strongly.

elevation: being in the air, either as a jump or a lift.

enchaînement: sequence of ballet steps.

en dehors: circling outwards away from the body.

en tournant: while turning.

esquiva lateral: movement in capoeira: escape or dodge sideways.

evaluate: observe and analyse the success of any task.

explain: in a GCSE exam question, give reasons for particular features being as they are.

expressive: describes movements that communicate feelings, e.g. grief, joy.

extension: stretching; reaching out into space.

external moderation: a moderator from the exam board visits the exam centre to watch and grade GCSE work alongside the teacher.

feedback: comments given by an onlooker to a dancer/choreographer on his/her work.

feet positions:

first position — feet together with heels touching, legs in turnout position from hips.

second position — legs apart; legs facing forwards in parallel, feet parallel or facing sideways away from each other in turnout.

third position — one foot in front of the other, front heel touching back instep, legs in turnout.

fourth position — legs apart, one in front of the other, feet facing forwards in parallel or sideways in turnout.

fifth position — feet together; front heel touching back big toe in turnout, or feet close with feet facing forwards in parallel.

FH: forwards and high.

flex: the ankle is contracted so that the foot is no longer pointed; or, the wrist is contracted, bringing the hand into a right angle with the arm.

floodlights: large lights that give a wide beam.

focus: where and how dancers are looking at any one moment in a dance.

fondu: smooth bend on one leg.

form: structure/outline of a dance or accompaniment.

formation: group shape made by dancers as they move in relation to each other.

fouetté: a whipping action of the leg.

fragmentation: breaking a motif into pieces, which are performed by consecutive dancers.

general space: area in which dance activity happens.

gesture: action in a dance space that does not take weight.

ginga: movement in capoeira: swing or sway.

group dance: dance for two or more dancers.

group performance piece: coursework task in which each student performs in a dance that expresses an idea and dances in a particular style, linked with a set work.

highlight: exciting, dramatic moment in a dance.

hitch kick: jump with legs gesturing in canon (forwards, backwards, straight or bent).

HL: high, to the left.

HLB: high, to the left and backwards.

HLF: high, to the left and forwards.

hop: jump on one leg.

HR: high, to the right.

HRB: high, to the right and backwards.

HRF: high, to the right and forwards.

identify: in a GCSE exam question, name or list information that is requested.

improvise: try out actions to see if they are appropriate for a motif in a dance.

instrumentation: instruments playing a piece of music.

internal moderation: when a dance teacher assesses the set dance, group performance piece, solo composition task and choreography.

jeté: jump from one leg to the other (throw the weight).

juxtaposition: using two dance ideas at different places in a dance, or performed by different characters or to different musical themes.

Kathak: style of classical Indian dance.

level: height at which an action is danced: low/deep, medium or high.

lighting design: colours, brightness and areas of stage lit.

lindy hop: style of dance with jazz and African-American influence.

lock: street movement that is strong, direct and sudden.

locomotion: travelling from place to place.

logical: progression of a dance from start to finish, with a clear, understandable structure.

lunge: position with one leg bent, one straight and both feet on the floor.

matching unison: dancers perform identical movements exactly in time with each other.

meia lua de frente: movement in capoeira: half-moon kick to the front.

moderator: external visitor who checks that coursework marks are in line with the national standard.

modern ballet: style of dance created with both ballet and modern dance vocabulary.

motif: short sequence of movements that makes a statement. Often repeated.

motivation: impulse or reason for choosing a movement; performing well in GCSE Dance.

movement memory: skill of learning and being able to remember and repeat taught dances.

movement vocabulary: range of action ideas that a dancer/choreographer uses.

musicality: a dancer's sensitivity to the rhythms, melodies and tempo in music.

mutual coexistence: when dance and music exist at the same time without being dependent on each other.

narrative: style of dance composition that tells a story.

negativa lateral: movement in capoeira: escape or dodge sideways press-up.

non-metric: sound that does not have a particular beat or repeated rhythms, e.g. breath rhythm.

orchestral music: music played by stringed, brass, wind and percussion instruments.

parallel: limbs in line with each other.

> **parallel arms:** arms in the position of parallel lines (like train tracks), e.g. forwards and high.

> **parallel legs:** legs in the position of parallel lines (like train tracks), in first, second, fourth and fifth. Used in modern dance.

pathway: journey between two points, on the floor or in the air. Can be linear, curved etc.

pedestrian gestures: everyday actions included in a dance.

performance style: way a dancer performs, e.g. classical, modern, jazz.

periphery: edge of the personal space a dancer can reach.

personal space: area that the body occupies (also known as a personal balloon).

phrase: sequence of movements.

physical contact: leaning on, lifting, carrying or holding another dancer.

physical setting: space where a dance is performed — the stage, site and what it contains.

pirouette: movement in ballet: a turn on one leg.

plane: two dimensional movement occurs in door, table and wheel planes.

plié: bend of both knees.

point: fixed zone that can be extended towards or a gesture of foot as used in ballet.

point method: approach in choreography, often improvised, using points in space or on another person.

pop: street dance movement in the centre of the body.

posé: a step onto demi-pointe.

position: shape or design made by a dancer when still.

posture: way a dancer holds his/her body and limbs in a style of dance.

project: to convey the intentions of a movement clearly and powerfully in performance.

proscenium arch: a style of theatre design including an 'apron' in front of the arch.

pure dance: choreographic style that focuses entirely on one dance style.

queixada: movement in capoeira: step into reverse half-moon kick.

rabo de arraia: movement in capoeira meaning stingray tail.

relationship: ways dancers face and place themselves in relation to each other.

release: counteraction to a contraction. A Graham term. Also a performance style.

relevé: rise onto demi-pointe; can be a quick, sliding action.

repertoire: range of professional works that a dance company can perform.

repetition: doing a sequence or a part again.

retiré: leg bent in the air with the foot close to the other knee or ankle.

retrograde: reversing a motif — performing it from the end back to the beginning.

rework: to look at a motif or phrase and alter or improve parts of it. Choreographers rework sections of their dance works.

rhythm: sequence of beats, with accents, within a phrase of movements.

role: particular character a dancer may portray in his/her part in the dance.

rolê: movement in capoeira: a grounded cartwheel.

roll: turning movement around an axis, either on the floor or in the air.

rond de jambe: leg makes a circular gesture.

rondo form: dance with repeated chorus and verses, in the possible form ABACADA (A is the chorus).

rotation: any turn — quarter, half, three-quarter and full — on any part of the body.

scoop: leg gesture in which the foot 'licks' the floor behind the other leg, then lifts, circles out, and goes round back to its own side. Used in *Front Line*, and with arms scooping forwards (gathering air in front of the body) in the 2007–08 set study.

scuff: sole of the foot brushes the floor quickly, with weight.

second parallel: feet apart, legs and feet facing forwards.

section: large part of a dance.

set design: plan of what will be on stage or at an off-site venue.

set work: professional dance all GCSE dance students are expected to study.

shunt: shift weight strongly, accented on the ball of one or both feet, which are close together in parallel; weight usually moves forwards or sideways. Used in *Front Line*.

SL: stage left.

solo: dance for one person.

space: area outside the body (personal or general).

spatial: adjective derived from 'space' that is used to describe levels, direction, size, shape etc.

spiral: Graham action involving twists within the trunk.

SR: stage right.

stimulus: starting point for a dance idea.

street: popular jazz style of dance.

structure: form a dance takes (e.g. binary, rondo, ternary).

style: identifiable manner/feature of movement or choreography, e.g. Asian, African, ballet, jazz, modern.

subject matter: theme of a dance.

suspend: hold weight up, 'hanging high'.

syncopation: rhythmic sequence with off-beat accents.

tap dance: style of dance using the taps of shoes to make rhythms.

technique: physical skill and shaping of actions in a particular style of dance.

ternary form: dance in three parts, e.g. ABA.

theme: subject matter or idea on which a dance is based.

time signature: number of beats to a bar.

transition: link from one movement or motif to another.

turned-out second: legs apart, knees facing over the toes, with turnout from the hips, as in classical ballet.

UK premiere: the date and venue of when and where a professional dance work is first performed in the UK.

unison: moving in time with each other.

unity: clear, balanced and logical structure of a dance.

use of contact: dancers have sight of, or are in touch with, other dancers, either visually or physically.

use of the feet: feet perform rhythmic phrases.

USL: upstage left.

USR: upstage right.

variation: when a motif is changed spatially, dynamically or performed in a different order.

venue: place where a dance is performed.

visualisation: when a dance expresses physically the qualities of its accompaniment.

voguing: a style of street dance.

warming up: process of moving aerobically, stretching, swinging and bending, to get blood flowing to muscles and increase the heart rate.

weight transference: moving weight from one foot to another, or to a hand etc.

world premiere: first time ever a dance is performed.

Index of dance companies, dance works and choreographers

Dance companies

Dance works

Choreographers